Running the Gauntlet

Running the Gauntlet

The Private War in Iraq

———◆———

LUKE DUFFY

authorHOUSE®

AuthorHouse™
1663 Liberty Drive
Bloomington, IN 47403
www.authorhouse.com
Phone: 1-800-839-8640

First published by AuthorHouse   07/13/2011

ISBN: 978-1-4567-8719-6 (sc)
ISBN: 978-1-4567-8720-2 (ebk)

Printed in the United States of America

Any people depicted in stock imagery provided by Thinkstock are models, and such images are being used for illustrative purposes only.
Certain stock imagery © Thinkstock.

This book is printed on acid-free paper.

Because of the dynamic nature of the Internet, any web addresses or links contained in this book may have changed since publication and may no longer be valid. The views expressed in this work are solely those of the author and do not necessarily reflect the views of the publisher, and the publisher hereby disclaims any responsibility for them.

To Liam Carmichael,

Gone, but never forgotten.

"Remember us, for we too once laughed, once cried and we too once loved. Remember us, for we too once lived."

GLOSSARY

2ic—Second in Command
50cal—Browning .50calibre (.5 inch) Heavy Machinegun
AK47—Russian 7.62mm Assault Rifle
BIAP—Baghdad International Airport
EFP—Explosively Formed Projectile; Shaped Charge IED
FOB—Forward Operating Base
Head Shed—Bosses and Management
IDF—Indirect Fire (Mortars, Artillery etc)
IED—Improvised Explosive Devise
IP—Iraqi Police
M4—5.56mm Assault Rifle (shortened version of M16)
OM—Operation's Manager
Peshmerga—Kurdish Militia/Army
PKM—Russian 7.62mm Belt-Fed Medium Machinegun
PSD—Private Security Detail (Team)
QBO's—Quick Battle Orders
QRF—Quick Reaction Force
RPG—Rocket Propelled Grenade
RV—Rendezvous
SAW—Squad Automatic Weapon, 5.56mm Belt-Fed Light Machinegun
SOP—Standard Operating Procedure
SVBIED—Suicide Vehicle Born Improvised Explosive Devise
TL—Team Leader
USACE—United States Corp of Engineers
VBIED—Vehicle Born Improvised Explosive Devise

FOREWORD

I was the first in my family to join the Parachute Regiment. It had been an ambition of mine after first learning of 'The Paras' when I was eight years old. I had always wanted to be a soldier, as most boys do at some point, but it was a dream that stayed with me throughout my school years. That would explain why I had no interest whatsoever in the academic side of my life and I left school with nothing in the way of an education.

I was the second oldest in my family with an older sister, a younger brother and two younger sisters to my parents, Frank and Colette. We grew up in the north west of England in a town situated between Manchester and Liverpool named St. Helens, and the idea of leaving school and working dull or dead-end jobs, just didn't inspire me.

One Sunday afternoon, while watching 'A Bridge Too Far' with my dad, I asked who the nut jobs were that were throwing themselves out of planes and fighting the Germans.

"They're the Paras son." He replied, "Hard as nails they are and the best in the army."

I decided then and there, that was the job for me.

I joined up at eighteen, and from the outset I knew it was where I wanted to be. My parents gave me their full encouragement and never once doubted my ability to see it through the tough training. Of course, they wanted their son to be safe and away from danger, but at the same time they knew it was something I'd always wanted to do and that I would make more of myself as a Paratrooper than I would as a factory worker or a labourer on a building site.

The training was hard and we had very little time to ourselves. If we weren't running about like lunatics with packs on our backs or attacking assault courses as though our lives depended on it, we were being subjected to inspections where the smallest discrepancy would earn you a thrashing from the Corporals and then a re-inspection at ten o'clock at night.

It was all about pushing us to the limit and beyond. Breaking us as boys, still clinging to our mother's apron strings then, rebuilding us as soldiers, ready to face and fight any enemy we were sent against.

It's almost a cliché to say it, but what we went through as recruits built our character and made men of us. Before I joined the army, as did many other recruits discover, I could hardly stand up straight by myself, let alone iron my clothes or even consider being able to administrate myself in field conditions with an empty stomach, lack of sleep and the rain pouring down the back of my neck.

A lot of people couldn't hack it and dropped out of the training course by their own accord. Others were kicked out for not reaching the mark and many more fell out through injury during the hard physical training. At the time, roughly seventy percent of the recruits would not pass out successfully at the end, for one reason or another.

After going through the Depot and passing out as a young paratrooper, I was sent to the 1st Battalion which, at the time, was based in Aldershot in southern England. Right away I settled into a life of exercises that took me all over the UK and worldwide. I had never been abroad before and to find myself in North Carolina and Florida on my first trip overseas, was something of a novelty.

The usual tours of Northern Ireland, which nearly every soldier in the British Army has experienced at some point, came and went. The first couple of years were routine and I began to wonder if I was ever going to get to experience anything more than patrolling the streets of Ulster and playing war with the Americans in Germany and the U.S.

As many others had, I joined the Parachute Regiment wanting, at some point, to go to war. Typical of the young men we were, we were full of testosterone and wanting a scrap with anyone who had the nerve to take us on. Mostly, it was all done on the weekends down 'The Shot' or during the riots in Northern Ireland.

Things changed in 1999 during the Balkans crisis and, for the first time since the Falklands campaign, The Parachute Regiment, along with the rest of the British Army and RAF, were thrown into the limelight as we all prepared to cross the border into Kosovo and possibly face the Serbs and Russians in battle. We couldn't wait.

After that came Sierra Leone in 2000. The first time was to help with the evacuation of British Nationals and to secure the main airport at Lungi. And the second time, a few months later, was the rescue mission conducted by the SAS and 1 Para to free the hostages of the Royal Irish Regiment who were being held by the notorious 'West Side Boys'.

Things were looking better for our boys. We were now operating in different theatres across the globe, something that we had been wanting for a long time. The Paratrooper mentality is basically all about taking the fight to the enemy. Aggression was always a key part of our training and by our very nature, we revelled in it.

In 2003, 1 and 3 Para were sent to Kuwait to start the preparations for the invasion of Iraq. Rumours were rife and we couldn't help but listen to them, especially when we heard whispers that they were planning to parachute us into Baghdad.

An operation like that would've been a nightmare, but we were all hoping it would become a reality. To be able to jump into battle, from a mass overhead assault, was the ambition of every paratrooper I knew, even though we knew it would be costly in casualties.

It turned out to be nothing more than a rumour and we went into the war in pretty much the same way that the rest of the army did, by vehicle and helicopter.

Once the war fighting came to an end and the Iraqi army simply dissolved into the country's population, we took on a 'Peace-Keeping' role. The aim was to win the hearts and minds of the locals. It was around this time, while patrolling the streets of Baghdad, that we started to bump into old friends we had known in the past who, were now part of the Private Security Circuit.

Instantly, people started to take an interest in what they were being told by these men. Mainly due to the kind of money they were earning. In the early days, demand far outweighed supply and a lot of companies were taking on people who had very little military experience and paying 'Rock Star' wages.

The great 'Gold Rush' to Iraq had started. Many soldiers from all regiments including men who had glittering careers ahead of them, left the army and cashed in on the void in the close protection market. Before long, supply was catching up to demand as the circuit was flooded with ex-soldiers wanting a piece of the action.

The second front in the war in Iraq was opened and thousands of professional soldiers from all over the world joined the mass career migration to the Middle East in the hope of making big money in a short space of time.

I was one of them.

CAREER CHANGE

In early 2005, I said goodbye to the army to begin working in Iraq on the Private Security circuit. After spending a third of my life wearing the uniform and having the security of a monthly wage, three meals a day and a roof over my head provided by the Ministry of Defence, walking away from it wasn't an easy thing to do. It was time to make my own way in the world and I couldn't have picked a more unforgiving environment in which to start.

Iraq was becoming a boiling cauldron more and more every day. Since the honeymoon period, just after the war had ended, the insurgent campaign had gained momentum. Shootings, suicide bombs, roadside bombs, kidnappings, mortar and rocket attacks, etc. increased dramatically.

In the early days when I was patrolling Baghdad as a soldier, we moved about on foot, wearing berets and carrying belt kit and weapons. Within a six month period however, the streets had become so dangerous that to patrol the city, you needed armoured vehicles with air support and a Quick Reaction Force, QRF, on standby in case you got into trouble.

A lot of soldiers and private contractors were being killed on a daily basis across Iraq. So much so that most newspapers and news channels rarely reported them anymore because they were becoming merely statistics in 'The Fight for Iraqi Freedom'.

I knew what I was getting myself into and the risks and the dangers were something we all accepted. As private contractors, no one was forcing us into doing the job and everybody involved was more than willing to cash in on the opportunity.

For a month after leaving the army, I spent a lot of time chasing contracts and attending interviews. Then, all of a sudden, I was offered three contracts at once. Obviously, I took the best number and agreed to start working for a company that, at the time, was considered to be one of the best to work for in Iraq. Extremely professional, well equipped, well paid and well staffed, I couldn't have asked for a better job. I was walking on cloud nine, knowing I had landed on my feet.

The weekend before I deployed was spent celebrating the start of my new career and saying goodbye to my mates. On one night, while on the way home drunk, and with my hands stuffed in to my pockets, I tripped and fell, head butting the curb. I was unable to get my hands in front of me in time to break my fall, so my face took the full force of the hit.

I can vaguely remember a young man and woman running over to me as I tried to get to my feet. Being drunk and concussed, and still having my hands in my pockets, wasn't the best approach to standing up, so naturally I hit the floor again. The young couple managed to get me vertical and I staggered off home, instantly forgetting the whole incident.

The next morning, I woke with my face stuck to my pillow and a raging headache. I peeled the pillow away and instantly felt the stinging air hit the gash above my eye because the pillow had taken away the clotted blood.

The look of sheer horror on my Mum's face was alarming, "You look a bloody state Luke. Why do you keep doing this to me? I thought you were dead when I walked in."

It wasn't the first time I had done this to her:

Years earlier, I had arrived home during the early hours one morning after a night out, and fell asleep sitting upright on the sofa.

My shirt was stained with ketchup as the result of a food fight in a Kebab shop after a heavy drinking session. Furthermore, it was ripped and torn due to an accident I had had on my way home, involving my face hitting a wall after stumbling out of a taxi. My eye was swollen and there was blood smeared across my face and neck.

For some reason, the windows in the living room had been left open that night and a cool breeze blew in from the outside. So, when my poor mother came down during the middle of the night, she could be forgiven for her reaction.

I woke up to the sound of her screaming and crying over me as she shook me. I struggled to understand what she was saying as my drunken ears and eyes tried to tune in and make sense of what was happening around me.

When she saw my eyes flicker open, she stumbled back; clutching a hand over her mouth and sobbing. I scratched my head in wonder.

"What's up mam?" I asked.

When she had walked in to the room, she had seen me sitting upright on the couch and she moved closer. In the less than perfect light in the gloomy room, she saw the rips in my shirt, the ketchup which she mistook for blood and the state of my damaged face. Immediately, she had thought the worst and it had seemed confirmed to her when she touch my cold skin that had been cooled from the open windows.

She thought I was dead. She believed I had been stabbed and I then staggered home to die.

I got a slap across the face once she had recovered her composure. It hurt all the more because she caught me across my already damaged eye.

Now, all these years later, I was in another state. In the mirror, I looked as though I'd just come out of a horror movie. There was a two inch long open wound above my eye, pouring with fresh blood that trickled down my face as I stood staring at the idiot in the mirror.

I was angry with myself because I knew that in my new line of work, first impressions really do count. Companies aren't too keen on post bout Rocky lookalikes turning up to deal with their clients. It looks unprofessional and a guy with a bust up face on his first day of the job is only going to attract one opinion, dick head.

I had four days to sort myself out and minimise the damage. I didn't want stitches because I knew they would cause more swelling, so I decided on my own surgery with one stitch from my mum's sewing box and lots of ice and haemorrhoid cream which, I was told, would help reduce the swelling. Within four days the damage didn't look too bad. Or so I thought.

My kit was packed and my farewells were said. It couldn't have been easy on my mum because she already had a son working in Iraq and there was me knocking years off her life by going out to join him.

My younger brother, Martin, had joined the Paras a year after me and had even served in the same battalion. My mum was clearly proud of her boys, but I knew she worried. It's natural for a mother to worry, but when you have two lunatics for sons who want to throw themselves out of airplanes, go to war and then work in Iraq where the dangers are endless, it's more than a mother should have to deal with.

On the drive to the airport my mind was full of worse case scenarios. Already, the death toll was rising and a few people I knew had been killed out there. But it was never something I had doubts about. I wanted to get on with the job, making a good name for myself and not fucking up. I had a young daughter of five, and I didn't like the idea of her losing her dad. But, like I said, my mind was made up and I've never been a nine to five sort of guy anyway.

I got a flight from Manchester to London and once in the departures lounge at Heathrow, I headed for the Irish bar for something to eat. The whole terminal was packed and getting a seat wasn't easy. It was only then that I started to notice in detail, the people around me. In the Irish bar, I realised that there was a large number of men that were going to be on the same flight as me, bound for Jordan then Iraq.

In the PSD industry, everyone seems to have the same fashion sense and travels to and from home dressed as though they're about to walk up Ben Nevis. Everybody looked like they had covered themselves in super glue and ram raided an Outdoor Adventure shop. The only difference in the guys I saw were the colours of their clothes and their hair styles. North Face was doing well in sales just from the PSD guys alone.

So, while I sat there eating my steak and ale pie and watching the hill walker's convention, I took a little look at myself and realised I didn't exactly fit in. I hadn't had the money to do a supermarket sweep at Blacks, so I had purchased the finest walking kit that Burtons could offer. I looked like the poor cousin of the PSD world. I was happy enough though, because it meant that no one was going to try and become my new best mate and start giving me the low down on Iraq. I just wanted to get to the company I was joining and get on with the job rather than listen to war stories.

Once on the plane I watched the people returning to Iraq from leave. You could tell by the tans they had that they had been earning the big bucks in Iraq and living the high life at home during their time off. I wanted a piece of that pie too, and I spent most of my flight daydreaming about holidays and Gucci suits.

By the time I landed in Jordan, I had travelled the world in my head and spent more time on a yacht than any A-list celebrity. It was only when I was collecting my bag that reality started to filter through. I was about to fly into Iraq and I was going to be there for at least eight weeks, so I needed to get myself into work mode. I didn't like the idea of getting killed because my head was elsewhere in dream land.

I checked into the next terminal for my morning flight to Baghdad and watched the people going by. I was shocked when I saw they had a Starbucks there because in my ignorance, I'd half expected tents and dirty glasses of water. I should've known better as the big corporations get everywhere, no matter how obscure. Taco Bell and Pizza Hut crossed the border of Kuwait and Iraq just behind the American forward units during the opening hours of the invasion, even before most of the artillery and air strikes had finished.

The flight from Jordan to Baghdad was nothing short of a white knuckle ride. The seating itself was cramped and the air conditioning had long since broken down. Everyone was sweating and the little bottle of water we were given by the cabin crew only just took the edge off our thirst. I couldn't wait to get off the plane and get on the move.

As we closed in to Baghdad, I noticed that we were still at a very high altitude considering we were on the approach run. Then, suddenly, the plane banked left and nosedived. I had a death grip on the arms of the seat and I thought something had gone seriously wrong with the plane. It felt like the plane was being used as a dive bomber. The cabin rattled and the seats we sat in shook violently as the aircraft gathered speed and dipped its nose toward the tarmac on the runway.

Inwardly, I was well and truly pissed off with myself. I hadn't even made it as far as the arrivals lounge and I was about to die because some cowboy ground crew hadn't done his checks properly in Jordan.

It was only after we had levelled off at a much lower altitude and began the final approach that I realised what was going on. A few weeks before, it had been discovered, or believed, that the insurgents had managed to get themselves some Surface to Air Missiles. So the Standard Operating Procedure (SOP) for the pilots was to come in steeply so as to spend less time in the air over Baghdad. It would've been a huge PR coupe if they had managed to shoot down a plane load of private contractors. I spent the next five minutes trying to look calm and collected as though I knew the score. I don't think my red face and beads of sweat along with my Jujitsu grip on my seat fooled many people though.

If I thought the heat on the plane was bad, then the midday temperature in Baghdad was like a fist to the face. The moment I stepped off the plane onto the tarmac, my breath was sucked from my lungs. It was like stepping in to a furnace. I was losing a lot of fluid through sweat, I'd had virtually nothing to drink and I was becoming seriously dehydrated. All I could think of was an ice cold jug of water.

We were shuttled from the plane to the arrivals lounge on an old rickety bus and I was hoping I'd be able to get a bottle of water there.

I couldn't have been more wrong. The queue for passport control was enormous and before I was allowed through, I had to endure the whole visa application process which, consisted of a bunch of Iraqi security guards with large moustaches in a small room wanting a few dollars from you to pay for my visa.

The air was so thick with cigarette smoke that I needed a guide to find the right desk. Once I got my visa, I then joined the back of the line to show my passport and get it stamped. Some of the guys, with more experience in the ways of Iraq, slipped the guards a few dollars and they were brought to the front and were soon through to the baggage claim area. I thought I'd try my luck too and it worked. I was rather pleased with myself as I was learning faster than I expected.

In Iraq, you can save yourself a lot of time and effort just by putting a few dollars into the right hands. It's the same across the board from the lowest guard to the highest general or government official. Just the amount of money is steeper the higher you go.

I'd managed to get some water in me, and as I waited for my kit to come off the plane, I started to soak up my surroundings. I began admiring the deco of the terminal which, by the looks of things, hadn't been touched or re-decorated since the 70's. The browns and oranges of the carpets, walls and chairs made me feel like I was in a time warp.

Looking at the local security and airport staff, it also became apparent that the same went for the Iraqi fashion too. Tight shirts with pot bellies, hairy chests on show and bell bottom trousers with slip on shoes. The Ron Jeremy porn star look was everywhere. And every one of them stood around chatting and smoking. No one seemed to do much at all except checking the odd bag or passport.

My sports bag came through and I then headed for the arrivals lounge. I was travelling light, with just a few changes of clothes and a wash kit. I had no other choice really because I had nothing else to bring. Most of the other guys had huge amounts of kit with them, including their own body armour, assault vests and so on. Again I must've looked like I'd got on the wrong plane.

There was a four man ex-pat team from my company waiting to take me to the villa, based in the Green Zone, now known as the International Zone or IZ. After a quick introduction, we headed for the vehicles where I was given a quick briefing by the Team Leader (TL) on the ground we were covering, order of March and positions within the vehicles, routes, friendly forces, possible threats, and actions on incidents from contact with the enemy, all the way down to a flat tyre.

Then I was shown around the vehicles and the kit and equipment in them. It looked to me like everything was covered, including communications and medical. The team 2ic gave me a set of body armour and an AK47 with a grab bag full of magazines. I was put into the lead vehicle which was a fully armoured black Mercedes. The vehicle behind was a BMW, also fully armoured with another two ex-pats in it.

The idea was that we were low profile and our main effort was to blend in with the other traffic. We would travel with a couple of hundred metres between each vehicle on the open roads and generally go with the flow of the traffic, so as not to draw attention to ourselves. Every other car in Iraq is a Mercedes, an Opel or a BMW, so it wasn't difficult to go unnoticed. In the cities and built up areas, the profile would close up slightly to keep in sight of each other, still being careful not to look like a convoy.

By the time we left the last security check point of the airport, I'd started to get a feel for it. Without looking like a tourist with my face stuck to the window, I discreetly watched the road and surrounding areas, including the other vehicles along the route. We were now on the BIAP (Baghdad International Airport Road) also known as Route Irish, which at the time was the most dangerous road in the world and only small sections of it were covered by coalition forces.

The blackened hulks of destroyed military and Private Security vehicles littered the roadside along the route. Already, many men had died on that road and the sight of the broken and twisted vehicles was a stark reminder to me of where I was. This was real. It wasn't a film and it wasn't a game.

High profile teams and U.S convoys were getting hit daily as they travelled the BIAP because it was too easy for the insurgents to run, with the slip roads and flyovers as perfect escape routes. Additionally, there were many ideal opportunities for them to plant roadside IEDs, Improvised Explosive Devices.

I sat with my AK47 between my legs, listening to the team giving instructions over the radio and pointing out general information on the road. It's important that everyone in the team is aware of what's ahead and what's behind, as well as everything that is to the left and right. That way, you can build a mental 360 degree picture of the whole environment and there's less chance of surprises.

A couple of hundred metres ahead we had a scout car with two trusted and trained local guys to give us a heads up on possible situations during our journey. Guys like them in the teams were a great asset because, not only did they know the routes better but also, being local, they would normally be able to tell if something wasn't right or out of place and could be an advanced warning to us. They were usually experienced men too. They had friends and contacts all over so they could always get you around the red tape of the young Iraqi guards and police who wanted to search us and our vehicles at the checkpoint and completely ruin our low profile by showing too much interest in the vehicle itself.

As we continued down the BIAP, I could see the city getting closer. Everything was covered by a low green/brown haze above the buildings and I couldn't help but think that the tree huggers and environmentalists back in the UK would love to do some sit down protests in Baghdad over the amount of green house gases and other pollution the locals were throwing into the atmosphere. Saving the planet and keeping the streets tidy were the last things the Iraqi people were interested in. Just trying to get through the day without getting killed in by a VBIED was enough to contend with for now.

Between the BIAP and the city we passed the Baghdad suburbs. Roof tops, doorways, windows and parked vehicles were everywhere, and so were my eyes. Rather than monging it in the back of the vehicle, I wanted to be proactive and if something was going to happen, I wanted to at least be able to react effectively.

As we approached, we hit more traffic and things slowed down. Check points in the city were near enough at every junction, and I soon realised that our main threats weren't just the insurgents. The Americans have always been very trigger happy and there have been numerous occasions of blue on blue (friendly fire) incidents between U.S and other coalition forces.

But it wasn't just the American Army, other PSD teams in high profile vehicles tore around the city like it was the Wild West, shooting up anything that moved. Some high profile companies were professional and conducted themselves in a much more controlled manner, and these tended to be mainly British companies. Some of the American companies behaved like they were in the Mad Max films.

I was in the Green Zone one time when I saw a huge guy from one of the American companies. Judging by his sheer size and look, I could tell he was obviously on steroids. He looked like a silverback gorilla with alopecia, carrying a sawn off shot gun across his back, a huge knife strapped to his leg, a pistol on each hip and an AK47 with enough ammunition slung around him to invade Iraq all over again, on his own. To top it all, he had a bandana with a skull and cross bones on his head. He looked a twat and he was clearly wrapped up in his own bad arse self image.

Driving through Baghdad was like one of those junk yard rallies. Every car was either dented or scratched, and broken windscreens were plentiful. Most didn't even have wing mirrors, and the ones that did were mainly used for adjusting the driver's moustache and hair, which I noticed on many occasions while travelling through the city.

It was every man for his self on the roads. People would cross over to the other side of the road and dodge the oncoming traffic, just to avoid the lights. Others would nudge their way in front of each other to jump the queue. Cars were filled to the brim with as many as three generations of the family crammed into it, and it was a common occurrence to see children on the dashboard. If you opened the door, they would all just tumble out.

The drive from the airport to the Green Zone was a big learning curve. Horns constantly sounded and exhaust fumes choked us. The surrounding buildings were dirty and had improvised air conditioning units hanging off them at crazy angles, and in between the buildings were rubbish tips, full of rotten food and unwanted household waste, left to fester in the heat. Dogs were constantly sniffing around them and young children would use the dumps as playgrounds. The whole city was one huge bio-hazard in my eyes.

In between the traffic, pedestrians walked amongst the static vehicles selling boxes of tissues, cigarettes, warm cans of Coke and sweets. Many earned a living by doing this and some simply begged. It was a pitiful sight to see Iraqi women, dressed completely in black with young children hanging off them, asking for a few Iraqi Dinar or U.S Dollars. When they approached our vehicles, we had to ignore them through necessity. We couldn't open the door and break the seal of the armoured protection, compromising the team, just for the sake of a goodwill gesture. Besides, I had no change on me.

We made it through the city and into the Green Zone. Once through the final check point we could relax and take a breath. The drive in had been hectic and my eyes and head were sore from overuse. The roads in the Green Zone were more civilized and ordered. People gave way, used their signal lights, stopped at junctions and lights and even travelled on the correct side of the road. Because it was a secure area, it was controlled by the American Military and they even had traffic cops who could give you speeding tickets or breathalyse you.

The whole of the safe area was surrounded by a twelve foot high reinforced concrete wall and guard towers along the entire perimeter. The place was well protected, and it needed to be. It was in the Green Zone that the process of putting the country back together took place. The new Iraqi parliament met there with foreign delegates from all over the world including the U.S, Great Britain, France and Germany. Security was of the utmost importance.

As well as the military and administration staff, the area was flooded with Private Security companies. It was an ideal base to operate from and, for insurance reasons, most clients needed to be within the protected areas of the city.

Travelling to the villa, we passed the huge palaces and monuments along the main road. They were quite impressive to look at, with massive wooden doors and large domes with once beautifully manicured gardens and manmade lakes. I'd had the chance to get a closer look and steal a few trinkets a couple of years earlier when I was there with the army, based at the British Embassy in the city. Since then, the embassy had moved into the Green Zone, as it was much safer and probably because the staff had wanted more comfort than was available at the old place. There, in the Green Zone, were barbeques and pool parties.

We arrived at the villa that was our company HQ. There were more armoured low profile Mercedes and BMWs in the parking areas, and teams were coming and going with their own tasks and concerns. The street was lined with villas and most were occupied by other PSD companies, clients and teams. Military helicopters were constantly flying over and the occasional burst of automatic gunfire could be heard from beyond the walls within the city, reminding us that not too far away, an internal war raged within the country.

In the Green Zone, the streets were much cleaner and better maintained. They had to be because when Saddam was in charge, I'm sure he would have had something to say if he walked out of his palace and stepped in dog shit. Since the coalition forces moved in, they brought their western ideas of street order and cleanliness with them too. I wasn't complaining because the inner city stank.

We walked through the gates and into the villa's courtyard. There were more vehicles parked in every possible space, people talking, laughing, briefing and generally getting on with things. I was taken into a porta cabin and introduced to the Country Manager who dealt with the running of the company and operations from Baghdad. He was a tall guy with a goatee beard; he also went for the hill walker look. He walked over from behind his desk, shook my hand and welcomed me onboard.

He took one look at my still slightly black eye and gashed brow and said, "Looks like you were talking when you should've been listening mate," then offered me a cup of tea.

So much for me looking healed then.

I was given a rough introduction to the company; how they worked, what the situation on the ground was and the upcoming tasks and political considerations that may have affected us and the circuit as a whole. He informed me that, for the first month, I would be assessed and if I wasn't up to standard, I'd be given the choice of a window or isle seat for the flight home. I'd only just got here, and I had no intention of being fucked off. I knew it was time to switch on.

From there, I went to the equipment stores and collected my kit. I was issued an AK47 of my own, a Glock-19 9mm pistol, a set of body armour, a hand held radio and ammunition and magazines for both weapons. Having come fresh from the British Army, I hadn't had much chance to use a pistol. Although I knew how to use one, I wanted to get as much hands on live firing with it as I could, and as soon as possible.

Using a pistol isn't like in the movies, with people firing one handed, jumping all over the place and getting head shots every time from one hundred metres. Pistols aren't very effective beyond twenty metres, and even that is pushing it. To be able to get accurate rounds on target consistently from as little as ten metres takes practice and more practice. So when I heard that in an hour's time a team was going to the ranges, I immediately asked if I could tag along so I could get my weapons zeroed and magazines tested.

I quickly dumped my bag in an empty bed space and grabbed what I needed for the trip across town to Camp Shield, where the ranges were located. I sorted myself out as best I could, which wasn't much considering all my personal kit was crap. But I managed to secure it and keep my weapons and ammunition in practical and easy to reach places on my body. The hunt for better kit would come later. 'First my weapons then myself' was a quote I always remember from my days in the army, and I saw no reason to change my attitude now just because I was no longer wearing green kit.

The drive across town was the same kind of wacky races as the trip from the airport, but I was surprised at how easily I was settling into it. By no means did I consider myself a seasoned veteran, but I didn't have the 'little boy lost' feeling anymore. All I needed now was to get placed in to a permanent team and start getting to grips with how things were run.

We got to the ranges and I instantly realised there was no shelter and it was hideously hot. I had no hat to shade myself either, so it was just a case of getting on with it and drinking plenty of water. I have the world's weakest bladder at the best of times, so after drinking gallons of water in that kind of heat, it was inevitable that I was going to end up pissing every ten minutes and looking like a plonker for having a bladder capacity less than my Grandmother. Even so, I managed to get my rifle zeroed, got a brief feel for the pistol and tested out my magazines.

A lot of stoppages are caused by a weapons magazines themselves and I needed to make sure each one of them worked correctly. Afterwards, I fired the AK47 from different positions and ranges to get used to it and start the process of the drills becoming second nature. The British Army don't use AK47s so we didn't get much hands-on experience. It was going to be my main weapon out in Iraq, so I needed to be able to handle it as well as I could handle the British and American weapons. When I was happy and had managed to swamp the whole of the ranges with my toilet trips, we loaded up the vehicles and headed back into the mayhem of Baghdad traffic.

Back at the villa, I was informed that I would become part of a team that was going to be sent to the north of Iraq and we would more than likely be making the trip in a few days time. In the meantime, we were free to sort ourselves out and adjust to our surroundings. I immediately gave my weapons and magazines a good clean, then I went on the hunt for better equipment.

First on my list was a holster for my pistol. I found one in the market in one of the compounds where the engineering projects were run just around the corner. While I was there, I bumped into a couple of close friends of mine from our days in the Paras. They had been on the same contract as me for a few months before I turned up, and right away the banter started and everyone took the piss out of the fact that I looked like a tramp and had a black eye too. Marc, Gaz and I had a few cup's coffee and a catch up that evening in their rooms.

I first got to know Gaz when he was a young paratrooper just before we deployed to Kosovo. He had a typical broad Yorkshire accent and was the kind of bloke you couldn't help but like from the start. During patrols in Kosovo, he would be constantly picking up pieces of wood and would tell me the names and properties and what they were best used for. He had an infatuation with Tabasco sauce; he put it on everything. His ability and skill were soon recognised within the battalion and he was sent to the Patrols Platoon. Like me, after Iraq he cashed in on the PSD scene.

I managed to collect a few bits and bobs that I'd find useful from them and also made new friends amongst the other teams. It was great to see Marc and Gaz again, and they offered me a few tips on how best to operate within the company. These guys were close friends and so the information they gave me wasn't just a case of 'waffle to the new guy'.

Marc had been on a task that day with his team and it very nearly went wrong when what they suspected were Iraqi Police, or IP, wanted to kidnap them and sell them to the highest bidder. However, because of the professionalism within the team, they realised before they even got to the site that things weren't as they should have been and they immediately aborted the mission and returned to base. With a combination of alertness, well practised drills and good local knowledge coming from their scout vehicle, they managed to save their own necks as well as their clients.

Marc and I had become close friends when he came to my platoon in B Company 1 Para, early in 2003. We had known each other a while already from playing Rugby League together in the battalion team, but it was only after the close work conditions of being in the same platoon for a while that we really got to know one another. Everything to Marc was funny, even serious stuff, which I think was the main reason we got on so well. He could make even the dullest of stories seem interesting and hilarious. On top of that, he was extremely professional and hard as nails. He was a great guy to have close by at times when the shit was about to hit the fan, which had become apparent on a few occasions.

On a night out in Deal just after we returned from the Iraq invasion, we became what could only be described as a tag-team as we took on a couple of the local 'wannabe' hard knocks. Unfortunately, Marc lost one of the sleeves from his shirt in the brawl, so I helped him rip the other one off in order to give the impression that he just had bad dress sense. With the cowboy boots he was wearing and his sleeveless shirt, he looked like one of the Village People.

By now exhaustion had hit home and I couldn't remember the last time I'd had a good sleep. I told Marc and Gaz I would catch them later and I walked back to my villa and jumped in the shower. I was feeling much fresher and ready for a sleep to recharge me.

I couldn't help but feel as though I should be doing something. After a while, sleep overwhelmed me and I drifted off. I woke a few times during the night with the low flying helicopters passing over the villa and the occasional alarm over the speaker systems as rockets or mortars came in and landed somewhere within the Green Zone.

Their low concussions, as they thumped in to the ground and buildings within the safe zone, made the walls vibrate and windows rattle in their frames.

Suddenly, the alarms sounded and people began to sit up in their beds, grumbling at the prospect of having artillery shells disturb their sleep. I, on the other hand, was wondering what I was supposed to do next. No one had informed me of where to go for cover in the event of a mortar or rocket attack. I was pretty sure that the villa couldn't withstand a hit.

Then, there was a loud whoosh as a round came in just above the building, followed by an almighty deafening bang. I ducked, involuntarily, cringing and gritting my teeth as the explosion rocked the villa. The entire room shook violently and bits of plaster landed on our heads as it was dislodged from the ceilings. Windows cracked and door frames buckled as the invisible shockwave of the blast ripped through the building. My ear drums popped and I felt the sudden vacuum caused by the explosion.

It had landed close. I guessed, just outside of the gate to the villa.

I jumped to my feet and followed the rest of the people from my room, now headed for the door. We crammed ourselves in to the reinforced concrete shelter along with everybody else, at the back of the building.

For an hour we sat and listened as the bombardment continued. Some shells landed close, causing the ground to shudder under our feet, others landed in the distance. I began to wonder what I had let myself in for.

The next day I was joined by the other three members of the team that I would be travelling north with. Spence, Steve and Andy seemed like a good bunch, and we immediately got our priorities in order; we had a brew. We discussed our backgrounds and experiences so that we could get a feel for each other. I was the only guy on the team that was new to the circuit so naturally, I was the Tea Lady.

We then took a look at our vehicles and checked them over mechanically. Both had just come back from the company garage and had been fully serviced, but we wanted our own peace of mind and there was no harm in double checking. Both were in good condition. They were B6 armoured Mercedes, and after an hour of scrutiny, we were happy.

I actually heard later that most of the vehicles the company used had been driven during the Cold War by the KGB and East German Secret Police. It made sense to me because the age of them was about right and everything was written in German and was metric.

Andy was going to be the TL with Spence as his 2ic. Different jobs were dished out amongst the team and my job was to sort out the vehicle equipment and medical kit. I needed to make sure we had all eventualities covered. To change a tyre, we needed the correct tools and jacks. To tow vehicles, tow chains had to be close at hand. Chains or kinetic tow ropes were best to use because the vehicles weighed around four tons due to the armour.

The medical kit was the same; lots of trauma treatment and fluids for blood loss and vehicle extraction kits in case of an accident.

Spence and Steve cracked on with the communications kit, vehicle and personal radios as well as the satellite tracking systems that all our vehicles were fitted with.

Equipment-wise we were all set to go. Now we needed to plan the mission. We were heading to Erbil in the north, which was roughly a seven hour drive away.

Erbil has become a beacon of northern Iraq. It's the Iraqi/Kurdish capital and is a mixture of many different cultures. There are Muslims, Shea and Sunni, Christians, Atheists and Turks in Erbil, not to mention many westerners these days, and they seem to mostly get along just fine. The majority of the trouble that the Kurds have tends to be tribal and low key. Now and again, there will be a shooting or an IED going off, but compared to Baghdad or Mosul, it's a completely different world.

The Citadel at the centre of the city is the oldest, still inhabited, building in the world and it's said that Alexander the Great stayed there to rest after the defeat of Darius at the battle of Gaugamela, an hour to the east of Erbil, in 331 BC.

Since the fall of Saddam, the Kurds had finally got to grips with their cities. They were being transformed into modern, more comfortable places to live at a phenomenal rate, with supermarkets, hotels and even Chinese restaurants and bars cropping up. Every time I've travelled through the northern regions over the years, I've noticed the place expanding and becoming more up to date with their road systems and buildings. Life was getting better for the Kurds now and rather than spend all their efforts in making car bombs and destroying their cities and people, they focussed their skills into making a better future for themselves and the generations to follow.

However, our main concern wasn't Erbil itself; it was getting there. We had to travel through Baghdad, north through Ballad and countless other towns and villages along the way, including the town of Tuz and the city of Kirkuk. Both areas were not the sort of places you would want to draw attention to yourself, so sightseeing was out of the question. We had to study maps, aerial photos and intelligence reports on the areas we were to travel through.

There were always significant actions, or sig-acts, to read up on and that way you could work out what the general feeling was in an area at that time. If the sig-acts reported that everything that went through an area was hit, then it would be prudent to consider alternative routes or even scrap the mission altogether.

The planning took some time, and afterwards, we had a quick brew and smoke break before we went into the mission orders.

Andy gave a full set of orders covering everything we needed to know for the task including the routes, general local knowledge of each area, ethnic makeup of the populations, enemy forces, friendly forces, and safe areas such as FOBs (Forward Operating Bases) manned by the Americans. We then went onto the communications plan for the trip, and Spence was to keep in contact with Baghdad and Erbil throughout the drive. The whole orders process took roughly an hour. We stopped for yet another brew before running over the actions on and the SOP's.

Every company has their own SOP's (Standard Order Procedures) but in general, they follow the same guidelines. You practice them within your team, in much the same way as we did in the army so that everyone knows what needs to be done in certain situations. If you come under fire or get hit by an IED, or even something as simple as approaching a checkpoint or a vehicle breakdown, there is a drill for everything. If you don't have

SOP's or practice them, and something goes wrong, you have guys all over the place doing their own thing. If you're in a contact and under fire, then things will go pear shaped very rapidly.

So we went through our actions on and then we practiced them as a team, which took a while as there were a lot of scenarios to be covered. But it's better to take your time and cover everything, rather than to go half hearted and unprepared.

By the time we finished, we were happy and knew what needed to be done. This was a world of grownups, and if you had something to add to the pot then a good TL would never say, "shut up, we're doing it my way or it's the highway."

We were all trained and experienced soldiers, and the company hadn't taken us on for our good looks. So over a final cup of tea, we had a chat to make sure everyone was happy and if anybody had had any last minute ideas to make the job run smoother. With that done, we all relaxed for the evening and I popped round to say farewell to Gaz and Marc.

The next morning at six o'clock, we met at the vehicles and Andy gave us a set of QBO's, Quick Battle Orders. These are a condensed version of the orders we had gone through the evening before to refresh everybody on the main points of the task and to inform us of any changes.

Good to go, we set out into the city. I was driving the rear vehicle with Spence as the commander in the passenger seat beside me. Getting out of Baghdad didn't prove too difficult with it being so early. We hit the usual check points, but with a quick word from our scout vehicle ahead, the guards were warned off on our approach and didn't show us too much attention as we passed. The city was still very much asleep with a lot of people still in the Mosques or just starting to open their shops and market stalls. Everyone was too busy in their own little world to notice us as we slipped by. With the profile we used anyway, we just looked like any other vehicle on the road.

Once clear of the city, we increased the speed and the distance between our vehicles. As long as we could still have limit of sight and good communications, we were happy. There was still a low mist in the open areas and fields either side of the road after we had passed through the suburbs, it seemed hard to believe that within the next hour, the usual bombs and small arms fire would be heard within the built up areas. It was very peaceful, but we knew not to get complacent. Insurgents would sneak out during the night to set up IEDs and ambushes at the sides of the roads because they knew that U.S Military call signs would be doing their early morning sweeps of the routes, to clear possible road side bombs and command wires.

Luckily for us, we passed through Ballad without a hitch, and the route to the north was long and open. As the day heated up, so did the traffic and it became a similar game of whacky races like in Baghdad but in a more linear sense.

My biggest concern became, not so much getting caught up in an ambush, but having an accident. On the open roads, oncoming vehicles would pull out to overtake with no warning and at extreme risk. By flashing their lights rapidly and slamming their foot to the floor, I think they believed it created some sort of protective force field around them because that's all they would do, rather than wait until it was clear to overtake. I decided to keep my speed manageable and stay at a good distance from other vehicles in front. However, that didn't stop people from screaming up behind at break neck speed and trying to run us off the road to overtake.

U.S Military and high profile PSDs were always going to be a concern. The general rule they follow is; if anyone approaches to within one hundred metres of their rear vehicle, the rear gunner would let them have the good news in the form of a belt fed machinegun firing 7.62mm rounds.

The problem was, the military call signs travelled at the same speed as a startled slug. In our vehicles, we carried British and American A4 sized flags, so the lead vehicle would slowly approach them from the rear and the TL would have his face stuck to the wind screen, flag in one hand and giving a huge thumbs up with the other hand like they were long lost buddies. We always used the U.S flag because most Americans didn't even know what Great Britain was, never mind what the flag looked like. To them, it was just a t-shirt design.

Normally after a few tense moments of the TL trying to communicate with the nineteen year old rear gunner who would point his gun at us as though he was about to open up, we would get a thumbs up and be allowed to pass. The message would be then passed from the call sign's rear vehicle to the rest of the convoy that, 'there's a low profile American PSD team coming up on the left and they're okay to pass.'

Sometimes, however, the rear vehicles would mong it and forget to inform all the gunners of our presence and then there would be dramas resulting in bullet holes in our cars. I actually saw this happen on the BIAP once as we were travelling to Camp Victory with some of our company head shed.

The young American soldier who was manning the gun on top of their lead vehicle gave our front vehicle a burst from his gun along the drivers and rear left passenger door as we passed. Luckily, the armour soaked up the rounds and as we got to Camp Victory one of our guys, who happened to also be one of the directors, got out of his vehicle and waited for the American call sign to catch up.

The American sergeant approached with an arrogant cocky apology, holding his arms spread wide as if to say, "hey, shit happens." He left with broken sunglasses and a smashed nose. You have to admire the British no bollocks approach.

As we came close to Tuz, we began to see destroyed and burned out vehicles left and right of the road, their charred and smashed frames stood as testament to the savage warfare being conducted throughout the country and the craters and blast marks from IEDs were visible everywhere.

I could even see where they had set up a daisy chain to take out a whole convoy. A daisy chain is a string of IEDs along the roadside, which are normally command wire detonated. The insurgents would wait until the entire or, majority of the convoy is within the kill zone then they let them have it.

Sometimes they are followed up by a small arms attack with machineguns and rifles to maximise the damage to the call sign they've hit.

Our alertness was on full by this point as it was midday and busy as we passed through the checkpoints of the town. Fortunately, the same road we were on ran straight through, without us having to turn off, so we were out of the built up area pretty quickly.

We kept our eyes wide once clear because we knew we were still in a very anti coalition area. After another hour, we started to approach the city of Kirkuk where we would meet two Kurdish scout drivers that would take over from our Arab scouts.

At the RV, which was just outside an American Air Force base called FOB Warrior, we met Siwan and Seaman. They were ex Kurdish Militia, known as Peshmerga, who had fought against the Iranians during the Iran/Iraq war in the 80's and then fought against the Iraqis not long after.

Siwan was very polite and kitted out in typical Kurdish traditional dress, which looked like a cross between a suit and an MC Hammer outfit.

He spoke good English and immediately began to give us a heads up on what was happening in Kirkuk at the time. There had been a number of IEDs that morning along our intended route through the city, but he explained to us that, it was pretty normal for a Saturday anyway.

Where I come from, Saturday mornings are for seeing people staggering home, still wearing their disco shoes after they had got lucky the night before and now doing the 'walk of shame'. Here, in Kirkuk, you would see cars and trucks exploding and people being blown to pieces on Saturday mornings. What a country.

Seaman was a little rounded guy with a big moustache and a permanent grin on his face. He giggled at everything. Even when I pointed out what Seaman, pronounced as 'semen', meant in English and gave him the nickname 'Spunky', he found it funny. I liked him. We had a pee break and then loaded up and set off through the city.

We came out the other end and we were now only an hour from Erbil. I couldn't wait to get there and sort myself out. I was hungry and my arse and legs were killing me.

Once you get north of Kirkuk you hit what's known as the 'Green Line'. It's an imaginary line at a certain grid, and north of that is considered Kurdistan and friendly. You keep your vigilance but you can afford to relax a little.

Spence and I had been talking on and off during the journey, and I learned that he had been in the Royal Navy and after that, he worked on cruise ships. He admitted to being involved in the Cabaret for the entertainment and, naturally, I had taken the piss and accused him of being a bandit. He took the piss in return for me being a stupid lump hammer Para. Within a team, you need to be able to have a laugh and joke, and the banter is important. You're living side by side and in each other's pockets for eight weeks at a time, so if you don't get on, it's going to be a long rotation.

The further north we got, the greener the country became and at a push, you could look at the rolling hills and fields left and right and imagine it being somewhere in the UK.

We came into Erbil and hit the road system that rings the entire city like a spider's web, with roads filtering closer into the city centre. Traffic cops were doing a fine job and people in general obeyed the rules of the road, with the odd moment of driving Tourettes thrown in to remind us that we were still in Iraq. All would be orderly and calm then, suddenly, a car would race across a packed junction, oblivious to the dangers. Or someone would decide that they've changed their mind on where they're going and turn 180 degrees in the middle of the road. But, on the whole, Erbil was much more organised.

We were heading for a district called Ankawa where there was a compound that was rather like a mini Green Zone, about a mile square. It was protected with large walls, towers and guards with dogs. Within the compound, there were rows of streets, lined with villas, and most of them were occupied with other PSD companies and clients.

All the villas were rented out by their owners to the companies and they were making a fortune from it. At least I wasn't paying the bill. They all had well kept gardens with trees and garden furniture to sit and relax in. Everywhere within the compound, there were young Kurdish women in tight fitting clothes who were obviously hired by the management staff of the different companies for their eye candy value, and any administration skills came as a nice bonus.

The Kurdish people are much more liberal and tolerant of other cultures and the majority of the men and women, dress more like westerners. Further south, women are expected to dress completely in black and walk around looking like ninjas in baggy clothes. I knew right away I was going to enjoy being based in Erbil.

Our villa was at the far end of the compound, and the Op's Manager for the northern teams was waiting to greet us. As we got out he walked over to us and shook our hands telling us, "get in lads and chill out. I've put the kettle on."

He was only a temporary OM for us, as he preferred to be out on the ground as a Team Leader. Unfortunately, he resigned shortly after and left the company to work elsewhere.

We were given a quick tour of the grounds and I was impressed from the start. We had our own rooms, a gym, garden furniture and plenty to eat. Life was sweet and it just got sweeter when I learned that while we were having a quick intelligence briefing and general heads up of upcoming tasks and the area, our rooms were being fitted with Cable TV and internet connections. It was better than I had at home.

I had been sleeping on my Mum's couch since leaving the army and all my personal belongings were in her garage. Here, I had a bed, Sky, internet and air conditioning and no chance of waking up with a cats arse in my face.

As it turned out an old mate of mine from 1 Para was also there on the team. Tom had been out a few weeks longer than me and true to form, I made use of the fact that I knew someone who was already there and scrounged what I needed.

The other guys were Stu, Spike and Gilly.

Spike was also ex 1 Para, but well before my time. Though to look at him, I don't think he realised that he wasn't in his teens anymore. Every time he went home on leave to Manchester, he would come back with bits missing. He had half an ear and a rough and ready look about him. Great guy all the same. We soon got to know each other and the banter flowed.

We spent the next couple of days settling in and making ourselves comfortable, both in our rooms and around the villa and compound. The vehicles were inspected and the kit was readjusted and checked for deficiencies.

We were introduced to our clients; a group of engineers working for a western construction company. They were overseeing the building of clinics throughout Erbil, Kirkuk, Mosul, Dihok and Sulimania which are the major cities in the north of Iraq. They were mainly middle aged Americans with one local Iraqi.

Our job was to escort them to and from the sites safely, advise them on security issues and generally look after their well being. They seemed easy enough to get along with, and I was looking forward to cracking on with the job.

THE LEARNING CURVE

For the next two weeks we spent most days training local Kurdish PSD teams. Recently, the contract had been changed and now called for a third armoured vehicle in the profile. They would travel at the back of the group at a distance of a few hundred metres, acting as what we referred to as a CAT or Counter Attack Team. The idea was that an ex-pat would command the vehicle, with a local driver and two more Kurdish guys in the back with heavier weapons, preferably a PKM; a Russian belt fed medium machine gun which could give a much heavier weight of fire, at a more sustained rate, than our AK47s.

The word had been put out by the head shed that local guys were required to train and work as security teams. When the first recruitment day started, with dozens of Kurdish men turning up hoping to get a job, there was an abundance of cliques going on already.

Within Kurdish culture, everyone has cousins and brothers they want to help out and people were bitching from the start about whom they wanted to work with and who they wouldn't. The majority of them had come from Kirkuk and Erbil. The guys from Erbil didn't trust the guys from Kirkuk, and vice versa.

Each and every city in Kurdistan has its own mini government, run by opposing political parties from the next town along. I could never tell the difference myself and the Kurds trusted the Arabs even less.

Right away we got down to conducting interviews and sifting through who would be kept on for training and who would be binned on the first day. Some even brought proper CV's, whereas others came with so-called letters of recommendation from the government. The majority came with pretty much nothing and we made judgements on how they conducted themselves during the interview and amongst the rest of the applicants.

With Kurds and Arabs, it's all about being the dominant male and the boss. Every one of them claimed to be a commander of some sort. I knew we had our work cut out for us.

We needed twelve men to be used as two teams of four with four guys on leave at any one time. About thirty had turned up hoping for a position within the teams and by the end of the first day, we had whittled them down to about eighteen, knowing more would either drop out or be pushed out. We preferred to keep hold of the blokes that had previous PSD training, military service or English speakers for obvious reasons. But that didn't necessarily mean they were in. The Iraqi idea of military training far differed from ours. Once we had the pool of men we wanted to work on, we started with the training.

Our main training concentrations were driving, weapons training including live firing on the ranges, medical and general tactics and vehicle drills. Before we could allow them to work with us and the clients, we had to bring them up to scratch as best we could. Not an easy task when each and every one of them wanted to be the boss of the local guys.

We started with medical and driving training. We wanted to assess their aptitude for the other aspects of the job before we would let them loose with weapons.

The medical packs were like the Holy Grail when I showed them to the locals. Their eyes lit up and they instantly believed that no matter what the injury, even if it was just a mild headache, it could be cured by wrapping it in a field dressing.

I kept the training very basic and focused mainly on the principles of First Aid and the treatment of trauma and gunshot wounds. Over the next few days, they started to grasp an idea of how to treat and react to different scenarios. Considering they didn't know the difference between a First Field Dressing and a neck brace to start with, they learned remarkably quickly.

During a cigarette break in the lessons, I was stood talking to Gilly about the job and the training. He had been working in Erbil quite a while longer than me. He was from the city of Sunderland in the north east of England and spoke with the typical 'Mackem' accent of the region.

"Ah, it's pretty peaceful here in Erbil mate. Nothing much happens except for the odd little drama. But it's never anything bad like."

Just as he finished the sentence, a loud explosion echoed through the neighbourhood. It was a fair distance away from what I could tell, but I could also tell that it had been a big one. We both looked at each other as if to say 'spoke too soon'. The bang sounded like it had come from somewhere within the city. Right away, there was an atmosphere of panic in the compound. People were everywhere trying to find out what had happened. It took an hour or so before any information started to filter through to us.

The Kurdish Police had been holding a recruitment open day at the football stadium in the southern end of the city. A man had approached on a bike, packed with explosives. He had driven in and blown himself up within the crowd, right outside the gates where all of the potential recruits and recruiters were gathered. Dozens were killed, including police and civilians.

A couple of our own recruits had brothers and cousins that were attending the open day and the look of worry on their faces was apparent. We sent them all home so that they could do what they needed to do and check on loved ones and friends. The next day, we found out that a couple had lost someone close to them. But in true Kurdish style, they cracked on and got on with the job.

After the first week of med training, tactics and learning the SOP's, we were ready to start with the weapons and live firing. Most had experience already with the weapons we used because they were the same ones the Iraqi army used. But their idea of weapon handling and operating drills were far removed from ours. The first thing we drummed home to them was safety.

It's all too easy to accidentally shoot a team mate and it's happened a number of times over the years, with ex-pats too and not just locals. As in the British Army, weapon safety was the first thing they were taught. From there, we went on to how to load the weapons, unload them and the drills we conduct when there is a stoppage from either empty magazines or jammed rounds in the loading chamber or the magazine itself. These drills need to be done quickly and smoothly because if you're under fire and your weapon stops for whatever reason, you need to be able to get it working again as fast as possible. So we went over the drills again and again. We wanted them to be as efficient with the weapon systems as we were. We always took part ourselves, mainly to show the guys that we train the same way they do and that we're efficient and slick with the drills we teach. It's also important to keep on top of your own skills as well, so we killed two birds with one stone.

The range was set up on the local militia training area on the outskirts of the city amongst some low lying hills. It was ideal for our purposes, and wasn't completely unlike the live firing ranges you find on UK military training areas, with small rises and long grass, only the sun was shining. The Brecon Beacons is the only place on earth I know of, where you can experience all four seasons in one day during July.

We found a good spot where we could fire our weapons without having to worry that if they missed the targets, they wouldn't continue into the built up areas and take out people as they went about their daily business.

It was a large dip in the ground, like a re-entrant, where the hill folded in on itself creating a sort of bowl area with slopes to either side. It was a couple of hundred metres across and wide enough for the teams to conduct some realistic training without being too bunched up. Later in the week, we would even use the road we came in on behind us to practice live firing vehicle contact drills.

Our first priority was to get the weapons zeroed and test fired. Most of them had been supplied to us from Baghdad and every one of them needed to be in perfect working order. Everybody had their own personal weapon assigned to them, and the care and maintenance was their responsibility. It's no good just picking up any weapon to use because everyone's eye relief and the way they hold the weapon is different from the next man. This needs to be taken into account when you zero the weapon, and it can take a while to get right.

A weapon that hits the bull's-eye every time for one person might completely miss the target for the next due to his eye being closer or further away from the sight or slightly up or down. It took us a whole day to get everybody zeroed and we even managed to check our own weapons while demonstrating to the recruits how to hold and fire the weapons correctly.

During the day, we had the chance to speak and mingle on a more personal level amongst our recruits. There were a few real characters amongst them, including some veterans of the Iran/Iraq war. They were never afraid of laughing, and we soon found out that the Kurds are as willing to take the piss out of each other as we Brits are.

Through the fluent English speakers, we managed to build some banter with them which helped to break the ice and bring them out of their shells and relax a little. It was important that they understood who was in command, but at the same time we didn't want to have an 'us and them' feel within the team.

I was still struggling to remember who was who at this point, not easy when most of them had the name Ahmed or Mohammed, but one or two were starting to stick in my mind. Very early on, we were beginning to get an idea of who we would be keeping. The rest of the training would just confirm it for us.

Toward the end of the week we started to introduce more movement into the drills on the ranges. Safety again was the main issue; once you start moving about with loaded weapons, the thought of someone falling over with his finger on the trigger and letting off a burst of rounds into someone, isn't my idea of a good day out. So we started off by conducting contact drills in pairs, then building up to groups of four.

The principle idea of the contact drill is to extract yourself and the team from enemy fire using the 'fire and manoeuvre' method. Its best described as 'keeping one foot on the ground'. Between two guys under contact, one will be static and firing into the enemy positions while the other moves back a few metres and then stops and turns to give fire support while his partner moves back level with him. All the time there is suppressive fire towards the enemy while one guy is moving back. With each tactical bound, you put more distance between you and the bad guys. You could be firing and manoeuvring for a while before you find suitable cover to rally behind and sort yourself out, so the sooner you can break contact, the better.

Our budding recruits soon discovered that a life style of kebabs and constantly smoking cigarettes wasn't good for their fitness levels. Even when you're fit and strong, with the kit you're carrying and the running, stopping, firing, shouting and running again, soon takes it out of you in just a few bounds, especially in the heat of Iraq.

Spike and I did the first live demonstration after we had explained to the locals what we wanted from them. The results of wearing heavy body armour while carrying weapons and ammunition combined with the intense heat meant that, I was soon sucking in the air from China and soaked to the bone with sweat after just five minutes of running and firing. It was mid spring by now, and already the heat was getting unbearable. By that time in Iraq, it was reaching around forty degrees Celsius and coupled with the hot wind, it felt like you had your face permanently stuck under a hand drier, the type you find in public toilets.

Afterwards, one of the recruits asked me, "Mr Luke, why are we are running away from the enemy and not attacking?"

He didn't quite grasp that we weren't the army and our main objective is to protect the clients and avoid injury to ourselves, so the idea of taking the fight to the enemy, would be counterproductive to our aims.

The first group of pairs to go through the range were nothing short of a gang fuck. They were all over the place and moving when they should've been firing, falling over, dropping weapons, forgetting their weapon stoppage drills and so on. It took a lot to control them, and after many hours of shouting and running around like lunatics in the blazing sun, they started to get the hang of it.

We had given them 'walkthrough talk through' training of the drills and movements without firing, but once guns start to make big bangs, some people become flustered. That's the reason why we train and train with as much live firing as possible. The more realistic the training, the more effective you'll react when it happens for real.

We progressed onto four man drills, which work the same as the two man drills only this time, two men are firing and two men are moving instead of one and one. The Kurdish recruits were coming on in leaps and bounds, and by the end of the week, they were ready to put the same drills into practice using vehicles and a number of scenarios.

We drummed into them that every vehicle can act as fire support if needed. In the new profile with the CAT, they were going to be our main weight of fire. If the team was hit during a task and any of the vehicles immobilised, they would provide fire support while the men in contact would extract to a safer area or cross deck into one of the other cars.

Whether you're moving away from a contact or taking the fight to the enemy and attacking, one of the most important things is to gain fire superiority. By returning a heavier and more accurate rate of fire, you keep the enemy heads pinned down. It's no good firing from the hip thinking you're Rambo; the rounds go everywhere that way and they're not effective. What we wanted was rapid, controlled aimed shots landing on target, making the enemy think twice about sticking his head up thus, giving the guys under fire a chance to get back into safe cover.

By the end of the week, we had the teams we wanted. They were a good bunch and well trained. They weren't super troopers by a long shot, but they were better trained and equipped than they had been. Now they had steady work and the money they were earning in just one month was huge bucks for them. They were happy with us and we were as happy as we were going to be with them, but their training wasn't over. During easy days back at the villa, we would keep on at them with medical and weapons training as well as fitness.

Our adventures on the range had brought to our attention that a fair few of them weren't exactly athletes, so whenever possible, we would have them huffing and puffing around the compound in their kit to build up some level of fitness. It was always amusing to watch the dramatics of them collapsing during the runs and on the verge of death with arms flailing and hands clutching their chests. Stamina is not a Kurdish strong point.

We were given a task of travelling to Baghdad to pick up another armoured Mercedes that would be kept at the villa in Erbil as a spare. Al, our temporary Op's Manager, would act as the TL in a three vehicle move and Stu was his 2ic. The mission itself went well on the way in. We stayed overnight and in the morning, headed back for Erbil with the extra car. It had very little in the way of communications kit and was therefore placed in the centre of the convoy with me as the commander and a local guy named Jamir driving.

By the time we reached the outskirts, the traffic had built up and people were taking chances and overtaking one another at high speeds and risk. As you leave northern Baghdad, you come to a large blue arch type foot bridge that spans across the main road heading north, with a gap just after it in the central reservation for vehicles to cross. By now our speed was around 60kmph and all seemed well.

As we approached the gap in the reservation, a large heavy goods vehicle suddenly pulled out, intending to cross from the opposite carriageway, and stalled in the centre lane. With the build-up of traffic left and right of us, we had nowhere to go and even with Jamir stomping on the brakes, the weight of the Mercedes caused our momentum to carry us forward with smoking tyres and screeching brakes.

I saw the whole thing in slow motion as we closed the gap and even noticed the bewildered look on the truck driver's face as our vehicle slammed into his side. I watched, as if witnessing the event from an outer-body experience, as the hood of the car folded towards me. I was instantly thrown from seat to windscreen to foot well and landed in a crumpled mess under the dashboard.

I think I may have been momentarily knocked out and, as I climbed back in to the passenger seat, I realised blood was dripping into my eyes from a gash on my head, caused by my sunglasses becoming fused with my scalp on impact with the windscreen.

I grabbed the radio and yelled, "Stop, we've had an RTA. (Road Traffic Accident)"

Immediately, we started to draw a crowd, and I looked up to see faces pressed against the windows checking to see if we were okay. They were trying to open the doors but thankfully, Jamir had followed the SOP of locking us down as soon as we got in the vehicle.

Once the locals outside realised who and what we were, more people started to clamber around us all shouting and gesturing to one another. Some seemed pretty worked up and agitated and began beating against the windows and the doors. I had visions of being lynched the same way the American contractors had been in Fallujah the year before.

They had been caught out and attacked while driving through the city. After killing them, the locals then strung their bodies from a bridge and set them on fire. I didn't fancy the same fate.

Stu called me on the radio to let me know he had managed to get alongside me, but due to the size of the crowd, he couldn't get eyes on. I told Jamir to grab his kit and his weapons and be ready to follow me out through the door.

"Don't fire unless I do," I told him.

He looked at me, fear in his eyes and he nodded sternly. He knew as well as I did that things could go terribly wrong at this point and all it would take was for someone within the crowd to shout a certain command or slogan, and it would fire up the crowd in to a lynch mob.

I had to kick the door open because the crash and impact had buckled the frame. Right away, I let everyone in the immediate area see that I had weapons and the way I was holding them said I was willing to use them. They may have just wanted to help, but I didn't want to take any chances and so, I barged my way through with my AK47 in my hand and Jamir close on my heels. I ran with my head down and my eyes ahead and on the ground. I didn't want to misplace my footing and take a tumble. If the crowd turned hostile, I'd be pinned to the ground and unable to break loose.

We made it into Stu's vehicle. I slammed my body against it and ripped the door open, bundling myself and Jamir in to the rear seat. We moved off to join the rest of the team further ahead, leaving the noisy and ever growing crowd behind us.

I had gone dizzy by now and I suspected a mild concussion. At least I hoped that was all. We headed straight back to Erbil and sent a sit-rep to Baghdad HQ, informing them of what had happened and what actions we had taken.

Luckily they had a team in the area and the vehicle was soon secured and recovered. I was pleased because I didn't like the idea of paying the one hundred and fifty thousand dollars for a new one. We got back to Erbil and received praise from everyone for our drills and conduct during the incident, but we still didn't have a spare vehicle so it was a costly trip in all.

We now had two teams in Erbil. Dave, Paul and Ash had just come into the country, and a guy named Stan was to be their TL. Stan and I would end up working together for quite a while, and a friendship developed that we still have to this day. He was a stocky guy of about medium height and covered in tattoos. He looked like a kids colouring book. He had served in the Foreign Legion with their paratroopers, so we automatically had something in common and once you got past his rough exterior, you soon discovered a very likable and friendly man.

I had a chat and a brew with the guys and learned that Dave was an ex Royal Marine who had to watch his sugar levels otherwise, he would become restless and you'd find him cleaning the cars at midnight. We nicknamed him 'the Womble'. If something stayed still longer than five minutes, it got a full valet from him. He was an extremely professional and clever guy. He had a very dry sense of humour and unless you had similar traits, you wouldn't realise he was making a joke half of the time.

We worked pretty much every day and the drills within the team became as slick as snot on a door knob. Every man knew what was needed of him before, during and after a mission. Most people think it's a case of get in the cars and turn up for the job. But in fact, each and every task takes a lot of planning.

Before we went out on the ground, we needed to study the areas, the locals, routes, previous missions there and any sig-acts for that area. If there were IEDs going off and regular shootings, then the mission wasn't likely to go ahead, or we would at least recommend to the clients that it should be left for another time.

For the next couple of months, we worked separately as two four man teams with four locals as our support. All in all, each team consisted of eight men and the clients were more than happy with the level of protection we provided them. Most of our jobs were spent in the partially constructed clinics around the northern regions. Most of them were nothing more than construction sites with bare concrete frames. Nobody wanted to wear hard hats or harnesses, and our clients spent more time reprimanding people for safety reasons, rather than inspecting the progress and workmanship of the project.

All the time we were on the sites, the client would have a minimum of two ex-pats as close protection. Another would stay with the CAT vehicle, keeping an eye on the surrounding area while maintaining communications with the team on the ground. The CAT commander would keep us updated with the comings and goings and be ready to give support if we had a drama on the site and needed to make a fighting withdrawal to the vehicles.

One of the projects was in the hospital in Erbil. On one trip, I had a real eye opener when I walked into the main building. The place stank to high heaven of rotten blood and human waste. Broken floor and ceiling tiles were everywhere, the paint was falling off the walls and the smell of decay seemed to physically claw its way in to our nostrils.

The place didn't have the disinfected feel we were used to in the UK. Used dressings and blood-soaked bandages were strewn on the floors of the corridors and, on a counter top in the reception area I saw a glass bowl, full to the brim with used needles and other sharp implements.

Sometimes, in dental surgeries or doctors clinics, you see a bowl full of lollipops or sweets. In Kurdistan, you get used syringes. The thing had flies swarming around it and no one seemed to pay much attention. It was obviously the norm for this place.

"It's like summat out of the fucking Dark Ages. It's fucking gopping," I remarked to Gilly, screwing my face up and swatting at a cloud of swollen black flies.

"Mate, you've seen fuck all yet," and he pointed to a big pile of shit-filled nappies in the corner of the waiting room. They must have been there for a while because the bundle had even begun to develop its own eco-system.

The whole hospital was like a huge case of Black Death in a can waiting to happen. I felt like scrubbing myself with bleach as soon as we left, but at that time, it was par for the course in Iraqi hospitals.

During our visits, I always noticed there seemed to be more administration staff than doctors or nurses. I think it was still very much a case of friends of friends and cousins making jobs for one another. The clients always needed to meet and discuss points with the hospital head shed and that's when the tea and biscuits would be brought out for us. I use the phrase 'tea and biscuits' in a loose sense. It was more of a block of sugar and a cup of sugar. But I'd always play the good guy and stand there with a shit eating grin on my face, pretending they were the best I'd ever tasted.

We had the evenings to ourselves, and I tended to spend my time training in the gym or drinking brews and talking rubbish with the other guys on the team. There was a bar and restaurant in the compound, and now and then, we would go over and have a few beers and a pizza with the lads. Of course, if there was a job on early the next day, then a drinking session was out of the question. Turning up half cut for a task was not only unprofessional and irresponsible, it was also dangerous. Regardless of where you are in Iraq, it's still Iraq and what can go wrong, will go wrong.

Mosul was a shit hole and not the place you wanted to go and try getting friendly with the locals. It's situated a couple of hours to the west of Erbil, and the difference in the dangers and threats is in stark contrast to Erbil itself.

For anyone planning a task to Mosul, the threat levels were high and therefore, when we were given a task to go there it had to be planned to the letter. Teams were constantly getting hit passing through. We blended in much more than the overt teams and we were less likely to be noticed. This didn't make us complacent in any way though, and we had to bear in mind that even though we were less conspicuous, we had less support than most overt teams had.

High profile teams normally run with around ten to fifteen ex-pats, all heavily armed and with military support on call at the push of a button. Our saving grace was that we had American clients and a QRF, Quick Reaction Force, from the base in Mosul were more likely to come out and help their fellow countrymen if we hit the panic button.

There were two FOBs in the Mosul area, and our client needed to meet the commander of the US Corp of Engineers stationed there. I knew that one of my best and closest friends, Liam Carmichael, was based there working for a high profile company. I was looking forward to a brew and a catch up with him. We had been in the army together and Liam, Marc and I had been thick as thieves.

We had the two scouts in their soft skinned vehicle in the lead, with Gilly and Steve in the first armoured car with the client. I was in the second armoured with my driver Ahmed, and Spike was in the CAT vehicle at the rear with three locals. My vehicle was a fully B6 armoured Mercedes, as was Gilly's, and at the rear with Spike, was an armoured SUV.

Every vehicle had fitted base sets for the radios and that way had a much greater range than the handhelds that we had on our belts. We used the hand radios once we were out of the vehicles to keep communications with each other and the CAT commander who, would be acting as our support. Even these were kept out of sight by way of being fitted to our belt along with our weapons and ammunition. We had earpieces, and everything, including our body armour was kept underneath our shirts. To the untrained eye, we just looked like everybody else.

In addition, each car had an MTS, Mobile Tracking System. This was similar to a mini laptop attached to a transponder which was linked to satellites and wherever you were, your position would show up as a blip on the big screen back in the Op's Room in HQ. It was similar to a Sat-Nav system but more advanced. We could actually send texts through it to our Op's Manager and each other and even call for immediate support from the Americans if we hit the panic button.

Of course, you give a bunch of British guys the means of real time communications to and from one another over vast distances and it is bound to be abused. I remember Spike sitting in my car and while I was distracted, he typed out a message calling the Op's Manager a 'knob' from my MTS and hit the 'send' button. Naturally, the Op's Manager thought I had a problem with him until he saw the bewildered look on my face and Spike laughing like a child in the background.

I had managed to get my driver into the habit of starting the vehicle up well before we were due to leave so that the air conditioning was running at full speed. Getting into a vehicle that had been sat in the sun, even for just a half hour, was like getting into an oven and immediately, you would begin to pour with sweat. So, I always ensured that my driver had the temperature just right, freezing.

The route in took us past the area where the battle of Gaugamela, between Alexander the Great and Darius, had taken place over two thousand years earlier. To look at the place though, you wouldn't have thought it was such an historic site. Rubbish tips and mud huts were scattered all around the area, with flocks of goats with herders moving through the fields.

A lot of people think the whole of Iraq is nothing but desert, but when you get into the northern parts, it becomes much greener. Fields and trees are abundant, and I'm yet to see my first camel in the north.

Whenever we approached a built up area, the sides of the road would be full of people selling cheap fuel in jerry cans. They always managed to make me gasp as I watched them pouring petrol into car fuel tanks, spilling it all over themselves, with cigarettes hanging from their mouths.

During one winter, we were passing through a town called Dianna where I saw a group of men seated around a gas canister. They had cracked the valve open and lit the escaping gas to act as an instant fire to keep them warm. Judging by the look of the rust and dents, the canisters were older than the Ark and if the valve was faulty, they would have the darkest and crispiest tan achievable.

In the outskirts of Mosul things started to look bleak. There was a noticeably increased presence in security and police check points. Blast walls and barriers were at every junction and heavily armed guards checked vehicles and people as they entered the control points. Every position was covered by towers and bunkers with heavy machine guns.

In the open waste areas to the left and right of the roads, the results of attacks and IEDs were clearly visible, burnt out vehicles and bomb craters here and there. I remember noting one vehicle in particular and thinking that no one could have survived it. It was on its roof and burnt throughout. It was obvious that it had been a PSD vehicle because even from a distance, I could see it had been an armoured SUV.

The buildings were closer together and the traffic got heavier. Slowing down in heavy traffic was always a vulnerable time because people are naturally nosey and look at the other vehicles they are side by side with. All we needed was to get noticed by the wrong person, then it would be a case of a quick phone call to his mates, and there would be an IED set up on the next junction or choke point, ready to detonate on us.

The rules of the road were treated with the same contempt as they were in Baghdad; if there's a gap, then go for it and it doesn't matter if it's on the wrong side of the road.

Once we were into the main part of the city, it became a nightmare. The traffic was hideous, and people who owned the market stalls at the side of the roads would inadvertently look in our direction. Sometimes I would notice a second glance and just had to hope they were a goody and not a baddy.

There were very few SUVs in Mosul at that time and so ours attracted a few stares. The best we could do was to ride it out and stick to our drills. We all wore civilian clothes with our armour and weapons concealed underneath. I had my pistol under my thigh for quick access whilst in the vehicle. My AK47 was at the side of my leg, out of sight, but easily brought to bear if we suddenly had trouble.

As we travelled, we constantly spoke over the radio. The lead scouts would be feeding us information on the road and possible obstacles ahead, and we would be giving our own observations over the net. Obviously, we kept the radios out of sight. It's no good trying to stay low profile and be clearly seen talking on a radio. Right away, we would be compromised as a PSD. So when we needed to speak to one another, we would keep the handset in our lap and speak down into it, without making it obvious. I had also grown a beard at this point and hoped it would help me pass as a local at a glance.

The central reservation doubled as a rubbish tip and a grazing area for cows and sheep. The livestock were actually sifting through the piles of filth, looking for food. I saw a cow eating a plastic bag and wondered how healthy a steak from it would be. The place was disgusting.

Everyone has had a moment when they've walked into a room or been somewhere and the whole atmosphere felt wrong. That's the feeling you can't help but get from Mosul. It was like a boiling lake of lava, bubbling away just beneath a thin crust of calm. Just from the sig-acts we read, we knew that at any moment, things could erupt.

Regular location reports were passed between the vehicles over the radio. We always tried to keep a few civilian vehicles between our own within the city. As long as we had line of sight with each other and could provide mutual support, it made sense to keep our distances. This was mainly to stop us from being noticed and also because if an IED went off, at least the whole team wouldn't be caught in the blast.

"Luke, three back, right hand lane," meant that I had two vehicles between myself and the client vehicle and I was over the commander's right shoulder if he needed to get eyes on with me.

"Roger that," was all that was needed in reply if the TL was happy.

On the open roads, it was given in distance rather than the number of vehicles between us.

"Spike, three hundred," meant he was three hundred metres from me and I would reply with my distance to the client car.

"Luke, two hundred,"

Then the reply from Gilly, "roger five hundred," meaning he's aware that the distance from himself to the CAT is five hundred metres with me roughly in between.

Everyday there were bombings, shootings and kidnappings in Mosul. Recently, the local Chief of Police had been abducted from outside his own home and found beheaded a few days later. No one was safe in Mosul. Even the different terrorist cells were constantly bumping each other off and a lot of men within the city, who had shaved their beards, were getting slotted because they weren't appearing Islamic enough.

A couple of months later, we received a chilling report of a young woman who had been found dead and mutilated in an alleyway. She had received a couple of prior warnings because of the way she dressed and demands were made for her to wear the usual Islamic clothes expected of women. She preferred to dress in a more western style and refused to change. One day, she was snatched and taken away and tortured to death. They had beat her half to death then, cut out her sexual organs including her breasts and beheaded her.

I had seen a beheading video on the internet and it's not a case of a swift blow to the neck with a big sword and the head comes off. They would tie the victim's hands and legs and with a butcher's style knife, they would hack away at the throat until they had cut right through the spinal column and the head had come clean off. During the whole ordeal, which took up to a minute, the person is awake and fully aware of what is happening to him or her, a horrific way to go.

We cracked on through the city, and to our relief, we hadn't encountered any trouble. Getting into the FOB was like pulling teeth. The American troops on the gate wanted to know even our shoe sizes and Grandmother's favourite colour. Each vehicle and man was searched top to bottom. It took almost two hours before we were given the thumbs up to pass through the gate.

Only a month earlier, a local worker who was contracted to work at the base, smuggled in a suicide vest and detonated it in the canteen during lunch, killing a large number of soldiers and civilians. We could understand why the soldiers were being extra vigilant.

Once in, we could relax and remove our body armour. The whole FOB was built around a palace and now instead of servants and marble floors inside, the place was full of soldiers and PSD companies, all in a maze of Operation's Rooms and communications equipment. While our client met with the Corp of Engineers Colonel, I went looking for Liam.

I found him sat outside his accommodation block, smoking a cigarette and chatting with another mate of ours, Jules. Jules had also been in 1 Para with us and as soon as they saw me, it was big group hugs and handshakes and man slaps on the back.

"Hey hey, Fun Size Frankie, what you doing here?" He shouted in his thick Geordie accent.

"Fuck off Fatty," was my usual reply to his references at my 5'7" compared to his 6'1".

Liam was as big as ever. Built like a barn door and from Newcastle, he was a monster of a man. He took the piss out of everyone and especially me. He was an excellent soldier and someone you could always rely on in a tight spot. However, Liam could never keep himself out of trouble and spent more time in front of the Company Commander for one atrocity or another than anyone else did.

No matter what the crime or how guilty he was, he would always give the shocked raised eyebrow look, as if the charge was something out of the blue and the last thing he expected due to his impeccable conduct.

With Liam, friendship was everything. If I asked him for his last couple of pounds, he would happily hand it over, even if it meant going without and being hungry himself. He was one of those types who could smoke and drink as much as he liked and only had to look at a gym to gain muscle. His fitness and strength were awesome and I hated him for it. So even though I always called him 'Fatty', he was far from it.

At the time, he was married to Lyndsey who he had met in Dover when we were based there. He had two young boys with her, James and Stewart, who he referred to as his 'little Spartans', and they were everything to him. He pulled out a picture of them and started gobbing off about how they were going to be in the gym everyday when they were old enough and learning how to fight the older boys.

Liam was an out and out rogue, but a lovable one at that. Back in battalion, he was constantly in trouble. Watching your step was never a consideration to Liam, and he wouldn't think twice about speaking his mind. If he thought you deserved it, a confrontation would be followed up with a crack in the mouth. He could start a fight in a monastery, and probably did at some point.

In the space of a couple of hours, we drank about eight cups of tea and smoked twenty cigarettes, swapping stories and jokes. Over the recent months, Liam and Jules had had a rough time of it and both thought themselves very lucky to be still breathing.

Jules asked me, "Did you see that burnt out SUV on your way into town?"

"The one on its roof, yeah I did, why?"

"I was fucking in it when it got fragged," he beamed.

They had been hit with an IED, followed up by small arms fire. The vehicle had been blown off the road and while it was on fire, he and the other three guys inside had to fight their way out while they were getting shot at from roof tops of surrounding buildings. Luckily, the rest of the team had reacted quickly and managed to take out the enemy positions while Jules and his teammates fought their way to safety. From what I was hearing, they were getting whacked near enough every time they left the FOB. But typical of Liam, he found it hilarious and told his stories as though they were lottery wins. None of us had ever been considered full shillings, but Liam wasn't even a half penny.

The company that Liam and Jules were working for had a contract with the U.S government. The Americans' had the best of everything, including weapons and equipment. Liam managed to grab our team some extra ammunition and medical kit from the stores, and even threw in some morphine and a few flash bangs.

A flash bang is a dummy grenade that makes a big flash and a loud bang, hence the name. The worst they can do is burst your ear drums and maybe crack your windows, but they're very affective at causing shock and confusion, especially in a confined space like the hospitals and sites we visited. If there was a drama and we needed to make a sudden exit, then a flash bang would help give us the time to withdraw.

After a few hours in the FOB catching up with old mates while the client finished his meetings, it was time to head back to Erbil. I said goodbye to Liam and Jules and we mounted up for our trip. We intended to take a different route through the city but we were limited on the rural roads. There were two that were practical without taking a massive detour. One of them was considered 'BLACK' at that time, which meant that no military or private security would be advised to use them. So we were left with one choice.

As we came through the city, we hit an overpass that ran over the road roughly west to east and we were travelling south. About four hundred metres ahead was a U.S military call sign travelling at their usual speed, super slow. We decided on staying with the flow of the traffic because we didn't want to be waving American flags in our windscreen in a place like Mosul. As far as everyone around us was concerned, we were locals, caught up in the usual traffic jams that lay in the wake of an American convoy.

Even from this distance, we could clearly see the large white warning sign on the back of the U.S vehicles, warning us in both English and Arabic to stay back one hundred metres. The Browning .50cal machinegun mounted above it broke the language barrier and spoke a thousand words.

Still, there were locals that for some reason, believed that the warnings didn't apply to them and they would approach at speed and try to overtake. A burst of half inch diameter rounds into the engine would normally be the end of their efforts.

The Browning .50cal is a fearsome heavy machinegun. Not only with the size of its rounds, but also its reliability. It has been in service with both the British and American Army since not long after the First World War, and even to this day, it's a great comfort knowing you have one or more of them supporting you.

The first time I had seen them used was when I joined my battalion after completing my recruit training. On a night time live firing exercise, we were told that the .50cals would be supporting us in the attack. When H-hour came, all we could hear was the big thundering boom of the guns opening up behind us. Because they were using tracer rounds, we could actually see them lit up red as they travelled towards the target. To me and many others, they looked like luminous tennis balls; they were so big compared to our 5.56mm ammunition.

So when a vehicle pushed out onto the outer lane and began to speed up towards the Americans, I thought right away that they were a suicide bomber or SVBIED that had a date with Allah and his very own seventy two virgins in Paradise.

It was a rusty old Opel saloon in the local taxi colours of orange and white. From where I was sat, I could see that the friendly call sign had spotted him and the .50cal had traversed and was pointed towards the possible threat. The problem was however, that we were also in his line of fire. If the young gunner let off a burst, there was a chance the rounds could always hit us too.

Most of the traffic had slowed to a crawl as soon as they had seen the convoy anyway, so it was easy enough for the TL to give, "Stop stop, go firm and stay in the vehicles."

Our scout car pushed over to the hard shoulder, roughly fifty metres ahead and we began to move to the right too when we heard the distinctive thudding of the heavy .50cal opening up on the suspected SVBIED. The rounds punching into the vehicle and the area immediately around it were clearly visible. Chunks of metal, rubber and tarmac flew all over the place in clouds of dust and holes the size of a fist appeared throughout the car.

Spike was about fifty metres back from me in the CAT vehicle, and I wasn't sure if he knew what was happening. As I watched the taxi disintegrate as it ground to a halt with its tyres, windows and engine shot to pieces, I gave Spike a sit-rep.

"Shots fired, shots fired. Not sure if you have eyes on Spike, but a local taxi just got splattered from the Yanks up ahead."

"Roger that mate. Have they done the driver too?" Spike asked.

"Not sure mate, but he got a burst of about thirty rounds into his car, so probably yes."

With the Americans now clearly jumpy after the shooting, we didn't fancy the idea of taking the same route the taxi had just gone. Too many times there had been blue on blue incidents because the young American soldiers were hyped up on adrenaline. Gilly gave us the word to turn back and we decided to pass through the town, taking the same route that we had taken coming in.

Travelling the same routes is setting patterns and a big NO-NO, but we had little choice at this time and we didn't want to be caught up in the incident. A lot of the local vehicles were turning at this point, so we followed suit and drove down the hard shoulder in the direction we had come.

As we turned, I glanced towards the chewed up taxi and saw no movement within. All the windows were gone and smoke and steam rose all around the vehicle. Whether he was a martyr or just a dickhead, it didn't matter but either way, he was pretty dead. I felt no pity or sorrow for the guy. This was Iraq and by now, everyone knew the rules. Plus, if he was a suicide bomber, then he deserved what he got.

After that, the journey back was uneventful and pretty easy going. It was the same route we had travelled but it was a different time of day. We got back to our compound and sorted out our administration. Weapons were cleaned and vehicles were fuelled and made ready for the next tasking.

After each mission, the cars needed to be prepared for the next one as it would be no good doing it in the last minute before a task. If there was something wrong with them, which often there was, we could get it repaired in plenty of time prior. Also, if something happened in the meantime and we needed to bug out, then they would be good to go.

After almost nine weeks in country, it was getting close to me going home for my four weeks leave. I couldn't wait. Even though I enjoyed the job and I got on great with my teammates, being stuck in each other's pockets and working near enough every day had started to take its toll and we all needed a break from each other.

On top of that, I wanted to get back home for some serious spending of some well earned money. I'd never had money like that before, so the idea of holidaying anywhere I wanted and walking into a shop and buying anything that tickled my fancy, was something I wanted to experience and experience a lot.

But until home time, it was work as usual and letting your guard down in the last few days isn't a good idea. I didn't want to end up like one of those cops in the movies who always seem to get killed the day before he retires.

We cracked on with the tasks and dreaming of home was for the evenings.

After a few more missions to the septic tanks they called hospitals and a few half built clinics, we had packed our bags and were waiting for our flights home. We were flying out through Erbil, which was easy and relaxed compared to Baghdad and not as corrupt. We flew from Iraq to

Jordan, stayed overnight in the Sheraton Hotel and got drunk beyond words.

The next morning, with a hangover that could cripple a Rhino and still with alcohol affecting my judgement, I went and bought the world's biggest watch for a ridiculous amount compared to my usual standards from the Duty Free shop in Jordan Airport. It felt great though, to just be able to do it. I felt like I'd hit the big time.

TEA PARTIES AND IEDS

———————◆———————

Wealth is relative. Compared to when I was in the army, I was rich and my leave was a hectic one. I spent most of it ensuring myself and the people around me, lived the high life and had the best of everything. But after four weeks of partying and spending like a man possessed, I was ready to get back to work. Even during my army days, I got restless easily and after just a couple of weeks of doing my own thing, I got bored and craved the adventure. Iraq wasn't exactly a playground but it was by no means dull.

It was the height of summer and before I landed this time, I hadn't realised it could get any hotter than when I had first arrived. It knocked the wind out of me and immediately I had a river running down my back.

Stan had been on the same flight and from what he was telling me, he had had a rather quiet leave with his wife and kids. He'd been doing this work a lot longer, so the novelty of the shopping sprees and high life had pretty much worn off for him and he used his money in a more prudent manner.

I was back in my old room again in the villa. With the money I was earning, I should've been looking at buying my own place while I was on leave but me being me, I decided to live in hotels and fancy holidays. So being back in our villa was more like my home.

There was a knock at the door as I was unpacking my kit and when I opened it, I thought I was in the shit. A huge guy of about 6'3" was stood before me with a completely shaved head, a football hooligan face and a look that said, "Hi, I'm your new roommate and my name is Bubba, now turn around and drop em."

Andy, as it turned out, wasn't half as scary as he looked. In fact, he was one of the most pleasant people I had ever worked with. Behind the football hooligan exterior was an extremely friendly and mild mannered guy, and as I was living in a small box type room, I was glad he wasn't to be my roommate and was just introducing himself. Still, I couldn't help picturing him playing the part of the stereotypical big guy with learning difficulties in a movie adaptation of a Stephen King novel.

A couple of other guys had joined us from other companies and, together with me and Stan; the four of us were to make a new team. Our call sign was P1, pronounced as 'papa one'. I was the baby of the bunch at just twenty eight years old, and the other three were in their early to mid forties.

Stan was to head up the team as the TL and I would be his 2ic or second in command. But the team itself was a single entity and everybody had their own skills and input to bring to the table. I also doubled up as the team medic, and in time, this job would become a real pain in the arse, especially where clients were involved.

Stan threw us straight into some training to shake off the cobwebs from leave and to help us gel as a team. We hadn't worked together before, so going out for a run around the compound in the midday heat was a good way to break us in.

For me, it was easy to do. I was young and fit and I spent the next thirty minutes listening to the Herefordshire accent of Paul as he huffed and puffed his way around the circuit, threatening to die on us. With both of us being ex Para Reg, Parachute Regiment, we had something in common and the fact that he could take a slagging really helped. Naturally, I gave him both barrels over his accent and from then on referred to him as 'Pointy Head'. Instead of getting upset, he played along and every now and then, he would make a stupid remark to make his self look like a bonehead. Already, I liked the team I was in.

We test fired our weapons and after Andy and Paul had zeroed their AK47s, we did a couple of hours of live pistol firing and went through a number of scenarios. Stan was big on his pistol training and I started to learn a lot from him. After leaving the Foreign Legion, he had joined 23 SAS, so his weapons training was a great asset to the team and every opportunity we had, we would get to the ranges to work on our skills.

Seaman and Semand would be our lead scouts in the team, with Stan and Andy in the lead armoured vehicle with the client. I was to be the chase car commander with Paul bringing up the rear with the CAT vehicle. Once again, I had Ahmed as my driver and by now, we had started to develop a good working relationship. He knew how I worked and what

I expected and even though he didn't speak English as well as some of the others, I found it easier to communicate with him. With the little Kurdish I knew and a great many hand signals and body language, we got along just fine.

We were in a gold armoured Mercedes and I had named it Polly. My idea was that if I made it personal to him, he would look after it and take pride in making sure everything was running smoothly. I didn't want my vehicle letting the team down due to neglect on my part. He even used to give it friendly pats on the dashboard and tell me, "Mr Luke, Polly is very good today."

We continued to visit the same sites as before, and the clients oversaw the construction and progress of the projects. Occasionally on the site, things would get pretty heated between the client and the construction managers. All of the projects were being built with U.S money, overseen by American engineers and contracted out to local construction companies.

Very often, the client wouldn't be satisfied with the progress of the building or the standard of the work so, arguments would break out between them. At these times, we would have to be on our guard because it wouldn't take much for someone to say the wrong thing. Near enough every man and his dog in Iraq carry some sort of weapon, be it a pistol or even a knife, and if they feel their honour is being insulted, there's always a chance they would use it.

One of our clients was a big American named Randy and he took about as much crap as the grease proof toilet paper you get at school. One day, he shut down a whole site because the standards were below what is required and was dangerous as far as he was concerned. He resigned over the following argument that ensued with his company management a short time later. I had to wonder what the point was in bringing these western construction and electrical engineers to help out, when they are subsequently given a hard time while trying to do their jobs.

Other than the odd little glitch during tasks, things went pretty smoothly for our team. When we weren't working or training, we would be drinking tea. We were like a group of little old English ladies sat in the garden having tea afternoons. It was good for the team moral, and being able to sit on the loungers, gobbing off at each other or discussing upcoming jobs under the trees in the garden feeling the grass under your feet, was a small taste of home to us. Paul deliberately made himself the butt of most of the jokes but Andy, just from his appearance, attracted a lot of remarks. For some reason, he always had one trouser leg riding four inches higher than the other. I never could work out why.

It was a run of the mill task to a site on the southern outskirts of Erbil. As usual, I was in the second armoured vehicle. We had visited a clinic that was under construction and were on our way through the town, back to the villa. The streets were packed with vehicles crammed bumper to bumper. In this area of the city, most of the regional administrative offices and buildings were located for the Erbil region. I was midway through giving our position to our HQ over the radio when, a huge whooshing noise mixed with a thunderous bang rocked the call sign.

The blast wave hit our vehicle, causing us to rock violently and throwing us about in our seats. My ears burst and my head felt like it was caught in a vacuum for a moment as all the air was momentarily forced from the car. It was a big explosion and enough to rattle my brain and leave my hearing impaired for a while afterwards. It was hard to focus for a few seconds as my eyes rolled around in their sockets and my brain tried to sit still from bouncing about inside my skull. The loud ringing in my ears sounded like a whistle being blown close by my head.

We were enveloped in a cloud of debris and nothing could be seen other than the brown and grey billowing swirls of dust around us. I automatically thought we had been hit by an IED. With ears ringing and eyes squinting, trying to see through the cloud of smoke that was quickly surrounding us, I tried to get an idea of what had happened.

I shouted over the radio to the other vehicles and our Op's Room, "IED left, IED left," knowing that when something like that comes over the radio, all other teams in the area will go silent in case we needed to use the net to call for medical and fire support or send situation reports.

I could see figures moving through the haze and by the looks of things they were very disoriented and confused. Bouncing off bumpers and car bonnets, just trying to put some distance between the danger and themselves. No doubt many were injured in one form or another. Ahmed steered us to the far right lane in case we needed to mount the curb for a quick bug out if there was a follow up with small arms and machineguns.

Paul was closest to the explosion and reported that from what he could see, a VBIED had gone off over the other side of the central reservation in front of one of the government building.

The whole team reported in and we confirmed everyone was okay with no injuries and all vehicles were still good and mobile.

"Push to the right lads. There's a police checkpoint up ahead so we'll see if we can get out of the immediate area with the client," Stan ordered through the radio.

We knew the police and Peshmerga guards would be a little twitchy considering what had just happened, so we let our scout drivers approach them first to explain who we were and due to having western clients with us, we needed to get to a safe zone in case of any follow up.

Once we got the thumbs up over the radio from Seaman, we moved up and got waved through the barricades. The guards looked nervous and gave us a good look over as we passed through. No doubt they would be soon feeling anger and rage because more than likely, they had friends in the guard force protecting the building that had just been hit.

Other than us, no one was permitted to leave the vicinity. For all they knew, there could have been terrorists in a vehicle initiating or filming the whole thing, which they very often did with a view to posting it on the internet, claiming a great victory for Islam and praising the martyr who had just blown his self up.

Our main concern was the safety of the client and the team, so we headed back to the protection of the compound. On the way, we gave George in the Op's Room a sit-rep, letting him know everyone was okay and we were returning to base, RTB. Other than that, there was no information we could give him on what had actually happened.

The whole city had come to a standstill. Very little traffic was moving, while all the pedestrians were glued in place and looking in the direction of the explosion. I just hoped that no one thought we had anything to do with it because we were the only people heading away from the scene. The smoke and dust still hung in the air around the area of the explosion as I looked back. It was chaos.

When we arrived back at HQ, even the compound guards were on edge and their security checks of us and the vehicles were a little more thorough than usual, even though they knew us by sight. Still, it's best to be on the safe side and I was grateful they weren't likely to let anything in that could put a hole in our villa or swimming pool.

The client was clearly shaken and asked question after question about what had happened. We told him he would receive a full briefing, along with the rest of the clients, as soon as we knew the details. In the meantime, as the team medic, I advised him to go and pour himself a large whisky and thank his lucky stars we were on the other side of the road when his 'come to Jesus' moment happened.

"Fuck this, I feel a little shaken too and I've a bottle of whisky in my room so I'm off for a wee nip and a lie down," Paul announced.

I had brought back a large box of Yorkshire Tea with me from leave; a habit I still have to this day in fact. Just a few weeks into the rotation and with the garden tea parties, I was running low, so I joined him for a 'wee nip'.

Until the full details of what had happened came out, the whole compound was on lock down. This meant that no teams, from any company at all, were to travel out. It was very rare that something like this happened in Erbil, so when it did, it was a huge to do. There was nothing for us to do except sort out our kit and vehicles and of course, have a tea party with Stan, Andy and Paul. Speculation on what had happened was rife. Later we were given a full heads up on the day's events.

A dumper truck, packed with explosives had been driven through the security wall of one of the government buildings and into the foyer then, detonated by the driver. The explosion ripped through the building killing dozens of workers and guards. It was unknown who had actually done it at the time, but later, a particular terrorist cell claimed responsibility. It seemed to me that in the Kurdish regions, including Erbil, where everything was generally peaceful; the bad guys from further south would now and then hit them big just to prove that they can if they wanted.

Erbil soon recovered and within no time, it was up and running again. It never ceased to amaze me how easily people in Iraq accepted things and got on with it.

It was around this time that the bombings in London happened. America had had their introduction to Islamic terror, and now it was the turn of Britain. For over thirty years the British people had been used to terror attacks from the IRA, and now there were these fresh attacks in the name of Islamic Fundamentalism. The difference in these bombings was the sheer scale and the indiscrimination of how they were carried out. The IRA tended to have specific targets, but Islamic terror in my eyes, seemed completely random and aimed to cause as much death and destruction as possible to the people themselves. There were no warnings and the attacks killed dozens of innocent people as they commuted to work.

One of the worst twists that came out afterwards was that the people responsible were British Muslims living in the U.K. It disgusted me that Islamic groups from Britain even praised and encouraged more attacks like 7/7 and 9/11, but nothing was ever done to stop them from spreading their hatred. Locking up or deporting the odd rogue Imam doesn't exactly instil confidence in the U.K's fight on terror for me, especially when there were Muslim protesters turning up on the streets, dressed in mock suicide vests, and threatening the country with fresh attacks.

As far as I was concerned, the protesters making the threats should have been arrested and charged with High Treason and then executed by hanging.

Guards were brought in to provide security for our villa. Even though we were in a secure compound, our company head shed didn't want to take any chances. It was a prudent move, and soon many other companies in other villas followed suit. Most would hire local guards and police as static protection. Our company splashed out and brought in Ghurkhas from Nepal. These guys were great. No matter how long they had been standing there on duty, they still had huge grins on their faces, as though they had just done something they shouldn't have.

There was never a middle ground or cutting corners with Ghurkhas. If they were given a job to do, they did it to the full. Even if there was an easier way of doing it, they would stick to their original instructions and see it through to the letter. And on top of their professionalism, they never had a glum moment.

They all lived in a four man room just a couple of doors down from me in our villa and I could always hear them singing their songs and giggling like little kids at each other. The whole villa soon took on the aroma of The Ghurkha Village restaurant in Aldershot from the cooking they were constantly doing. Instead of using the kitchen like the rest of us, they would insist on cooking in their rooms as a group. One or two dishes they knocked up smelled highly suspect, more so after I'd noticed that there were several dogs and cats less than there had been before in the compound. In spite of this, their scoff was great and I would always ask for a taste.

I had worked with Ghurkhas a few times during my army service and always found them to be a good bunch. They were natural jungle soldiers and I learned to admire them during a Long Range Patrol course I attended in Brunei. We nicknamed them 'Tree Frogs'. It was never a racist slur as some people may see it; it was more of an acknowledgement of their natural ability in the jungle environment.

I'm no giant, but their average height was about 5'4" and we could never find uniforms to fit them properly. So in the end, to save them from looking stupid while trying to do a serious job, we took the uniforms they had and got them tailored in town. The look of gratitude on their faces afterwards was a picture. After that, they had the habit of saluting us and holding car doors open as we loaded up to go out on task. We explained to them it wasn't necessary and eventually they stopped.

After a while, they became comfortable enough with us to just give us a wave and a grin. Not bad going considering none of them spoke a word of English except the word 'yes'. You could ask them anything at all and they would answer, 'yes,' while nodding their heads as though their life depended on it and grinning inanely at you. If only they knew half of what I was asking them.

Mark insisted he needed to go to Mosul to check on a site. Mark was a client who never really understood the risks and the nature of our job and assumed that if we were there to look after him, then all would be right with the world and there would be no problem.

Part of our job was Risk Assessment, and travelling to Mosul just for the sake of Mark getting out of the office for the day, was an unnecessary risk in our eyes. But he insisted it was mission critical and he needed to go. So in the end, we had to give ground.

It was never a case of us not wanting to do the jobs or being scared, but more to do with us doing our job correctly and avoiding risks to the clients and ourselves. On top of this, every time we visited places, we were watched and there was then a risk to the workers themselves for collaborating with westerners.

Nevertheless, we went into the planning and preparation of the task and like always, it was thorough and nothing was left out. We aimed to spend no longer than twenty minutes at the site, then bug out back to our HQ so there was minimum exposure on the ground. We explained this to Mark over and over to try and hit home the need for him to get a move on once we had debussed from our vehicles, and not to bother with the big handshakes and chit chat with the locals.

The site itself was a hospital that was already in use and currently being renovated, so it was going to be a whirlwind tour of the place then back to the vehicles. Mark assured us he knew exactly what he needed to see and that he would stick to our timings.

Paul was to control the outer security cordon while Stan, Andy and I would take the client in. We borrowed two extra local guys from the other team to act as additional protection on the ground once we got there. One would travel in my vehicle and the other, would be with Paul in the CAT. Both would debus once we went static and protect the entrance to the hospital as we took the client inside.

Everything was covered and set to go. It took us two days to plan and prepare for the job and everybody knew what was expected of them.

We took a longer route into Mosul this time and approached from the north. That way, the hospital would be on our side of the road and there would be no need for any U-turns that would give us away as a team in convoy. Travelling through the built up areas was the same as before; a nightmare. Even though we had set out from Erbil at first light, by the time we reached Mosul, it was mid morning and everywhere we looked there were people and cars crammed into every available space.

Getting to the hospital was no problem in itself, but when we got there we found out the view from the road outside, led straight into the main car park and the front of the building. Once we turned off the main drag, we were pretty much on top of the hospital and the parking areas and entrance were below the level of the surrounding buildings, giving anybody who was interested a perfect over watch.

We knew right away that we were compromised and that before long, certain sorts would be getting phone calls, informing them of the activities going on at the hospital. The vehicles were parked as close to the exit as possible and the CAT car pretty much blocked off the entrance to the car park. The locals weren't happy, but we couldn't take chances. We had gone from a low profile vehicle move to a high profile security team once we were static; with weapons visible and our guards covering all possible firing points.

As we pulled up to the entrance, I got out first as always to give the area a once over, before giving Stan the all clear to bring the client in. This time, Andy was to get out too and one of our locals would take his place behind the wheel of the client vehicle. Every car needed to be manned and ready to move at the first sign of trouble.

Mosul had the same hygiene problems as everywhere else in Iraq, and their hospitals were no exception. As I started my clearance of the immediate area, I noticed the smell of raw sewage.

The septic tank was only a few meters from the entrance and was more of an open pit, lined with bricks, and filled with shit. Though I didn't relish the idea of it, I still had to stick my head over to make sure there were no surprises waiting for us and right away, I wished I hadn't. It was like I'd snorted the stuff and wedged some in each nostril. As I walked away, gagging, I made a mental note to hold my breath in future when checking unknown areas.

The outside of the building was dusty and dirty, and near enough every window was cracked or covered up with cardboard. Weeds grew everywhere and if I hadn't known better, I would have thought the building was derelict. I made my way to the entrance and Andy was stood between the doors and the client vehicle, waiting to escort Stan and Mark through. I gave him a nod and informed Stan over the radio that I was about to clear the foyer.

Once inside, I checked the corridors left and right and the main offices and reception that were directly in front of me. When I was happy the area was secure, I called Stan in and within a few moments he and Andy were in the building with Mark. The interior was stuffy and had the same smells as the Erbil hospitals, rotten blood and human waste.

Andy and I were carrying our AK47s running down the right side of our bodies, on a short sling attached to our shoulder, so that they could be brought to bear in a split second. Stan carried just his pistol in the holster on his hip. This was mainly because, if he was trying to handle a flapping client during a drama, he wouldn't be able to use the AK47 effectively so, his main job was to protect the client and extract him while Andy and I gave fire support with our AK47s. All of us were made ready, meaning the weapons had a round in the chamber and it was just a case of bringing the weapon up and at the same time, flicking off the safety catch to fire.

I took the lead as we travelled through the hospital and Andy brought up the rear, Mark was safely in the middle with Stan close on his right hand side wearing him like a pair of underpants. If anything happened, the first thing Stan would do would be to push Mark down into a crouch, making him as small a target as possible, while me or Andy dealt with the threat, depending on the direction it came from.

I was thankful I'd managed to get the flash bangs from Liam because they were perfect for this sort of scenario. If it was to suddenly become unfriendly and we were attacked, I could quickly pull the pin and there would be a huge flash and bang, instantly stunning everyone in the immediate vicinity, no doubt including the client. All we would have to do then is extract as quickly as possible while everybody else was wondering what had just happened.

Moving through the hospital, I had to constantly let Stan know what was at the next turn in order for him to build up a picture in his head which would in turn, help him to make better judgements if it was called for. The place was packed with people. Mainly women, but there were groups of men here and there, smoking and talking quietly as they always seemed to be in these places.

As soon as they saw me enter a room or corridor, they would go silent, then as Stan and Andy came into view, there would be whispers and muffled talking between them. I didn't get the impression they liked us all that much. But whatever they thought, just the sight of us and the AK47s was enough to let them know we weren't there for a check up.

It was the generators that Mark needed to overlook and once there, I stayed in the open area leading into the corridor, while Andy guarded the entrance to the generator room. Stan proceeded inside with Mark and the hospital site manager to do what he needed to do.

Five minutes later, through my ear piece I heard Stan informing, "Task complete, that's us heading back towards you Luke."

"Roger that. Stan's towards me. You get that Pointy Head? We'll be out in roughly five mate." I informed Paul.

"No worries. All's good to go out here."

At best speed, we moved through the hospital and once again we had the same looks of surprise from the patients and visitors as though we had just landed in a spaceship. We gave them no time to admire us and moved on as quickly as possible towards the exit. As we approached, I gave warning to Paul that we were about to leave the building and that was his nod to have the protection ready to mount up once the client was in his vehicle and secure. I moved straight to the rear left passenger door of Stan's Mercedes and opened it. Mark, without stopping, slipped in and buckled himself up. Stan moved to the front passenger side and Andy relieved the local guy in the driver's seat.

All the team were heading to their vehicles and Paul and Stan stayed at the side of theirs to cover me as I made my way to mine. I heard the distinct loud crack of rounds going overhead.

When bullets pass over, you hear a loud snap, like the crack of a whip. This is the bullet displacing the air as it travels. Then you hear the thump, which is actually the sound of the bullet leaving the barrel of the gun. The round travels faster than the speed of sound, so you hear it's crack first and, depending on how far away the firing point is, the thump can be as long as a couple of seconds after it. This way, you can judge the distance between yourself and the firing point. If all you hear is the crack of the bullet and no thump, it's normally because they're firing from close by.

They didn't seem too close but they were close enough for Stan to call, "shots fired, shots fired," over his radio.

My weapon was brought up in to the shoulder and I thumbed the safety catch to fire as I turned, checking rooftops for the firing point. At the same time, I was headed for my vehicle, to safe cover. All vehicles locked down with everyone loaded up safe inside, and we headed for the exit with haste. Once there, we wasted no time and hit the main drag leaving whatever was going on, far behind in our wake.

The drill had gone as smooth as we could have wished for. Because we weren't actually taking fire or the rounds weren't landing around us, then it was ineffective and there was no need for us to react by shooting back. On top of that, we didn't know where they had come from or who they were intended for. For all we knew, it was just some guy celebrating his oldest son's birthday by firing a burst off, or a guard giving warning shots to someone. Nevertheless, we didn't know the intent of whoever fired them so we bugged out. Murphy's Law of Combat: 'Friendly fire isn't all that friendly'.

We got back to our villa and Mark was over the moon with his little adventure. As far as he was concerned, we were the dog's bollocks and the best security team in the world. So much so, he arranged a barbeque for both our teams and the clients later that night. He even bought the beers.

Two days later, we received a report that the site manager for the Mosul project had been abducted. A ransom was then demanded, and only due to his family selling their house, his car and cashing in the business, were they able to pay the hostage takers and get him released. He lost everything, but managed to keep his head on his shoulders.

At the end of each month, the local project managers from all the sites would meet at the villa in our compound. They would receive their pay and at the same time, meetings would be held to discuss any important matters regarding the construction.

At the end of that month, the manager from Mosul came along with the others. It had been agreed that he should receive some sort of compensation for his loss, so he was given a bonus. The clients themselves even chipped in to help pay him off and asked if we, the security teams, would also donate.

Personally, I thought it was a load of crap and didn't throw anything into the pot, but one or two others with much larger hearts than me couldn't bear to see the poor guy down on his luck. It wasn't that I didn't care, but I was there to make money for myself, not to be a charity for the down and out of Iraq.

At least two expats were always in the immediate area with concealed weapons as the payments and meetings were going on in case somebody got upset with a client. Even in our villa, we were still on standby and ready to protect our principal. I sat in the garden with Paul and Stan as we watched the contractors file in and out of the office receiving their pay from the administration staff.

It was shameful so see the guy who had just lost everything he had worked his whole life for, leaving the office with a few thousand dollars as compensation and many pats on the back from the clients, who were still sitting very pretty but pretending to care.

I may have not donated, but at least I wasn't false. I wanted to suggest that they each give half their monthly salary to him, in order for him to begin rebuilding his business and home.

Stan kept me in check and I bit my tongue.

After this incident, it was discussed with the clients about future jobs to Mosul and only mission critical tasks would be considered. It was an unnecessary risk and someone had ended up paying with his livelihood. Luckily, it wasn't his life. Afterwards, Mark had to wind his neck in and didn't ask to go to Mosul again.

After returning from a job in the city a few weeks later, I walked into my room and was hit with a blast of extremely hot air. Somebody had turned my air conditioning on full heat. Outside in the street it was in the late forties Celsius and in my room, it was roughly the same temperature to cook a Sunday roast. Only after I switched it off did I realise that everything in my room had been gently and neatly placed upside down. I knew right away it was an old mate stitching me up, but I couldn't think of who it could be.

We used to do similar things when we were in the army. One guy even deployed onto a two week exercise during the middle of winter to discover that, someone had replaced his sleeping bag with a few scabby dog blankets.

Nothing had been damaged and great care had been taken to even tie extremely tight knots into the sleeves of the shirts and trousers in my wardrobe. I headed for my laptop in the hope it had been left alone. I couldn't have been more wrong. It was now flooded with gay porn pictures and whoever was responsible had gone to a lot of effort. It was going to take me a long time to put everything back to normal.

I went into the Op's Room to see who it could be and I ran slap bang into Liam, standing there with a huge grin on his face.

"Alright Frankie, have you been to your room yet?" It was typical of Liam.

"Yeah I have you fat twat. You must've spent hours doing that. What you doing here anyway? I thought you were still based in Mosul."

Liam was in his element knowing his efforts were going to cost me an entire evening stumbling across more of his handy work as I put my room back together.

"I'm with your lot now. I cross decked and I'm going to be working in Suli. Cushy number too, because we're based out of the Palace Hotel."

"Great stuff buddy. We sometimes stopover in the same hotel so no doubt I'll be able to get my own back."

Liam, being the big hearted guy he was, decided he would sit and have a brew while he watched me rearrange my room back to how it had been. He even sat pointing out things I had missed, like the fact that he had nailed my flip flops to the wardrobe floor.

Nevertheless, it was great to have him onboard and working for the same company as myself. Especially seeing as he would be based in the next city along, just a few hour's drive from Erbil. At least once a week we would visit the Sulimania sites and because of the distance involved, it was normally close to last light by the time we finished so we would usually stayed over in the Palace Hotel because it was against company SOP's to travel in the dark.

The Palace Hotel was considered to be secure. It was surrounded with blast walls. Armed Peshmerga guards controlled who came in twenty four hours a day. Very often, government officials and foreign delegates would meet there to discuss matters. Even by western standards, it was a pretty good hotel. The rooms and the service were of a good standard and I never had any complaints.

Other Iraqi hotels I've stayed in have claimed to be five stars, and I think the reason for this could only be because they had running water. One hotel we stayed in was up in the mountains and had no heating. During one winter night we were so cold I almost asked Andy for a cuddle.

I did manage to get my own back on Liam. A couple of weeks later, during a visit to Suli, I managed to get into his room and removed the plugs from any electrical equipment he had, including his laptop and TV. He hit the roof, and it was only after leaving the next morning to head back to Erbil that I gave him a call, telling him where he could find the map leading him to his plugs.

I couldn't make it that simple for him though, and one map led to another map and to another until eventually, he discovered his treasure on the far side of the car park behind a skip. It wasn't until the morning after when he realised I had also stolen every pair of his socks too, so he travelled around barefoot for the next day or so before he managed to get replacements.

All in all, I saw Liam regularly and we never failed to have a laugh and a catch up together. For the next couple of years, we would be working in the same areas and sometimes in the same security bases.

Ramadan is a Muslim festival that lasts for thirty days in September and October and is always a dramatic time in Iraq. During these days, the locals would fast themselves from dawn until dusk every day and feast at night. Some of our lads would of course be fasting too, though I once caught one of them hiding behind the CAT vehicle, eating a tuna sandwich. He seemed to think that God couldn't see him so he was okay.

There were certain days during this period when the budding martyrs and heroes would happily throw their lives away because they believed that if they died in battle during the 'Night of Power' for instance, in the latter stages of Ramadan, they would receive three times as many virgins in Paradise.

It's not hard to do the math, and I could never understand why anyone would want two hundred and sixteen inexperienced women to party with. I'd prefer a little variety myself and go for a mixed bag option of one third virgins, one third experienced and the other third, complete sluts. At least that way I wouldn't have to teach them all from scratch and I could treat myself now and then.

During these times, we would be locked down and the sites would be closed. Even the American army would think twice about patrolling in some areas because Ramadan was like a full moon to lunatics for some. Terrorist groups would increase their attacks in frequency and scale and with the promise of rewards in Paradise; they would be much braver also. So the lockdown periods were a sort of holiday for us. Our locals wouldn't be brought in and the time would be our own to train, relax and generally take a breather. Though being in Erbil and the relatively easy going environment of the Kurdish city, the lock downs weren't all that often. Still, they were appreciated when they came along.

On one occasion, the clients decided they all wanted full medical checks from the team medic. I was there to patch bullet holes and such, not a General Practitioner.

Most of them had some sort of ailment or other. A life time of chilli fries and super size everything had taken its toll. One client, a hugely overweight and unhealthy American guy, was complaining of having sore feet. So I was called across to have a look. I've never been a fan of people's feet so when I saw that he was wearing Gortex walking boots and thick woolly socks, I knew I was in for a treat.

"Firstly, tell me John, why are you wearing waterproof boots and winter socks during September while the weather is still in the forties?" I asked him.

He just sat there, with his big red puffed out cheeks, scratching his head. His whole attitude towards me was that I should just come in and cure him, and I had no right to speak to him or tell him off.

During the summer in Iraq, I always wear desert boots and thin sports socks. These were lightweight so my feet could breath. When I wasn't working, I would be walking around in just my flip flops and bare feet in order to get plenty of air to them. It was something that was taught to us from very early on when we joined the army. Your feet are your means of transport. If they're in a shit state, then you won't get far and before long, you'll become a casualty that others then have to deal with and look after.

Wearing Gortex boots and woolly socks during the summer was the worst thing anyone could do. Especially if you were just sat in an office and not going out on a task. I really couldn't understand it. While he was sitting there, his feet were sweating and the moisture was being trapped in the boot itself, making his feet slowly rot away.

I told him to remove his shoes and socks and he did so after looking at me as though he expected me to do it for him. I was losing my patience and I had to bite my tongue as best I could. As soon as his feet were out, I could smell the putrid odour from them and I felt even angrier for being put in that position due to his stupidity.

There was no way I was going to touch them, but I could see he had trench foot.

"John, your feet are rotting from under you. You've got trench foot and it'll get worse if you don't sort them out. Keep them dry and clean. Don't put your boots back on and keep your feet uncovered and in the open air."

"How?" He replied, sounding more confused than if I had just asked him to give an in depth explanation of nuclear fusion to a five year old, speaking in French.

I clenched my teeth and even considered drawing him a picture to explain.

"Get some sandals on while you're in the office and wash them twice a day, then use foot powder." It wasn't rocket science.

After that, I then had to attend to even the local administration personnel who were complaining of all sorts, from sore throats and in-growing hairs to headaches and upset stomachs.

Stan found it hilarious, and I could see him and Paul giggling and drinking tea in the garden as I set up my practice in the administration office. One local even came to me, asking about his bad eye sight. I was sure someone had put him up to it, but then I realised he was serious.

When one turned up with a cigarette in his mouth, complaining of a chesty cough and shortness of breath, I almost hit him. I decided I'd had enough and closed up shop for the day.

Things continued in a routine way for us and with constant site visits and meetings in FOBs, it was inevitable that people would become bored and move on. Thankfully, we had four weeks at home after every eight to recuperate and relax.

During a leave at Christmas, I met a girl named Lisa, from Sunderland. We had a great leave together, and I now had something to look forward to when I came home. It mainly consisted of partying, eating out and holidaying, but we were both more than happy with that. Most of the lads had either wives or girlfriends at home, and it could be a strain on a relationship being away. I knew many guys that left the job altogether as their relationship was crumbling because of it.

There were a few personality clashes within the teams and as a result of one Stan was moved onto another contract in another city. I was sad to see him go. The size of the teams was cut too, going from two teams of expats to just one team.

Paul and Andy also moved on and I was placed into a team with Dave and Ash. Matt had been brought in as our new TL and things continued as before. The workload however, increased because just one team was now covering all the sites with the clients. I was becoming worn out and short tempered through lack of time to myself.

During visits to Dianna, a town in the far north, we had to travel through the mountain passes. These roads were narrow and at some places there would be a sheer cliff face on your left and a straight drop on your right into the valley below.

Some people would think of them as beautiful and scenic, but I saw them as perfect ambush sites and accidents waiting to happen. Our clients would always want a five minute stop to stretch their legs and take photographs at the highest and best looking peaks. It always reminded me of the Lake District or Wales when we stopped at a particularly nice spot. I would look down into the void to see the rivers and lakes below. However, the big piles of discarded plastic bottles and oil cans at the side of the road always reminded me that, we were in Iraq.

We were in Kurdistan and our main threat in these areas, were traffic accidents. Even here, on the narrow mountain roads, people would still insist on overtaking at great risk to themselves and the other vehicles on the road. On more than one occasion, I found myself breathing in and holding onto the door handle as though I could actually bail out if need be.

Being British, we were all animal lovers, especially towards dogs. On one visit we noticed a pack of wild pups by the roadside on our way into the town. They couldn't have been more than a couple of months old and just looked like little balls of beige and grey fur.

On our return leg, from my position in the second vehicle, I noticed there was only the one pup now. I thought nothing of it and the drive continued as normal.

When we reached the villa, Dave who had been the CAT commander, jumped out with said little ball of beige and grey fur under his arm.

"I couldn't just leave him there. He looked well and truly pissed off so we stopped and I nabbed him," he offered as an explanation, "he's shit all over the back seat though."

One of my main gripes in Iraq was the way the people treated animals. Dogs, horses, donkeys and even birds of prey such as hawks and falcons were abused and beaten just for the sake of it.

I once saw one of the most stunning horses I'd ever seen, standing in the middle of a rubbish tip with a metre of wire around its leg and staked to the floor. It was a huge shiny black beauty.

It was midsummer and the horse had no shelter or even water. It didn't take a genius to realise the poor thing was suffering, yet people walked by it as though it wasn't there.

Driving from town to town you would see dozens of dead dogs at the roadside. Having been hit by cars, they were left to die. Even donkeys, an animal that tends to look pissed off whatever country they're from, look even more so in Iraq.

From then on, we had our very own dog that would never stop barking and leaving little presents around the villa gardens for us to step in.

We knew the contract was coming to an end but not the exact date. We guessed and heard around July time maybe, but towards the end of March, when we suddenly got told to close everything down and pack up, we were surprised to say the least.

We were shocked to be told that we had just three days to do it.

Worse still, was that the contract had come to an end and there were no more positions within the company for us to move to, so we were to be sent home. I was happy to get home and have a break because I was due for leave anyway, but I didn't like the prospect of looking for a new contract with a different company.

Our head shed told us that something may eventually come up but nothing in the immediate future, so it was a case of being prepared to work for another company. I'd been working for the same company for around fourteen months and for some reason, I felt like I'd just been kicked out of my home.

I went to Rome for a week long holiday. Life was still great, but soon, I would need to be on the hunt for more work and a return to Iraq.

High Profile and the Dirty Dozen plus Three

After I had taken a couple of months off, I was offered a contract with a high profile company. I didn't really need the break, but it was nice to be able to take some time to have a breather. Secretly, I was also hoping that during this time more work would come through with my old company. Unfortunately, they had hit a severe dry patch and the company as a whole was downsizing with men finding themselves in the same boat as me.

After spending most of my leave living like a pop star, I decided to take the contract I was offered. I didn't cherish the thought of working overt because, from what I had seen, they were nothing but bomb and bullet magnets. I had a few friends working for similar companies and what I was hearing, didn't fill me with enthusiasm for the job.

After working in Iraq for over a year, conducting my SOP's and tactics in a way in which the main aim was not to draw attention to myself and to blend in, going in the opposite direction felt alien to me. Nevertheless, I needed a contract and the company I was about to start with, had a relatively good reputation for their conduct and professionalism.

I was given a rough heads up via email on the job, the contract and what was expected of me. It was a U.S government contract and I discovered that I would be covering the same sites as I had already on my last job. When my last client company had closed down, the United States Army Corp of Engineers, USACE, had taken them over completely. At least I had advanced knowledge of the ground and a rough idea of what the locations we would be visiting would be like. Whether it was in the north or the south of the country, these clinics were built to the same blue print. It was just the environment they were in that was going to change.

I met a close army buddy of mine on the flight from Jordan to Baghdad and we ended up sitting together. Hutch had been working in Iraq for about a year longer than me and had been with the same company all the way through.

We had shared a room when we were in A Company 1 Para together and, like Liam, he loved to stitch me up. During the flight, the air stewards kept coming to my seat, asking if I was okay and after the fifth time or so, they were looking a little angry. I couldn't understand why they were showing so much interest in me until I realised that every time I wasn't looking, Hutch was pressing the flight attendant button above my chair. It made me remember how much I had to be on my guard around him.

When we shared a room, we couldn't leave each other's sight for fear of what the other would do to the other's kit in their absence. He once broke in to my wardrobe while I was out, and ironed razor sharp creases down the front of every pair of jeans I had, and this was while I was out getting a takeaway for the both of us out of the goodness of my own heart. I got my own back by pissing over his TV and when he turned it on, it exploded. After that, we called an amnesty.

I arrived in Baghdad airport during early summer. As I've already pointed out, even early spring in Iraq is like a heat wave in the UK, so it was back to shade hugging and drinking water like I was trying to break a record.

In just a year since I'd been travelling to and from Iraq, the airport had changed. It seemed more organised and less corrupt. This meant that I was going to have to queue to get through passport control, which pissed me off. I've never been the patient sort when it comes to waiting in lines.

This time, I brought plenty of kit with me. Instead of travelling light as when I started my last contract, I decided to make sure I had everything I needed. Having mates already working for the company helped and I could get their advice on what kit I needed and what they recommended. It was to be a twelve week on and four week off rotation and I didn't fancy the idea of roughing it for the duration so, I made sure I had plenty of everything.

My most important piece of equipment was my body armour. I had bought my own when I was on my first leave and it was the best buy I'd ever made. Though it was expensive, it was worth every penny. It was much more comfortable and less bulky than most sets we get issued and more importantly, I knew its exact condition and history. Sort of like a car with its services. Body armour is usually made of a Kevlar soft armour vest that can stop shrapnel and low velocity pistol rounds like 9mm and even

.357 Magnum slugs, with the armour plates fitted over the top. The vest I had could stop armour piercing rounds from an AK47, so I was happy to splash out.

When you join a company, you get issued standard kit and equipment from them and you can never tell what condition the body armour is in. For all you know, the last guy who used it may have dropped it at some point with the plates fitted. All it takes is a hairline crack in a plate and that literally becomes the proverbial chink in the armour. With having my own vest, I always made sure I treated it with the utmost care, being careful not to bash it about, and it went everywhere with me.

Even when I travelled through Dubai, back and forth from leave, the airport security staff would always try to confiscate it from me but I would argue the toss and eventually, they would give up and let me keep it. There was no way I was going to let some rag head bully my shiny GUCCI body armour away from me and keep it for himself to show off to his mates.

After collecting my bags and passing through security, I walked into the arrivals lounge and spotted my pick up team right away. I couldn't miss them.

Dressed in the company colours, both of them were around the same height as basketball players and built like shot putters. I made my way towards them.

They looked down at me and asked, "Are you Luke?" in Eastern European accents.

"Yeah, that's me."

I was trying to work out where they were from and before I had the chance to ask them, they led me off towards the car park area. It wasn't exactly a warm welcome, but I didn't expect banners and balloons anyway.

I tagged along as they both spoke to each other in their own language. The penny dropped after listening to them for a minute or two and I recognised a few words and phrases. They were Serbian.

I'd met many Serbs during the liberation of Kosovo, and even though we had been pumped full of propaganda, telling us that they were the bad guys, I soon discovered that they were more like us than the Albanians who we were apparently going in to save. Within the first day of the invasion I realised, along with many others in my battalion, we were on the wrong side, but that's a different story.

When we got to the vehicles, I realised that the whole team were Serbian. I would later find out that they were the HQ team for the company. Their job was to pick up and drop off clients and employees to and from the airport, and escort management to meetings within the city and the Green Zone.

They were all huge men. Not the pumped up steroid type, but naturally big. There was definitely something in the water in Eastern Europe. They were an unfriendly looking bunch and I couldn't help wondering how many of them were wanted for war crimes. I found out a couple of weeks later that many of them were ex Serbian army, and some of them were even Arkan Tigers at some point.

The Arkan Tigers were a paramilitary group that fought in the former Yugoslavia for the Serbs. They were considered to be akin to the SS Death Squads or Head Hunters who fought against the partisans in Russia during the Second World War and were accused of war crimes.

They gave me a set of armour and a helmet but to my surprise, no weapons. I think the TL noticed my confusion and looked at me grinning, "Today, you are client."

The expression on my face told him I that wasn't in the least bit impressed, so he gave me an AK47 with three magazines. At least it was something and if things went wrong, I could take matters into my own hands instead of relying on others.

It's funny how just having a means to defend yourself in an environment like Iraq can put you instantly at ease. The fear of being killed never came into my head in Iraq; it was always the fear of not being able to control my own fate if I got into trouble. I sometimes thought of being knocked unconscious during an IED or something similar, and waking up in an orange boiler suit on Al Jazeera television about to be beheaded. I'd at least rather die fighting and deny them the satisfaction.

I had the usual briefing that you get before you are escorted to HQ from the airport. Pretty much the same as when I had first come into the country with the last company. Only this time, I was craning my neck to look further up at his 6'5" height and it was in a different accent. They covered everything and then placed me into the second vehicle.

We were travelling in a four vehicle convoy with a gun truck to the front and rear, with two client vehicles in between. They were fully armoured Ford Excursions. The gun trucks were the same as the client vehicles but instead of windows, they had armour plating with firing ports cut out of them. The windscreen and the driver and front passenger side windows were made of armoured glass. Each gun truck had a driver and a commander plus a left and right gunner in the back passenger seats and a rear gunner sat in the rear compartment. All in all, there were five men in each gun truck with a driver and commander in each client vehicle. They were a heavily armed team with a large amount of firepower that could be brought to bear.

The rear gunners, who would deal with anyone approaching from the rear position, were carrying PKM's. As I've mentioned before, these are Russian belt fed medium machineguns; a formidable weapon to come up against. The side shooters covered the nine and three o'clock positions of the arcs with AK47s. The only part that wasn't covered by a gunner was the twelve o'clock position; a point I would argue about getting rectified for the next eighteen months.

Once we got moving towards the last checkpoints before we hit the BIAP road, the huge difference in tactics from what I was used to, became apparent. Rather than travelling with the flow of the traffic, we pushed our way through, blowing on the horns and keeping relatively close together, allowing no one to come too close or between the vehicles within the team.

Clear of the final checkpoint, we gained speed and before I knew it, every truck had its blue and red lights flashing and sirens blazing. I felt like I was in the president's motorcade. I was uncomfortable and to me, it seemed as if everyone on the road and the surrounding areas could see and hear us, and they could.

The profile was aggressive to say the least and by being so, inevitably the team itself would be pumped up with adrenaline. I could hear over the radio the chatter between the team members, and even though I couldn't understand what they were saying, I could tell they were doing similar to what we had done in my last company, calling out possible threats and details on the road as we travelled. Only this time, instead of being calm and cool as they spoke, they seemed much more excited as though everything was about to explode.

As best they could, they stayed in the left hand and centre lanes. The right lane is the closest one to the pedestrian areas and easier to plant an IED along.

Any vehicle in the lane ahead would soon hear and see us behind them and push across to the far right, putting as much distance between themselves and our call sign as they could. The last thing they wanted was to get shot up because they stayed too close.

In the back passenger seat of the second vehicle, I felt like putting my fingers in my ears, waiting for the bang. To me, it seemed like we were travelling way too fast and making too much of a song and dance about our presence and just asking for someone to take us on.

The journey, in a route sense, was very much like the one I had travelled earlier in the low profile team, with the same checkpoints and suburbs along the way. Only this time, we couldn't be mistaken for anything other than a PSD in convoy.

As we passed vehicles, I could see the rear gunner of the gun truck in front of us moving his PKM to cover us as we travelled at break neck speed. I knew he wasn't going to fire on the vehicles, but the locals could never be too sure. I had visions of them suddenly seeing the barrel of a machinegun pointing at them and flapping, thinking they were about to get the good news, and causing them to career off the road.

I made eye contact with the driver of a taxi as we passed and the look of contempt on his face was clear. It was hard enough trying to get through a day, running the risk of being caught in an IED or opened up on by a U.S or Iraqi Army patrol, without a bunch of Serbs pointing guns at him and bullying him off the road.

Whenever we approached a checkpoint, the lead vehicle would hit the sirens again and the civilians ahead would push across, leaving a lane free for us to travel through. No matter how congested the traffic was, as soon as they heard our sirens or saw us in the distance, rapidly closing in, the static vehicles would find a way of getting out of our path. Even if it meant bumping in to each other, they would clear a channel for us to pass through. Obviously, they had seen and experienced high profile PSD in the past and knew that they don't stop for whatever reason and if you're in the way, you'll be ploughed under, and probably shot up too.

The Iraqi Police manning the barriers would let us straight through with only a wave and that would be it. It would be so easy to be a bunch of terrorists pretending to be a PSD; all they would have to do is look the part and hit the sirens and they would be waved through without being checked over. Two months later, a particularly brave and daring terrorist cell did exactly that, with significant results.

As always, when we hit the suburbs, the traffic became more compact and things slowed dramatically. After the sirens blazing and fast travelling on the open road, this felt like we had stopped in our tracks and we were like a sitting duck waiting to be whacked. The commander said something through the radio and before I knew what was happening, we had mounted the curb and crossed over to the other side of the road, driving against the oncoming traffic.

They weren't slow with the speed and once again, sirens and lights were on and the whole city must have heard us. People all along the roadside were getting away from the curb's edge and vehicles were pushing over to the left to let us through. Every time we hit a junction, the traffic police would stop all traffic in order to let us pass. Our vehicles wouldn't even slow down and continue to plough through as though we were carrying a heart and kidneys donated for the Pope.

Nothing in Baghdad looked any different from when I'd last been there. It was still dirty and the majority of people lived in poverty, but because it was so widespread, it seemed normal.

When I had travelled through in a low profile team, I had felt almost part of the indigenous population to a degree and no one paid any attention. We were in the traffic jams with them and saw the beggars and filth up close and personal.

Now, flying through at warp speed, I felt completely detached and in my own little bubble. It was almost like glancing at pictures in an album as you flick through with disinterest; nothing seemed real and the people themselves were just a blur.

We hit the last checkpoint and turned in to Al Mansur, a protected district of the city a little like the compound I'd lived in while operating in Erbil. Blast walls and guarded barriers were everywhere and once inside, we came into a street filled with villas and little shops.

Ghurkha guards were providing static and mobile security within the compound and it was obvious that these guys were the inner cordon protection for the company HQ's, while the Iraqis provided the outer security.

I was unceremoniously dumped outside the gates to a villa and my bags were bundled out along with me. There was another Englishman there too, and I realised we were both the new kids on the block.

A Ghurkha led us through the gate and told us we could leave our kit in the shade by his guard box. He said this with the usual big smile a Ghurkha has tattooed across his face. We were both thirsty and helped ourselves to a cooler box by the door to the villa, packed with soft drinks, water and chocolate, grabbing what we could before someone was came out and told us not to touch it.

As we waited to be seen to, I chatted with the other new guy, Matt, who had come in with me. It turned out that he was ex 3 Para and had gone through the depot with my younger brother. It's a small world on the circuit and someone always knows somebody.

It was a good thirty minutes before anyone got around to dealing with us. We were led into the office and we started on the administration and documentation. Because it was a U.S government contract, they wanted every detail about us. Background checks, medicals, dental records, Army service etc.

Afterwards, we drew our kit from the stores and I was surprised at how much we were issued. On top of the usual body armour and weapons, we were given shirts and trousers in the company colours along with t-shirts and, fleece jackets for the winter. At least they weren't scrimping on the equipment side of things.

We were issued with M4 rifles, which are a shorter version of the M16, with around twenty magazines and SIG pistols. I was expecting to be given AK47s then I realised that it was an American contract and it wouldn't look good if we were running around using Eastern Block assault rifles instead of American ones. The Serbs in the HQ team weren't on the U.S contract, so they used AK47s and naturally, coming from Eastern Europe, they would prefer the weapons they are used to.

For the next four days, we were placed onto an induction cadre. We were taught pistol and rifle drills and tactics used by the company. Also, we had to go through a fitness test and I was shocked to see people failing it. It consisted of a sort of bleep test where we needed to do a certain amount of shuttle runs in a set time. The older you were, the more time you had.

I remember one of the instructors shouting as we ran back and forth, "You younger guys should be doing it easily. Try and come in well below the given time and even break the record."

I turned to Matt and mumbled with a grin between breaths as we ran, "Well, why don't you pay us extra for it and I'll put the effort in."

Afterwards we did our press ups, sit ups and pull ups tests. There were guys as young as me unable to complete the required amount on certain tests. They weren't particularly hard and even a very basic level of fitness could have been sufficient to get you through. The men, who failed, either sat a retest or were sent home.

Personally, I felt disgusted by these people who failed such a basic and rudimentary fitness test. We were all ex soldiers and regardless of age, I've always seen it as a man's personal responsibility to his pride and self respect to keep his physical abilities to a certain level. So, for the men who were told that they'll be on the next available flight, I felt no pity.

Listening to the lectures on the tactics, I knew it was going to be an interesting rotation for me. Even more so when the instructor turned to us and said, "I can guarantee that at least two of you will be involved in a serious contact before the end of the month when you go to your teams."

I glanced around at the people who were attending the course and counted ten of us.

"Great stuff, can you tell us who it'll be or are you not allowed to say?" Someone asked from the rear, drawing laughs and giggles from the rest of us.

The instructor didn't see the funny side however, and then lectured us on taking things seriously. It wasn't that we didn't take it seriously; it was just typical British squaddie humour. The man lecturing us was a South African who had a completely different humour to us.

After the induction cadre, Matt and I were informed that we were to travel north and that was where we would be based. I was being sent to Kirkuk which I knew well and because of this, they believed my knowledge of the ground would be an asset to the team. Matt was to join the Tikrit team.

Tikrit was a couple of hours drive south west of Kirkuk and was the town that Saddam Hussein had been born and raised in. There was never a dull moment there, and as we would soon discover, the Tikrit team needed to have one of the biggest senses of humour in the company.

We were to travel together by helicopter and the plan was that we would be dropped off in the Kirkuk airbase and Matt would then get a chopper flight to Tikrit.

Things didn't quite go according to plan. Even between Americans and English, there is a language barrier. When our helicopter came in to land I approached the door gunner, asking him to confirm if the flight was for Kirkuk. He gave me the big thumbs up, so Matt and I climbed on board and we took off with all of our kit.

Three hours later, we touched down in the pitch black of night. With the whirling of the helicopter rotors and the dust flying, we could see or hear very little. Again, the door gunner gave me the signal that this was our stop so we bailed out. The chopper wasted no time and took off right away, leaving us to take in our surroundings as the dust settled. It didn't feel right. We were at a FOB, sure, but it didn't look like what I had been expecting.

It seemed much quieter than the Kirkuk airbase I had remembered and worse yet, there was no one there to meet us. Someone from my team should at least have been stood waiting to pick me up and take me to our compound.

We grabbed our kit and dragged ourselves off the landing zone then began trying to get our bearings. I was hoping it was just a remote part of the camp we had been dropped at, but that still didn't explain why there was no one from my team to meet us. Was I expected to make my own way, with all my kit, around a camp that was ten square miles?

After a couple of quick phone calls to our HQ, we realised we weren't in Kirkuk. We headed for a large building that looked like it may be some sort of HQ and we soon started to see American military vehicles. At least it was a FOB and not some Iraqi Army base.

After asking a few stupid questions like, "excuse me mate, where are we?" we found out we had been dropped in a place called Kirkutche.

Kirkutche was situated in completely the wrong direction from where we wanted to be and worse still, the wrong end of the country. I was fuming. The door gunner hadn't heard me correctly with his helmet on, the rotors still turning, the engine running and my North West English accent hadn't helped.

Most Americans believe that all British men sound like Hugh Grant. I should have used my best American accent to make sure he had understood because he had obviously never watched Brookside on cable back home.

We stayed the night and the next morning, we were picked up by helicopter again. This time I even wrote our destination on a piece of paper, handing it to the door gunner when they came in to land. The pilot had heard the story and he saw the funny side and apologised.

"Sorry for the fuck up boys. Some of these Red Neck door gunners are as dumb as a bag of hammers."

At least no one seemed to be getting bent out of shape over the mishap, including our HQ.

By the time we landed in Kirkuk, it was dark again but no less cooler. Because of the open area of the airfield, the hot air blasted us as the heli took off again with sand and grit hitting us like thousands of tiny pins. It had been a long flight and we had made a number of stops and pickups along the way adding to the time.

A short stocky American guy, named Geoff, met me at the airfield and he informed me that he was the Operation's Manager for the Kirkuk team. He spoke with a strong accent and during the conversation I found out he was from Texas. He also informed me that an old friend of mine was on the team and that he had been singing my praises since he found out I was on my way.

Sean had come to my platoon as a new guy in 2000 and I had been the most senior private at the time, known as a senior Tom, in the Parachute Regiment. As keen as anything, he had wanted to look the part and be the part of a British Paratrooper right from the day he had turned up, so once again, I had someone familiar already in situ to scrounge from because I knew he would have plenty of kit.

Kirkuk airbase was huge. It had been an Iraqi Air Force airfield during the war, and the Americans had taken it over and turned it into a Forward Operating Base. Like the Green Zone, it was surrounded with high walls and barbed wire fences with guard towers running the length of the perimeter. Typical of the American Army, they needed their comforts and they were short of nothing. The base had a number of gyms, a swimming pool, a huge canteen and even Pizza Hut and Burger King.

British soldiers were lucky if they got mail, never mind somewhere to drop your laundry off or a supermarket. Every American base has a PX, which is a sort of mini shopping mall where you can buy pretty much anything, from magazines and snacks, to ordering a Harley Davidson to be delivered to your home.

We had a fenced off area of our own within the base known as the USACE compound. Our clients, as well as the team, lived there with all the administration staff and the offices. Geoff dropped me off outside a large prefabricated style cabin and told me it would be my new home. I couldn't believe what I was seeing. Everything was even better than I had on my last contract when I was living in a villa; I even had an en suite bathroom and a shower.

I dumped my kit and took a shower, then the next thing I needed to do was to get my operations kit sorted, including my weapons and assault rig. Gone were the days of carrying all my equipment out of sight under my shirt and trying to blend in. Now I would be wearing a harness style vest, known as an assault rig or operations vest, ops vest for short. That would carry my ammunition and personal medical kit.

I made sure it was all ready to go in case I was suddenly called out for a job, and then it was time to get some sleep. Geoff had told me not to worry about getting up too early, as the team didn't need me in the morning, but I didn't want their first impression of me to be that of a layabout, so I set my alarm good and early.

The next morning, I made my way up to the office that Geoff had pointed out the night before to me. The team was there, about to start a briefing for a mission that morning.

"Hi mate, I'm Dave," the Team Leader introduced himself to me with a handshake, "take a seat and I'll introduce everyone once I've finished the brief."

Everyone watched me as I made my way to the back of the room to take a seat while I listened to Dave give his orders for the task. It was a set of Quick Battle Orders, QBO's, briefly outlining the mission and tasks. It was obvious to me that he had given them a more in-depth set of orders the evening before.

The aim of QBO's is to refresh you on what's going on and to bring up any changes that may have occurred since the full orders were given. After he had finished, he introduced me to the guys, and the first to come up was Sean.

Like a little kid on a sugar rush, Sean was telling me how great it was to have me there and so on. The rest of the team welcomed me, and I started to realise that none of them were right in the head. They were a rag-tag bunch from many different backgrounds of the army and just to look at them, you would have thought they were the Dirty Dozen.

Only a few of them bothered to wear the uniform that they were supposed to. In the contract, it even stated that everyone was to be clean shaven everyday and military style haircuts. Every team member was breaking the rules to some degree. One had a full bushy beard, another had a hair do that made him look like one of The Beatles and, they were all wearing whatever they felt like putting on that morning.

Dave took me to one side and gave me a quick heads up. He already knew of me, and he informed me that I'd be pleased to hear that the team was made up of mainly ex Marines and Paras. I knew that meant rivalry and banter that would never cease.

It had always been that way between The Parachute Regiment and The Royal Marines. Both regiments were considered to be elite within the British military, and so it was inevitable that one would strive for supremacy against the other. It was all good natured though, and it rarely got worse than piss-taking. They looked like a decent bunch and everyone seemed to be getting along, so the atmosphere in the team felt like a good one.

They left to do their tasking and I returned to my room to settle myself in. I unpacked all my kit, and after an hour or so the team returned and Sean came to visit. He even brought me a kettle, so I broke out the Yorkshire Tea and sat down to have a chat on what he and I had been up to since we had last seen each other.

I gathered, from what he was telling me, that I had landed on my feet and they were a good bunch of guys. We were the furthest northern team in the company, which meant that we were away from the prying eyes of management. As long as we stayed on the good side of the clients, we were left alone. I liked the fact that the head shed didn't bother us. There was nothing worse than when top brass came to visit. That's when everyone had to run around, pretending that they spent twenty four hours a day in their kit and did nothing other than prepare for missions and training. Even on operations, when we were in the army, we couldn't get away from it.

During the Sierra Leone operation, we were told one day that our platoon would be getting a visit from General Sir Charles Guthrie. Everyone in the officer's club went nuts. They all wanted to put on a good show, and so we were all to look our best and appear to be doing something constructive.

After four weeks in the jungle, we had to find a way of cleaning our uniforms and we were even ordered to shave. In a jungle environment, you never shave because even the smallest of cuts will become infected, leaving you as a casualty that then has to be dealt with by other members of the platoon and therefore, weakening the fighting capability of the unit as a whole.

We searched high and low for a razor, and eventually a lad named Danny found a cut down disposable one amongst his kit. It must have been there for years because it looked blunt and used.

Thirty four men had to use it and by the time it got to the third person, it was like shaving with a house brick.

Normal harbour routine in the army consists of patrolling, sentry duty, administration and resting. No one was to be resting during the visit to give the impression that, as far as the General was concerned, we were the most energetic platoon in the British Army, even though we had been patrolling and taking turns on guard duty all night. God forbid he would see anybody getting rest.

Everyone was given a bone task to do.

One group of lads were to be digging a trench. Another group would be having instruction on the machinegun, and another group were poised, just out of sight within the trees to give the impression of them being a section on its way in from a patrol. The Section Commander even had to have a bluff report on his findings and observations during the patrol, ready to reel off to the Platoon Commander on his return to the harbour area.

I was told that I would be powdering my feet and making a brew as part of the normal daily routine in the harbour area when the General arrived. So before he was due to show up, I lighted my little stove and started to boil some water then, removed one boot and sock. You only remove one boot at a time, clean and powder your foot then, replace the boot before removing the other one. That way, if you get bumped, you're already halfway there and it's easier to slip the other boot on.

We were all shaved, cleaned and posing ready for the visit. He turned up four hours late with his entourage and by this time, my water had evaporated and my foot had enough insect bites to swell it to the size of a football.

When he saw me sat there nursing my itchy foot he asked me, "Why have you all been shaving? You're not supposed to in the jungle, are you?"

I glanced at the CO who was stood behind him, glaring at me, so I kept my mouth shut and nodded like a halfwit. However, I think he knew the score just by the slight grin on his face as he spoke to us and even remarked to the CO about how clean and fresh his men were looking, considering they had been out in the sticks for four weeks.

After that, half the men in the platoon developed ringworm in their faces, open sores became infected and all sorts of other uncomfortable skin problems developed due to sharing the same razor as everybody else.

Therefore, I was glad that the Kirkuk team was well out of the way.

Sean was half Iranian and half Irish, but he always insisted he was Persian. He was always easy to wind up; all I had to do was say that the Iraqis and Iranians were pretty much the same and he would go into a lecture about Persian history. Always one for kit and the latest gadgets, he showed me all the stuff he had hanging off him and his equipment when he went out on missions.

"You look like Buzz Lightyear Sean." I told him, and from then on the nickname was often used.

Nonetheless, he insisted it made the job easier. Personally, I was a minimalist and liked to keep my kit basic. Weapons, ammunition and first aid kit with one or two other bits and bobs. The way I saw it, the more gadgets you have, the more time you'll spend thinking about them and fiddling with them, rather than the job in hand.

There is definitely something about English men and tea. Within five minutes of me making a brew, another guy turned up at my door carrying an empty cup.

Toad looked like a throwback. If there was ever a missing link, then it was him.

"Are we having a brew then?" He asked me, helping his self to my kettle. "Sean told me that you're ex 1 Para, me too."

His shoulders were as wide as he was tall, and his chest was like a barrel. His hair never stayed on his head and just seemed to wave about doing its own thing. It always appeared as though he had just crawled out of bed and even with his kit on; he looked like he had just spent the night by a dumpster.

So far, that was three of us on the team that were 1 Para. Toad was the sort who could make friends and scrounge kit even if he was in a windowless cell all by himself. He was the Kirkuk team's version of 'Red', the character Morgan Freeman plays in 'The Shawshank Redemption'. On one occasion, I only mentioned that I wished I had a printer in my room and an hour later, he turned up with one for me. I half expected a picture of Rita Hayworth too.

It was always best not to ask him where he got the gifts from that he presented you with. But for a guy who could get anything, he never had his own cigarettes.

Toad had a million stories to tell, and there wasn't much he hadn't done. He had friends everywhere and one of them was Colin Farrell, the

Irish actor. Toad had done a fair bit of work as a movie extra, and one of his roles had been with Colin Farrell in the movie 'Alexander'. When I watched it, I couldn't help but laugh at seeing Toad's big ugly head riding on horseback into a charge alongside a Hollywood star. Apparently, they had become good friends and stayed in touch over the years.

Being the new guy on the team, everyone wanted to check me out and weigh me up. For the next couple of hours, I was the most popular man in Kirkuk. Dave came in and gave me a rundown of my job and position within the team.

I was to start out as a side gunner in the rear gun truck. He went over the tactics and the drills with me and told me that, the next day I would get the chance to do a little training with the rest of the team to get a feel for it.

Dave was a mild mannered ex Marine and he had a thing for big hair. To me, he looked like a big sheep dog with his bushy hairdo. He was also one of the best medics I'd ever come across. I'd always taken a great interest in medical subjects, but my knowledge compared to his was like a day one, week one recruit's.

I'd had a lot to take in on my first day, with getting to know everyone and sorting myself out while at the same time, making cups of tea every five minutes for visitors as they came to my room to have a chat. I was invited later to have a few drinks with the rest of them as a sort of 'welcome on board' party. Even though we weren't supposed to have any alcohol, the team was big and ugly enough to know when and when not to have a few. If we were on a mission the next day, then obviously the drinking wouldn't happen. But being in Iraq, it was nice to have a taste of home now and then and relax.

So later that evening the vodka, whisky and beers were flowing like water in the room of a guy named Smudge, also another ex member of 1 Para. The whole team squeezed into his room and the banter and slagging soon got underway. Everyone was laughing and things couldn't have been better.

We were a fifteen man team and from what I could see, there wasn't a guy amongst them that I didn't like the look of. Even Geoff, the Op's Manager, was in there gobbing off and ending up the butt of most of the jokes for being American.

There was only one other American on the team and that was Rick, a quiet guy who at first struggled with the British humour, but after a few months of working closely with us, he got the hang of it and even picked up on our slang.

"You wanker," was one of his favourites. He would shout it out of the firing ports in the gun truck to locals who were in the way, knowing they had no idea what it meant. He got a kick out of it.

It was supposed to be a few welcome drinks, but it soon turned into an all night party. I was stumped when even one of our clients turned up with a bottle and shook my hand. At first, I thought we had been busted and were in trouble. He was a Staff Sergeant with the U.S Army and he sat down next to me and introduced himself. By the looks of it, he had started a few hours earlier as his whisky bottle was half full and his speech was slurred.

"Man, you guys have killed more men than AIDS, so who the fuck are we to tell you that you can't have a drink?"

Smudge was a great host and he didn't earn the nickname Ollie Reed for nothing. It was the early hours of the morning before we headed back to our own rooms to sleep it off. No one had any intention of being up early anyway, so we could afford to enjoy ourselves.

Luckily, I've never been one to suffer from hangovers and the next day, after I had showered and with a coffee in my hand, I stood on my doorstep watching Smudge clean out his room across from me. The huts were all set up like a street you would find in the UK; two rows facing each other with a gravel path, instead of tarmac, down the centre. All the rooms were encased in layers of sand bags because the base was forever being mortared and rockets would sometimes land pretty close.

"Want a brew, Smudge?" I shouted across.

"Aye please," he shouted back in his Scottish accent. "Someone pissed in the bin in my bathroom last night and I bet it was Toad."

I smiled at the thought of Toad missing his aim.

We all met up at the office ready to perform some drills which were mainly for my benefit, so I could see them in action and know what was expected of me from my position.

We practiced contact drills, flat tyre drills, cross decking from one vehicle to another in the event of it becoming disabled, casualty extraction and so on. We were at it for a couple of hours and as always, at the end of each drill, we had a quick debrief and offered our own advice on how it could be done better if needs be.

Afterwards, we went to the local ranges on the outskirts of the base to check and zero our weapons. I'd never used the SIG pistol before, but the drills were very much the same as the Glock I had used with my previous company.

As usual, I made a point of testing out all my magazines to make sure none of them were going to give me stoppages. It took a while because of the amount I had been issued but once I was happy, we headed back to get some lunch.

The canteens in American bases are huge and there's nothing you can't get in them. If you want to live off burgers, fries and chicken wings, then you can. I however, tried to eat as healthily as possible, which was difficult considering they had great desserts including every flavoured ice cream you could think of. In the canteen we would all sit together on the same table, but Toad would always be getting up and going off to talk to someone.

I assumed that he knew them all but he didn't. He was just a big believer in making as many friends as possible because that way, he could always lean on them when he needed something. He was an absolute pirate.

The base had a ratio of roughly 70/30 men to women, and every American girl that he saw, Toad would be over talking to them. Very often, he would come back having arranged for them to come over to a barbeque that we would lay on the next time we had any time off.

The American soldiers weren't allowed to drink, and with no chance of getting their hands on any alcohol, the offer of good food and booze was always tantalising to them. Most girls thought that Toad was just being a friendly British guy when actually; he wanted to get in to their knickers.

Most of the Americans wouldn't even approach us. They seemed wary and a little afraid of us. Unlike them, we would sit at our table gobbing off at each other and generally being loud British soldiers. But they could never work out who or what we were. Even though we spoke English, most Americans didn't realise we were British. We found out why they seemed worried about us later, when I was approached in the canteen one day.

A young American female soldier walked over to our table and asked me who we were.

I casually replied, "Oh, we're dolphin trainers."

81

"Oh, that's really cool. Why are you in Kirkuk then?"

I couldn't believe she thought I was telling the truth. The sniggers and grunts from the guys on my table should have told her I was winding her up. I couldn't carry it on and make a fool of her though, so I came clean.

"Nah, we are a PSD team really, working for the Corps of Engineers."

She seemed shocked when I told her we were all ex British soldiers that now worked with a private security company.

They had been told by their commanders that, the men they would often see driving around in the black SUVs were ex Israeli Mossad, and that we now worked as mercenaries for the CIA, and to stay away from us because we were dangerous.

They were also told that our job was to drive into the city, conduct snatch operations and bring back locals for interrogation then, we would execute them afterwards in the desert.

We found it hilarious, and I think she soon realised how ridiculous the whole thing sounded now that she had spoken to us. From then on, we were in their cool books.

I already felt comfortable within our group. Even though I had never worked high profile before and the whole sirens, flashing lights and the general 'in your face' approach wasn't my cup of tea, from what I had seen of the team, they were well trained and experienced.

Most importantly, they behaved as a team and worked for each other. Now all that was left was to get out on the ground and see how I could perform for the guys.

THERMITE GRENADES AND PROBLEM CHILDREN

No one in the team had been working together for long. Up until a month earlier, the bulk of them had been South Africans. Then the contract had changed and they were no longer allowed to work for the company.

A new team had needed to be put together. Everyone had experience with other companies and like me; they had mainly come from low profile teams. No one knew the Kirkuk area as well as me and Sean, and so we would be relied upon for our knowledge of the ground. Sean had worked there with a previous company and had as much experience as I did within the city and surrounding districts.

Brian was the team 2ic and he was a real nerd when it came to navigation and computers. He would often bring us in on the mission planning, asking our opinions and recommendations on routes to take and avoid. Additionally, he would want to know about the locals in the area and the general feel of the place. He was extremely thorough and never left anything out when preparing for a mission.

To look at him, he seemed a mild and well mannered person but, as soon as he opened his mouth, every other word would be a four letter one. Even in normal conversation he couldn't help it, but I put that down to him being from Northern Ireland.

My first mission was to be a site visit in the heart of the city. I'd been there dozens of times and knew the place well. It wasn't in the best area you could think of and I knew that being such a big target as we were, there was a good chance someone would want to take us on. It was a clinic that was halfway through construction and, as I remembered, it was surrounded on all sides with rooftops that overlooked it.

I drew Brian a rough sketch of the area and what I had observed on previous missions. The site was next door to a fire station, with a main road on its eastern side and houses immediately to the west. To the north lay a large open area which was about the size of a football pitch and then more residential areas beyond that. Further to our north would be a t-junction and high rise flats.

It was an ideal position for a shoot. No matter where we went on the site, we would be exposed from at least one side. I explained this to Brian and Dave and the plan we came up with was to use the vehicles to block off the roads and have the machine guns on the upper floor of the clinic, covering the possible firing points.

Every man had a radio so communications between the team wouldn't be a problem. Each man would be a set of eyes and ears on the ground and we would pass information to and from the gunners regarding anything we thought could be a threat. With each gunner there would be a spotter with binoculars who could then adjust him onto a target should the need arise.

The mission was planned for mid morning. By that time, the day would be heating up and the roads would be busy. Not an ideal time for the mission but with the area we were travelling to, no time was particularly ideal.

The evening before the mission, we went through a full set of orders with Dave and Brian. We covered every eventuality and the support we had on call was better than anything I had when I was there during the invasion.

If we had to, we could call in helicopter and infantry support from the FOB. The American helicopters were constantly flying about in the city anyway, but it was comforting to know that they were aware of us and we were a priority if we called them. If it had been the British Army, the chopper would have either broken down or they would refuse to fly on account that the pilot hadn't had his full twelve hours sleep.

The Americans had enough helicopters to get an entire division off the ground in one go, whereas the British, struggled to get a platoon in the air. It was embarrassing during the invasion when our Brigade, which was supposed to be heli-born, had a few pathetic aircraft while the Americans had enough choppers even for their Burger King re-supply. Again though, that's a different story.

In the morning we all turned up suited and booted in our ops kit. With the amount of weapons and ammunition I was carrying, I weighed a ton. Even though there was a lot of weight to carry, it felt good knowing I wasn't likely to run out of ammunition in the first few seconds of a contact.

Dave gave us a set of QBO's and then it was time to mount up. I was to be the right side gunner of our truck with Omar covering the left. He was the pretty boy of the group and the youngest too. Fresh from the Royal Marines, he had come to Iraq hoping to make his millions like the rest of us. He was quiet at first but once he knew you, he was as sharp as a knife, and funny with it.

We would be sat back to back, leaning against each other as we travelled through the city, facing our arcs at right angles to the vehicle. I was glad he was a short arse like me; otherwise I would have been pushed up against my door with my head sticking out of the firing port.

Toad was our driver and Smudge was the rear gunner with the SAW, Squad Automatic Weapon. This was a belt fed 5.56mm machinegun. Not the heaviest calibre in the world, but the round was just as effective. They were enough to put holes in flesh so, we were happy.

Brian was to be in the commander's seat with his navigation kit, and he would give a steer to the lead vehicles on turnings and any other features of the route as we went. The more I saw him, the more I realised he was a nerd. In the truck with him, he had a laptop with FalconView on it so that he could trace the route and possible alternate routes as we travelled.

FalconView is a military mapping system, a little like Google Earth but it's much more in depth and specially designed for the military. Brian knew all there was to know about FalconView, and he even once tried to pass his knowledge onto the rest of us bone heads by giving us a lesson on it.

For a whole hour, all he received was stupid and ridiculous questions until in the end, he lost his temper shouting, "Fuck it, you're all thick as shit and I'll take care of the navigation from now on," as he stormed out of the room.

He was also a member of Mensa and I often gave him stick over it, asking him what they talked about at their meetings and if it was as much of a barrel of laughs as it sounded. He would reply with his usual Northern Irish charm and tell me what I could do with myself. He was ex Royal Irish

Regiment and after that he had gained a degree in computer science. To us lump hammers on the team; he was better than Bill Gates.

As the clients arrived we mounted up and gave radio checks between the vehicles. If we didn't have communications, then the mission would be scrapped until it was fixed. The checks had already been done earlier but it was good to double check. After the last vehicle had answered the radio check, we received the order to roll out from Dave.

At that stage, we were still a three vehicle team. We only had the one gun truck and that was to the rear which I was in, but we were about to become a four vehicle call sign with an additional gun truck in the lead.

Sean was in the lead vehicle and he would be guiding us to the site. Dave travelled in the second truck and the Ant Hill mob, that I was part of, was in the rear gun truck.

Toad was playing ABBA over the stereo as we travelled towards the gates. As soon as we were beyond the wire, the music would be off but until then, we were having a sing along to 'Dancing Queen'.

We had to obey the rules of the road whilst in the camp and so we travelled slowly and kept in the correct lane. Once beyond the gates however, we knew that we wouldn't be giving way and stopping at crossings and lights.

Omar was giving it his all, singing along and even doing some air guitar for us, followed by air drums. He looked a prat but it was amusing.

As we approached the gate, it was time to switch on, the music was turned off and everyone checked their weapons and ammunition and did a final communications check.

At either side of the gate there were large ridges that had been built to act as a blockade and cover from small arms fire. As we passed through the barrier, we gave the pretty American soldier who was on duty, a wave and she blew us a kiss and wished us luck. Toad made a mental note for future stalking.

Once clear of the first barrier, we made ready our weapons by pulling back the cocking handles and chambering a round so it was just a case of squeezing the trigger.

The entrance/exit to the camp was set up so that you couldn't drive up to the gate in a straight line. Chicanes channelled and forced you to slow down, and there were two barriers to pass through which were covered by machinegun towers before you got to the main gate. If you didn't follow the orders of the sentries to the letter as you approached the barriers while entering the base, you got a reminder through your windscreen in the form of a bullet.

After driving a hundred metres further on from the last barrier, we hit the main road running left to right in front of us. The two lead vehicles slowed and pushed to the left so that the gun truck with the team firepower could push past them before they came in sight of the road and block traffic approaching from the right.

The Iraqi police had a checkpoint immediately facing the exit, and halted the vehicles coming from the left. From my angle, I was covering the houses and open ground to the right of the road while Smudge and Omar covered the rear. Once Brian gave the all clear, the other two vehicles came screaming out of the exit point and hit a hard left onto the main drag and we followed on.

Whenever we left a FOB, we would always 'Hard-Target', meaning we would come out at speed. That way, if anyone was sat waiting with a Rocket Propelled Grenade, RPG, or a machinegun, it would be harder for them to gain a sight picture on us and more than likely miss their shot. That was the theory anyway.

We picked up speed and I could hear the sirens of the lead vehicle as they raced towards the next junction. Cars were moving sluggishly on the route ahead and had to pull over to the side of the road to clear the way for us.

Sean gave a running commentary on the way, pointing out vehicles, buildings and rooftops that we should be aware of. My SAW was pointing through my firing port and as I scanned the buildings and cars, the muzzle of my weapon went everywhere my eyes went. It was pointless having your weapon pointing in one direction as you looked in another.

Things were happening fast, and the surrounding area flew past me in a blur. As we approached the next junction, our truck pushed forward in the convoy to cover the rest of the team as they cleared the choke point. It was inevitable that we would have to slow down as we turned, and this would be the perfect place to mount an attack against us. Therefore, we needed to have the firepower in place covering the junction and traffic before the client vehicle made the turn.

When we were clear of the turn our gun truck latched back onto the rear of the convoy. Every man in the vehicle was shouting out what he could see, whether it was vehicles approaching from side streets or people on rooftops. Again, it was a case of every man having a mental picture of the area and what was occurring within it. Also, because Smudge was facing to the rear covering the six o'clock position, he needed to know what was going to be in his arcs as we passed so, it was important for Omar and me to call out the details to save him from any surprises.

We were approaching a bridge up ahead. This was a vulnerable time for us because once we were on the bridge; we would be committed to crossing it. We wouldn't be able to turn as easily in the middle of a bridge, so once again we hit the sirens and put our feet down. The bridge raised high above a river that runs north to south and cuts Kirkuk in half. On a number of occasions, there had been IEDs planted on the bridge and teams had been caught in the blast. Our best approach was to stay in the centre lane and get across as quickly as possible.

Because our vehicle had open ports, hot air rushed in from the outside and the truck soon began to heat up. Coupled with our kit and body armour, it was like a blast furnace inside. I had sweat dripping into my eyes from my forehead and the best I could do was to try and blink it away.

Smudge was keeping all vehicles a good distance from our rear and Omar and I kept them from approaching us from the sides. With the noise of the sirens and the flashing lights, we knew that anyone who approached us could only have bad intentions. Either that or they were from a different planet. Everyone in Iraq knew not to approach a PSD or military call sign; it was even written in big red warning letters on the back of every vehicle.

Once we had cleared the bridge we had built up areas to the left and right of us again. People were everywhere and I wondered how I was supposed to see if someone took a pop at us. In one ear I had Sean and the vehicle commanders giving commentary and in the other ear, I had Toad, Omar and Smudge, all doing the same thing inside the vehicle. All the while I was trying to cover my arcs and not miss anything that was a potential threat. I could feel a headache coming on after this trip.

Kirkuk had the same look and smell as the rest of Iraq. Everything looked run down, and even the buildings and roads had the appearance that they were never intended to be more than just a temporary feature.

What I found with the Iraq was that, if they could cut corners, then they would. Even when building their own homes. I was amazed at how some of the buildings stayed up at times when I saw them being constructed.

As always the central reservation was a sewage pit and grazing area rolled in to one. The cows and sheep had given up trying to distinguish the difference between the scraps of food and the engine oil or human waste and cracked on eating the lot. I was glad that our food was flown in from the States.

I heard Sean in the lead vehicle say, "approaching left turn," in my earpiece, which was our cue to push forward again and clear the turn.

This was our last turning before we reached the clinic and once we pulled up it was mine, Sean's and Omar's job to clear the site before we allowed the clients out of the vehicle.

The street was narrow with a number of side streets leading off to the left and right before we reached our objective. Because of the little space in the street, the rooftops of the buildings on either side seemed to tower over us. The sirens and flashing lights had been turned off once we had crossed the bridge, safe in the knowledge that we were approaching our stop point, and we didn't want to advertise the fact that, we were on our way.

As our truck stopped, Omar and I jumped out and Sean debussed from his own vehicle. Omar cleared the outside while Sean and I cleared the building. It was still a concrete shell with a roof and looked nothing like a clinic as yet. In fact, it looked exactly the same as it did when I had first visited the site a year and a half ago.

Sean pushed upstairs and we all continuously spoke through our radios, informing each other of the layout of the site as well as our own locations in relation to the rest of the team. If someone got injured, then at least the team would know their last position which would be a good starting point.

Sean gave the all clear to Dave. Smudge and Omar then pushed onto the roof with Sean acting as a spotter for their guns. Our gun truck pushed to the north of the site to cover the junction and the client vehicle stayed close to the clinic perimeter fence, ready for a quick bug out. I stayed on the outside of the building acting as cover for the vehicles and keeping an eye on the entrance, while Brian and Dave escorted the client through the site.

I was sweating like a fat kid in a cake shop and I had to pour water into my eyes to clear them of salt. They were stinging and my vision was starting to blur. At least now I had a moment to sort myself out, and it was only then that I realised how thirsty I was. I necked a whole litre of water in one go. I was soaked through with sweat and I could feel my t-shirt sticking to me under my body armour and ops vest. The sun was beating down and so I kept in the shade beside the client vehicle as I watched the entrance.

After ten minutes, I heard Brian on the net, "That's task complete and returning to the vehicles."

I moved to the door of the client vehicle, ready to open it so that the client could get in without being exposed for any unnecessary length of time.

Dave and Brian approached and the client jumped in. Once he was secure and ready to go, the rest of the team closed in to their respective vehicles and within thirty seconds we were moving again. It was all smoothly done and it was clear the drills had been practiced time and again.

As soon as we hit the junction, the sirens were on again, warning everyone ahead to get out of our way. We took a different route back through the city towards the FOB and came in from the north. Sean was doing an excellent job of navigating the different streets and turns and his knowledge of the area was obvious.

For the last mile before we got to the entrance of the base, it was pretty much a straight road with a couple of junctions along the way. We had no intention of stopping or even slowing before we were in and secure.

Because it was a straight road and due to the direction in which we were travelling, it was obvious where we were heading to and so we needed to cover the distance as quickly as possible before anyone could set up an attack further on. It would be all too easy for the bad guys to grab the RPG they kept in the wardrobe or the IED the baby had just been playing with, and whack us on our last couple of hundred metres before safety.

We made the final turn in to the base and immediately, ABBA picked up where they had left off when we had set out. I think we were on to 'Super Trooper' by now.

Brian informed Dave, "That's the call sign complete and we're in and closing."

"Roger that. Nice one lads." Dave answered.

My head was spinning and I was guzzling water like a man possessed. It was my first job in a high profile team and even adjusting my fire position in my seat as I covered my arcs and rolled with the movement of the truck so as not to fall over, was hard work.

Despite this, I actually found that I enjoyed it. I was working with a good team and from what I could see, even though we stood out like a sore thumb, the profile worked and we conducted high profile the way it should be done and not like some of the cowboys we had seen elsewhere.

We unloaded our weapons and slowly made our way through the airbase back to our compound. Compared to the speeding about with sirens and lots of gobbing off, the drive through the FOB was surreal. A sort of tranquillity came over our gun truck and everyone, for a moment, was quietly listening to ABBA. Even Omar had put down his air guitar.

It was now late morning and the rest of the day was ours to do with as we saw fit. I was used to working fourteen hour days and having minimum time to myself, but now I had time on my hands and didn't know what to do with it.

That was until Toad told me that him, Sean and Omar were off to the pool for the afternoon once they had sorted their vehicles and weapons out. At this point, maybe I should have passed on the offer, instead opting to do some weapon training or something similar but instead, I asked them what colour towel I should take.

My first mission had gone like clockwork and I was impressed at the level at which the team operated. I was feeling comfortable and a part of the gang. Our clients were also an easy to get along with bunch.

Most of them were American National Guard with the Corps of Engineers. When back at home, they would be doing normal jobs and leading everyday lives. The National Guard is a little similar to the Territorial Army in the UK; they would support the regular troops and it was obvious with the amount of National Guardsmen that were operating in Iraq that the U.S army was stretched of manpower.

Our clients worked with us as best they could and whenever it was given, they would take our advice into consideration. But there was always one black sheep.

From what I could tell, Joe looked Oriental but he had a Latin American style surname. Just by his sly appearance, I knew I wouldn't like him and the rest of the guys warned me that he was a problem child.

Our next mission was to take Joe out to a water project on the outskirts of the city. As always, we prepared and planned the mission to the last detail and made arrangements for air support accordingly.

Because of the flying time and fuel that needed to be taken into consideration, when we requested helicopter support we had to resolutely stick to our timings and couldn't afford delays. But one thing we hadn't taken into consideration was, the 'Joe factor'.

If he could trip you up, he would go out of his way to do it. On the morning of the mission, we had had our QBO's and everyone was in the vehicles and ready to go. Joe turned up twenty minutes late and as he passed us on the way to the office, he carried an almost smug expression on his face, knowing he had caused us to slip our timings and that we had been waiting at his pleasure for a while.

There were mutterings in our gun truck as he passed us with a slight wave of the hand as if to say 'good morning'. Between us and under our breath, we returned his greeting with desires of what we would like to do to him in a windowless room with no witnesses, and it wasn't to kiss and cuddle with him.

Yes, my mind was already made up, the guy was a knob.

I've always hated those kinds of people. He had absolutely no reason to dislike us and it was in his interest to work with us. There was no way I would put my life on the line for someone who I couldn't stand the sight of. But Joe didn't seem to realise this. His attitude was that he was untouchable and that Iraq was safe. I couldn't wait for the day he would be proven wrong and I just hoped that it wouldn't be at the cost of anyone on the team.

Dave had a quiet word with him about his time keeping and even while this was going on he had the same 'yeah, whatever' expression on his face. It was the first time I'd had dealings with him and already he was boiling my piss.

We did our final communications check and headed out towards the gates.

The camp had four main gates to choose from and it was prudent to vary them when leaving and entering. If we started setting patterns, then it wouldn't take a lot of effort for someone to set an ambush. This time we left through one of the side gates to the base. We didn't use sirens as we left because we had a few hundred metres before we hit the main drag, so again, in much the same way as when we approached sites, we moved quickly and quietly, trying not to alert people of our advance.

As we passed through the barrier, we all made our weapons ready and began covering our arcs. As soon as we left the FOB, we crossed a small culvert bridge and it reminded me a little of Northern Ireland. Very often, the IRA would plant an IED in a culvert and sit watching and waiting for a British patrol to cross. As they did, the terrorists would initiate the explosive device and bug out with an easy kill.

I just hoped that the Iraqi's weren't quite brave enough as yet to approach so close to the camp. There were piles of rubble all along our left and right as we approached the road. By the looks of it, they had been the barrack buildings for the Iraqi troops when the airbase had been in their hands. Civilians were now living in and amongst the buildings that hadn't been destroyed and I could even see satellite dishes erected above them. Clean running water was a problem but, watching Sky Movies wasn't.

We turned right onto the main road and then hit the sirens. Everyone could see us now and they knew we were there, so it made no difference if we made noise too. At least that way, for the short sighted people, they would at least be able to hear us coming and keep their distance.

As always we were passing information between us and giving Smudge, as our rear gunner, possible target indications as we went. Even though I was on the right side of the truck, because Smudge had his back towards me he knew that if I said, "people on roof tops right," he would automatically turn his gun to his left and scan the buildings I'd pointed out.

Omar was doing the same on his side and even Toad and Brian were pointing out details to us because they had a clear view ahead, whereas Omar and I were covering the left and right. It was all about communication and everyone singing off the same song sheet. At the same time, we were receiving a running commentary from Sean through our earpieces. It was a hell of a lot to take in, but already, I found myself adapting to it.

In one area of the city, heading towards the suburbs, there was a large monument of four swords on the left hand side as we travelled roughly north. I knew this area well and there were often IEDs planted there. I had seen the aftermath of the bombings many times when I had travelled through Kirkuk with my last company.

Sean knew this too and as we approached the area, he advised us to keep to the far right in order to put as much distance between ourselves and any possible threat as we could.

All along our route, cars were parked up and people were milling about. The usual fuel sellers with jerry cans full of cheap petrol were in abundance as we passed. The traffic was building up but with our sirens and lights, we paved a corridor for the team to travel down and the locals kept their distance.

Clear of the suburbs, we hit the open road. There was wasteland left and right of the road with residential areas into the distance. Our main threat now was roadside bombs and traffic accidents. With the speed we were travelling, it would have taken a Hollywood action hero to hit us with a rocket from the kind of range they would need to be at to have any form of cover.

There was a lot of debris and disused building materials at the side of the road and we did our best to stick to the centre lane. It would've been easy to plant an IED in amongst the rubble.

The road wasn't completely unlike motorways we have in England, with three lanes and even crash barriers. However, you were not allowed to ride a donkey on the M6 and a lot of the crash barriers had been removed so that people could cross onto the other side during a moment of Driving Tourettes, which every Iraqi seemed to suffer from.

A few miles out of the city, we passed the last check point and after that we were on the Erbil road. If we carried on travelling north we would be in the Kurdish capital within an hour. The stark contrast between cities, just an hour apart, was hard to imagine. They were different planets.

To the north of Kirkuk there is a prominent ridge line that runs from east to west and on the eastern side, overlooking the suburbs, was our water project. We turned off the main road and hit a rocky narrow road with steep outcrops on either side of us. Omar and I had our weapons pointing almost vertical trying to cover the tops of the hills in case anyone fancied their chances. It was down to Sean and the lead vehicles to spot anything planted in the road.

As we approached the site, Sean and I jumped out and jogged up the steep hill toward the objective. I was breathing through my arse by the time we got to the top, but I kept my composure and couldn't allow Sean to see I was sucking in the air from China. I would get a slagging for it. With the weight of the kit we were carrying and the heat of the day, I suspected that he was in the same condition as myself and was doing a very good job of hiding it from me. I caught sight of the sweat running down his face from his hairline and that made me feel a little better.

I headed around the site, checking the outer approaches and making sure there was no one hiding and waiting for us. Sean checked the water pumping station. It was only a small concrete building but needed to be secured all the same.

The site was on a sort of plateau and had a sudden drop off a cliff on its southern side which overlooked a residential area and the city beyond.

"All clear, Dave," I said once I had the thumbs up from Sean.

Dave and Joe debussed along with Brian and Omar while Smudge stayed with the gun truck to cover the road approaching us from the rear.

As Dave and the others came closer, I could clearly hear him telling Joe, "Don't get too close to the edge of the ridge Joe, because there *is* a sniper threat and we'll be in plain sight of the hundreds of buildings below."

So what did Joe do? With great haste, he rushed towards the cliff edge and stood there for all to see, with hands on hips, as though he was the ruler of the land.

My blood turned to molten rock immediately, and I looked across at Brian who had the same expression as me on his face. On that day, I was actually wishing that some rag-head down there had the balls to take us on and was a good shot.

Dave gripped him by the collar of his body armour and dragged him back forcefully.

"Joe, I've just fucking told you not to move near the fucking edge, there's no reason for you to be there."

"I didn't hear you and I wanted to see the view." He said with his usual manner of superiority.

Dave wasn't impressed or convinced. "It's the same view as the rest of Iraq; mud huts and breeze block houses with scabby dogs eating turds. Now don't move from my side."

Brian and Dave had to pretty much sandwich him between them because we knew, at the next opportunity, he would pull another stunt.

It was clear that Joe didn't really know what he was looking at; all he did was stand there for ten minutes, staring at a wall and scratching his nose.

Dave lost patience and told him he had two more minutes and then we were gone. We headed back to the vehicles and once the client was in, me and Omar jumped back into our positions.

"He's a knob isn't he Luke." Brian shouted over his shoulder to me.

"Yeah, a first class cock end from what I can tell." Everyone in the gun truck was nodding in agreement with me on this point.

"He's always like that, mate. He never shows up on time, always tries to do his own thing on site, and will *always* do the opposite of what you tell him." Brian's voice had its usual tone of aggressiveness, but he became even more belligerent when speaking about Joe. "He even claimed Chicago is more dangerous than Iraq. The prick isn't even from there."

Yes, it was universal within the team that no one liked Joe.

I have always tried my best to get along with clients as it makes for a better working environment all round. If you don't like each other, you'll be less willing to play ball. And when one side is considered to be your protection when the shit hits the fan, it would be prudent to try and get along with them.

Joe never saw it like this, and I became convinced that the man was a natural born shit head. A snake in the form of a man who would stitch you up the first chance he got. I made it my own personal mission from then on to avoid contact with him as much as possible. I didn't like the idea of losing my temper with him and turning his head inside out, I would get the sack and would then need to look for another contract.

We returned to base and, as always, Dave needed to go and see our head client from the Corps of Engineers. He wanted to specifically speak with him about the 'Joe factor' and how it scuppered most of our plans; from his lack of time keeping to his conduct on sites.

Speaking directly to Joe on the matter and trying to reason with him was out of the question. It had been tried before to no avail. Therefore, trying to iron out any creases between ourselves and the client where Joe was concerned, had to be taken directly to his bosses in the office.

Ten minutes later, Dave returned with the promise that Joe would be sorted out by his own head shed. So all there was left to do, as usual, was to clean our weapons and sort out the vehicles for our next mission. There was a higher risk in this job, but I was enjoying the relatively easy atmosphere amongst the team. If it wasn't broke then no one would try to fix it, and that suited me fine.

Personal fitness was left to us. I would go for a run every other morning and would train at the gym five times a week. Most of the team did the same, and it was clear that we were in an adult's world where we were expected to keep our own levels of professionalism to a high standard. I didn't want someone breathing down my neck and telling me to get up to go for a team run at silly o'clock in the morning. I did things in my own time and when I felt like it. I found myself actually looking forward to my early morning runs as the sun was rising and when the heat was bearable.

On the other hand, when it came to our tactics and drills, we always trained as a team. At least three times a week if we had the time. We would get onto the back road of the camp, out of the way from prying eyes and run through our SOP's and contact drills for a couple of hours, or conduct medical and weapons training. Once a week we would try and get to the ranges to do a little live firing and give our training more realism.

All in all, our team was a pretty well oiled machine. There was only the 'Joe factor' that could trip us up. He was like Kryptonite to Superman; he only had to show up and we were knackered.

Because of the good atmosphere in the team, most evenings tended to be a social event for us. Even if it was just sitting in each other's rooms drinking tea and watching movies. There was a whole bunch of different personalities, which meant we all got along better. If any of us wanted to be alone, then it was just a case of going to your hut and chilling out in your own company.

I kept in touch with Lisa as often as I could, and I would either phone her or speak to her through the internet most evenings. I was to be away for three months, so contact between us was important.

In this day and age, the internet is a lifeline when away from loved ones, so I made sure I took advantage of it as often as possible. I also spoke to my daughter as regularly as I could too. She was growing fast and I missed her a lot. But once I was home, I would always make up for lost time and spoil her rotten.

After a couple of weeks on the team, I found that I had settled into the high profile role much easier than I had expected. We continued to conduct missions within the city and although there was always a threat, we never gave anyone a chance to mount an attack because of our meticulous preparation and planning for each task.

With a good set of orders and rehearsals before a mission, you could achieve your objective in a more smooth and efficient way than if it had been done off the cuff. However, no matter how much you plan and prepare, some things are never foreseen. We had a drill for everything, but some occurrences could still be a big surprise when they happened.

We were still a three vehicle team with just the one gun truck at the rear of the call sign. We were expected to ramp up to four vehicles in the near future but in the meantime, we would continue as we were.

We were returning through the city from a task in the eastern outskirts; a school project that the American government was funding as part of the 'Hearts and Minds' campaign to win over the Iraqi population. The city was packed and we found ourselves in slow moving traffic.

Even though our sirens and lights were blaring away, the traffic had nowhere to go to let us through. We couldn't cross over the central reservation as the congestion on that side was just as bad. It was a tricky situation to be in because we were moving slowly, which meant we were an easy target. The lead vehicle was doing their best to push us through the jam, but we still weren't making much headway.

All along the right of us were shop fronts and high rooftops. Numerous alleyways filtered into the main street from between the buildings, and slip roads joined onto the main road in a number of places. To make matters worse, every man and his mate's dog were on the street as well, and they were all eyeing the three large black SUVs that slowly travelled by.

We were approaching a slip road that was joining us from the right. We had created an invisible bubble around our convoy that gave us a little space to play with, but if someone came at us from the side, we wouldn't be able to manoeuvre much to avoid them.

I could see the slip up ahead and to the right, and I scanned the vehicles that were approaching from that side.

"Vehicles approaching from the right Smudge," I shouted over my shoulder, and he turned his attention to cover the slip road once we had passed it.

I was waving a warning to a vehicle that was trying to approach and telling him to stay back when, our truck suddenly rocked violently. I snapped my head and weapon around to my left to face who had hit us and I instantly realised that they weren't a threat.

The twenty or so kids' faces that were pressed against the windows of the inside of a saloon car made that clear to me. Some prat, who had already cleared the slipway and wanted to join the main flow of traffic, had suddenly pulled out from our right without warning and his front left side had hit our front right wheel. Because of the weight of our vehicle, his car was pretty much written off and we thought we could continue. That was until Toad tried to steer the vehicle away; nothing happened.

When the car had hit us, it had snapped our steering arms on the inside of the wheel.

Brian called for the rest of the call sign to stop, and Omar and I jumped straight out to start keeping the traffic from approaching us. We were now completely vulnerable and all three vehicles were static in the road.

Fortunately, because the traffic was slow moving, we were soon the only vehicles on a two hundred metre stretch so we could see any vehicle borne threats approaching from a good distance.

We had started to draw a crowd of spectators from the roadside. I kept a close eye on them as Smudge covered the rear and the static vehicles to our six o'clock while Omar watched the rooftops and the other side of the street. Sean was doing the same with Dave further up in the convoy.

At the same time, Dave was on the radio to our Op's Room to find out if a recovery was possible and how long it would take.

Toad and Brian were checking the damage, and they informed Dave that it needed to be a low loader to salvage it and that it couldn't be towed because there was no steering. Geoff told us over that radio that it would take at least an hour to get a recovery truck from the base to us, but we weren't in an area where we could wait an hour.

Right at that moment, we knew that someone was probably checking his stash of grenades and rockets and getting ready to hit us from a rooftop or maybe from within the crowd. The street was full of civilians and more were showing up by the minute. I kept my weapon in the shoulder, ready to fire at the first sign of trouble.

"Right lads, strip all the kit from the gun truck; we're gonna have to burn it. We can't sit here much longer." Dave shouted to us.

I couldn't believe what I was hearing. We were actually going to set fire to a gun truck? This was a new one to me.

"At least let me get out first." Smudge grumbled from the back.

"This is how we send $200,000 up in smoke, Lukey." Toad shouted over to me as he stripped the radio and navigation equipment along with his own personal kit, including his CD collection, out from his side.

Brian was doing the same.

Omar and I continued to cover our arcs and once the vehicle was stripped of its kit and equipment, Dave approached with a Thermite Grenade.

The locals could see that we were abandoning the vehicle and they couldn't wait for us to be gone so that some lucky guy could have a nice armoured SUV to play in. Or so they thought.

I backed away towards the other two vehicles and covered Dave as he tossed in the grenade. He headed back towards me and a couple of seconds later there was a flash inside the gun truck and smoke started to pour out from the doors and windows. The looks on the Iraqi faces all around us was like that of a kid who had just had their toys confiscated.

"Mount up fellas and let's get back sharpish. We've no gun truck now, so we have fuck all protection." Dave gave a last glance to make sure the gun truck was fully ablaze.

Even the front windows were melting with the heat. Every man squeezed into the two remaining vehicles and both drivers put their feet down to get us through the city as quickly as possible.

I had Toad's arse in my face and Smudges' gun barrel jammed into my back. If we had been hit at that point, there was nothing I could have done from in there. Every available space of the interior was filled with men and weapons. It was like stuffing ten pounds of shit in to a five pound bag.

Dave had informed our Op's Room of the actions we had taken and that we now had no gun truck. Geoff had called the air-cell and two helicopters were sent out to meet us en-route to act as top cover for us as we raced back to the FOB.

The steady beating thump of their rotor blades announced their arrival overhead. From where I was sat, with a face full of Toad's arse, I couldn't see them, but just knowing they were there was reassuring. It was great to have, and all it took was to ask nicely and the pilots would always do what they could for us.

Over time we ended up developing a close relationship with the helicopter crews. They even told us that working with us, was much more exciting and adventurous than working with their own army.

They escorted us the entire way and they even hovered overhead as I fell out of the truck once we were inside the gate. Every muscle in my body was cramped, and we all seriously needed a leg stretch once we were in the secure area beyond the gate. The pilot gave us a wave and I gave him the thumbs up while Dave thanked them over the radio.

Once back at our Op's Room, I assumed there was going to be the holiest of shit storms coming our way because we had just burnt out a $200,000 vehicle. But to my amazement, Geoff had already informed our HQ and the USACE commander, and praises were coming in thick and fast for our professionalism and slick drills in a tricky situation.

That's when the penny dropped; I realised that the company didn't pay for the vehicles and the U.S government did. No doubt we would have been shot at dawn if the company had been footing the bill.

All we had to do now was write a full report on the incident from each of our perspectives, and then we were off until they got a replacement truck to us. I was told that it could take as long as a couple of weeks.

The vehicle that hit us was clearly no threat. My first reaction had been to turn and face the driver and I very nearly put a burst into him, but I had realised instantly that he was just a bonehead. He hadn't meant to hit us and clearly wasn't a suicide bomber or anything like that. Terrorists don't tend to take all of their kids with them when they set out to become a martyr, and that vehicle was packed with them.

He had just wanted to quickly get to where he was going and in his haste, hadn't noticed the big black four ton SUV to his immediate left as he pulled out.

Again, this was due to the utter contempt in which the Iraqi men view the abuse of a wing mirror for anything other than correcting hair styles.

But the consequences of that little bump had been huge. Luckily, it turned out to be just from a financial standpoint but it could have easily cost lives, had circumstances been different and explosives had been involved.

Again, I was impressed with the team that I was part of. No one had flapped or panicked, and the situation was dealt with without so much as the blink of an eye.

For the next two weeks, all we could do was wait for the new truck to be delivered. In the meantime, the army had recovered what was left of our gun truck from within the city. Nothing much was left of it except for a melted windscreen and a burnt out shell. Our answer to HQ when they asked if it could be salvaged, repaired and made roadworthy again was clear, "Could it balls."

Therefore, our days were spent doing a little weapon or medical training in the mornings and then going to the pool in the afternoon. Most evenings were spent in Smudges' room or down at the compound garage having barbeques.

SUICIDE TRUCKS AND MINE FIELDS

———————◆———————

A week later, two new trucks arrived, along with some additional team members. We were ramping up to a four vehicle SET, Security Escort Team, and so we needed each vehicle to be fully manned. At any one point there were always five team members on leave so, all in all there were now twenty men in our group.

The new vehicles were exactly the same as the one we had set fire to, but each still had to be checked and tested. Neither of them was new and had been used by other teams so we wanted to be sure that HQ hadn't sent us a couple of trucks that were likely to break down or fall apart on us.

The new team members also had to be trained up. Even though a couple of them had been working with the company for a while, they still needed to train with the team to make sure we were all the same standard.

Even on the circuit in Iraq, you still get people who haven't a clue what they're doing and shouldn't be there. Normally it was due to having a friend in management who would give them a job as a favour.

After a couple of days training and preparing vehicles, we were once again good to go. Because we had been unable to conduct missions for over a week, a back log of tasks had built up in the meantime and we knew we were going to be busy for the foreseeable future.

Our first task was to drop off a client in Sulimania. He was supposed to have gone the week before but, because we were out of action and the PSD teams in Suli were unable to pick him up, he had just had to sit tight and wait for us to be operational again.

Our mission required us to cut a direct route through the city and travel as quickly as possible towards the east and onto the open road leading to Suli. We were going to be travelling through some heavily built up areas and over the same bridge mentioned previously that cut across the river running north to south through the centre of the city.

Our intention was to get through Kirkuk as fast as we could before anyone even realised we were there. As usual, I would be the right side gunner of the rear truck but, instead of Omar sitting at my back, I had a huge Australian, named Guy. He needed the extra leg room and so I found myself sat a little closer to the armour plating of the door.

We screamed out of the FOB with the sirens and lights blaring but this time, because we had a gun truck at each end of the call sign, there was no need for us to push up to the front to hold traffic. The lead vehicle would do that, and as the client vehicles came out we would replace the front gun truck and cover the turning then tag onto the rear. It was much easier to control and that way, we had 360 degree protection at all times.

Once clear, we picked up speed and raced along to the junction further up. Sean once again was giving the commentary from the lead vehicle. We made the right turn and the road was clear ahead towards the bridge.

Weaving in and out through the traffic, our truck took on the feel of a sailing yacht rolling from side to side in a rough sea. I had become accustomed to it and swayed with the vehicle as though riding out a storm in order to keep on my feet. Only I was sitting, but I was still very much aware that I had to keep control of my weapon and by anticipating the bobbing and weaving of our vehicle, I was able to cover my arcs.

Guy was new to the circuit and he hadn't quite mastered the 'sailing technique' needed in the back of a gun truck and so I found myself, now and then, pushed against my firing port with twenty stone of Australian and his kit on my back as he lost his balance and slid to my side.

"Sorry mate. Not got the hang of this gripping the seat with your arse cheeks routine yet."

"No worries," I replied over my shoulder to him, "just give me warning when you're popping over to my side so I can stop my head from twatting the armour plating."

As we approached the bridge, the lead truck paved the way with the sirens to make sure we had a clear run. The last thing we wanted was to slow down at this point. Coming over the bridge, I could see the road on the other side and the surrounding buildings coming into view.

Market stalls were set up everywhere and people were selling their sheep and fuel as normal. All along the road, there were smaller tracks leading off between the buildings and houses. Vehicles pushed off the road and went static as soon as they saw us to avoid being fired on as we passed. The sight and sound of us was clear warning enough. Well, for some people anyway.

Brian screamed over his shoulder, "Watch this fucker coming in from the right."

I looked to where he was pointing and I could see a large white flatbed truck approaching us at speed at a right angle. He was coming from a side street and was roughly fifty to sixty metres to our right and slightly ahead of us. The dust coming up around his wheels and in his wake was a good indicator of the speed he was travelling at and he wasn't slowing. If anything, he looked to be building speed.

I immediately noticed that the driver was alone in the cab and on the back of his truck, was what appeared to be dozens of gas canisters. Everyone was passing the information over their radios.

The lead gun truck had no arcs to cover the approaching vehicle due to other cars and people in the way so, the only person who had a clear line on him, was me.

"Roger that Brian. I've got him," I shouted as I gripped the SAW tighter in my hands.

I adjusted my position in the seat and fixed my sights on the fast approaching truck. Everything else became diluted in to the background. The sounds of the engines and the voices around me became distant as I focussed my attention and weapon on to the approaching threat.

He continued coming towards us, even though he could clearly see who we were, and the fact that all other traffic on the road had come to a stop to let us through should have made him follow suit.

I was frantically waving to him and even screaming for him to stop, but I knew that he couldn't hear me. Just by the look of him, I could tell that even if he could, the driver had no intention of avoiding us.

From the moment Brian had pointed him out to me waving warnings at him, it had taken only a second or two. By now he was too close to us and if he continued, he would hit us side on. There was nothing left to do because the safety of the team was now in jeopardy.

I took aim.

"Stand by, stand by," I shouted to inform the others that I was about to fire.

I squeezed the trigger and let off a burst of five rounds into the grill on the front of his truck. The weapon shuddered against my shoulder as the rounds exploded from the barrel and the working parts were forced back and forth, forcing the next round in to the chamber and repeating the process. The report of the gun was loud within the confines of the vehicle, but the sound of it firing and the feel of its force as it pushed in to my shoulder, was reassuring.

Knowing the engine was directly behind the grill, I had hoped to immobilise the vehicle. It didn't. Because of his speed and momentum, the truck continued to plough towards us and even shooting the wheels would have made no difference at such short range. I aimed higher and in the sight of my weapon I could clearly see the driver in the cab.

He didn't look as though he was trying to slow down or even avoid us. He seemed concentrated, determined and I could almost imagine him saying his last prayer before he found himself in Paradise.

By now, he was about twenty five metres away and no matter if we swerved, slammed on the brakes or tried to turn, he was going to hit us.

I squeezed the trigger again and fired at his centre of mass, feeling the weapon jerk against my shoulder. I saw his windscreen suddenly spider web and cave inward and large pieces of it fell out as more rounds punched through.

Because of the damage to the window, I couldn't see if the driver had been hit but he immediately swung to the right and almost ran over a parked car before he hit a drainage ditch running parallel to the track he was travelling along then, coming to a complete stop.

Because the flatbed had changed its course, we were just able to pass without being hit. The threat was now behind us and I continued to cover my arcs knowing that Smudge would now have sight of him in the six o'clock position of our truck.

Brian was on the radio to Dave, giving him a sit-rep on what had happened.

"You nailed him good style there Luke," Smudge shouted from the rear. "He just slid out of the cab when some locals opened the door mate. Nice shooting."

"Cheers mate," was the only reply I could think of.

I was back covering my arcs and the incident was behind me. Regardless of the fact that I had just killed a man, I still had a job to do and we were still on task so, it was forgotten about just as quickly as it all happened.

The whole incident had taken no more than five or six seconds from the truck first being pointed out by Brian, to us being clear of the threat. If I had hesitated, the flatbed would have hit us and regardless if he was a suicide bomber or not, there would have been casualties and no doubt a few deaths, including my own.

The sheer weight and speed of his vehicle was enough to turn our gun truck into a crumpled steel mess if it had slammed into us. I had warned him and there was no doubt in my mind that he knew what and who we were. He had left me little choice but to fire on him. I wasn't about to lose sleep over him being dead at my hands, but I wasn't looking forward to writing the reports that would inevitably follow such an incident.

After a quick debate over the radio between Brian, Dave and Geoff in the Op's Room, it was decided that the mission would continue and we would go ahead as planned and drop the client off before returning to base. It wasn't a big deal to me or anyone in the team. We had all seen and done similar things in the past, and there would be many more incidents in the future, so we cracked on and continued on our way.

Once clear of Kirkuk, we found ourselves on a long open road with very little traffic and few built up areas. After a few miles we hit the Green Line. At that point we withdrew our weapons from sight to adopt a more liberal profile.

The Green Line is a point between Kirkuk and Suli on the map which is considered to be the demarcation line between hostile and friendly territory. We still kept the vehicles at a distance but instead of pointing weapons or shooting, we would wave to them to stay back. If they were clearly no threat, we would allow them to pass.

It was once we were clear of the green line that the banter started.

"I can't believe you shot up a bunch of orphans on a day trip, Luke." Dave said across the radio. "You're not much good at the hearts and minds are you."

"Yeah why did you light up a coach full of pensioners on their way to bingo night at the FOB, Luke?" Toad chipped in looking over his shoulder and grinning at me.

I sat listening to everyone's twisted version of events for a while before Toad drowned them out with a CD from his collection.

To my joy, when we reached the small FOB on the outskirts of Suli, my good friend Liam was there. After our last company had had to reduce in size, he had gone on to work for another high profile company that was also working the same contract as us. The workload and projects were shared out between the two companies and his team had been subsequently based in Suli.

I had known this but I was unaware that Liam had gone to work for them. While the rest of my guys waited around for lunch to be served in the small canteen, I went to Liam's room and had a catch up.

As always, he was playing the jolly fat man routine; dancing around his room, telling me animated stories of what he had been up to in both work and on leave since I had last seen him.

He also showed me pictures of his little Spartans, James and Stewart. They say a picture paints a thousand words, but Liam could paint a million words when telling you a tale, just from his hand gestures and tone of voice. I could imagine him as a children's TV presenter, although with the amount of trouble he would get into, he would be on the front page of the tabloids every week with yet another scandalous story about his drinking antics.

We headed back to Kirkuk after we had had some lunch and we made a point of changing our route from the original plan in order to avoid the scene of the shooting on the way in.

When we got back, before I could do anything else, I had to write out an initial report on what had happened so that Geoff could send it off to Baghdad HQ.

I was then required to write a full, more in depth follow up later, along with everyone on the team who had witnessed the incident, including Brian and Dave. Nothing came of it and as far as anyone was concerned, I had acted well within the 'Rules of Engagement' or 'Rules for the Use of Force' as it is now known.

As previously mentioned, it was something that happened on a daily basis in Iraq and no one was going to get their selves bent out of shape over the whole thing. We tried to find out from the police in Kirkuk what they had found when they attended the scene afterwards, but no one could give us an answer. No one seemed to care, so why should we?

A few days later we were tasked to take Joe back to the water project, only this time, it was a different facility that we needed to visit a few kilometres further north in a more open and flat area than the ridge line we had been to previously.

He assured us that he had the correct grids and that he would turn up on time for the mission. On the morning of the job, he arrived at the office only ten minutes late. He was still taking the piss. Dave threw a track and gave him a severe talking to out of ear shot of the team, but we all got the gist of what was being said just from the expression on Dave's face.

On the mission, I was to take a turn in the commander's seat of the lead vehicle as the communications guy. Therefore, it would be me giving the running commentary this time. Doing the commentary, especially in an urban area, is similar to being the commentator at the horse races. I had to speak at a thousand miles per hour and point out everything I saw as well as giving steers and informing the rest of the team of turns and junctions.

We set out and before long we were through the city and heading for the ridge line north of Kirkuk. Beyond the hills, the country was open and flat with sparsely scattered villages and farmland. The area we were heading to would provide no cover whatsoever from either an attack or the elements. Because of this, we were required to use our vehicles as a sort of 'steel ring' around the area in which Joe needed to operate.

When we arrived at the grid that Joe had given us, we could see no evidence of a water project or any other project for that matter. He swore black was blue that he had been there before with previous teams and that they must have moved it. We knew ourselves that they couldn't just move an entire site without the Corp of Engineers knowing about it and so we guessed, and as it turned out, correctly that Joe had given us the wrong grid again. We were all of the opinion that, Joe couldn't find his own arse with both hands. It wasn't the first, and by no means, the last time Joe gave us incorrect coordinates.

We found the actual site a few kilometres further on.

The site engineer and a few workers were already there waiting for us, to give Joe the heads up and help him with the inspection of the work. As per SOP, we provided all round defence as Joe, Dave and Brian walked the site.

The foreman informed us of a recently discovered minefield that had been unearthed a kilometre south of us. This was no concern of ours as it wasn't our job to deal with, but it was useful information for the next time we came to this location so that we knew to avoid it when planning.

During the Iran/Iraq war, both sides had used minefields extensively throughout the border regions. Even though Kirkuk was well away from the border with Iran, the wide open areas to the east of Kirkuk were ideal tank country. For this reason, the Iraqi army had laced the whole area with anti tank and personnel mines covering the approaches to the city should the Iranian Army ever make a breakthrough and advance westward toward the central cities.

Kirkuk is a large oil and gas city and would have been of major strategic value to the Iranians' had they got that far. In the hills all around Kirkuk you can still see, even to this day, the Iraqi trench systems and bunkers built into the rocks overlooking the low ground.

Joe informed us that he needed to inspect an area south of where we were and also check the pipes running between the sites. Dave spoke to the foreman, asking him if the route was clear and if so, could he guide us there to make sure that we didn't hit the minefield. My truck was to follow the pickup truck of the engineer.

As we mounted up, Dave opened the door for Joe to climb into the rear of the client vehicle. Joe saw his chance and quickly turned back and rushed to the foreman who was going to lead us. Before Dave could get to him, they had exchanged words and Joe headed back to his vehicle, with his usual smug smile on his face, avoiding eye contact with anyone. We all just put it down to Joe being Joe and his usual dick self.

The foreman set off and we followed at a distance. After a few hundred metres we then left the track and headed to the left, across open desert and plain area. We all assumed that we were taking a detour to avoid the minefield up ahead until, our truck slammed on and came to a sudden stop, jolting everyone in the vehicle forward.

Right in front of us was clearly a half buried mine. Everyone froze but to our amazement, the pickup in front turned around and started to head back to us. I opened my door and screamed and waved at the foreman to stop. He did so, then got out of his truck and started to walk towards me. I decided to close my door until he got to me, just in case anything went off beneath his feet. I didn't want to be caught in the blast.

He walked up to my door looking very pleased with his self and knocked on my window. I cracked the door slightly.

"Why are you walking around? There's a mine right in front of us."

He was smiling and nodding. "Yes, I know. Mr Joe told me to come here."

I was getting confused and couldn't understand why he was so pleased with himself. I looked at Sean, who was driving our vehicle that day. He looked just as confused and shrugged his shoulders.

"I'm not driving another fucking yard Luke," he barked. I agreed completely.

"Right, Mr Joe told you to take us into the minefield?" I asked the foreman, who now realised that I wasn't as impressed as he was.

"Yes, he said he wanted to see the mines." His smile had faded and a look of concern spread across his face as mine turned red and my eyebrows knitted together.

"Dave, the foreman here has led us right into a minefield mate. I'm not sure how far in we are, but he said it was Joe who told him to do it." I sent over the radio.

"You fucking what, are you sure?"

"Yes mate. We have a mine right in front of our bumper and the foreman insists that he's just doing what he was told."

Silence, then Dave informed me that he was going to change vehicles before he killed Joe. I watched through my side mirror as Dave got out and made his way to the vehicle behind. He was careful to walk in the vehicle's tracks, knowing that the path was clear. Once he was safely inside, he told the call sign over the radio that one man per truck needed to guide their respective vehicles back through to the main track and to make sure that the wheels stayed in the tyre prints of the vehicle behind.

Most anti-tank mines are set to only explode when a certain weight and above travels over them. That way, it wouldn't detonate when a man stepped on it or even a car and therefore wouldn't alert any armour approaching by going off under someone's foot. With the weight of our trucks however, we could have easily set one off.

It took a good hour before we retraced our tracks and cleared the minefield, and by then, Dave had composed himself enough to return to his original vehicle. The mission was scrapped and we headed back to base. I could only guess what was being said in the client vehicle, and I had a suspicion that Dave was doing all of the talking.

Once we were back in the camp, Joe was immediately dragged into the office and put before his boss. I would have loved to have been a fly on the wall as the commanding officer tore into him.

It was obvious that when Joe had quickly ran to the foreman and spoken to him prior to returning to his vehicle before anyone had been able to react, he had told him that he wanted to go and see the minefield. Whether he wanted to actually go into the minefield or not is irrelevant.

He put the team in danger by his actions and the mines had nothing to do with him or us anyway.

The whole team was fuming. If the mine we nearly ran into had been more difficult to see, the whole thing could have detonated below our gun truck, sending five men to their deaths instantly.

They are not like mines that you see in the 'A-Team', where they cause the vehicle to flip through the air after which the occupants climb out dazed and confused. They are normally a large amount of high explosives in a shaped charge that punch a hole through the underbelly of an armoured vehicle, destroying everything inside including living tissue. I had seen the results of such mines and the remains of men caught inside the vehicle were unrecognisable as people. Corned beef is the best word to describe them.

We all hoped that Joe would be on the next flight home but to our horror, he got off with a dressing down from his bosses. There was nothing else we could do but accept it, as the matter had already been dealt with. He walked out of the office with his usual smug look and slight smile, and even managed to give a nod in our direction as we sat looking on in shock.

Rab was beside himself. "That wee cunts gonna get someone killed."

He was pacing up and down and grunting like a bear about to go mental. He already looked like a guy who was about to lose it at the best of times. Rab was a big, angry Scottish guy on the outside but, I'd already come to realise, that he wasn't as bad as he looked. Still, with his size and his fieriness, you knew there would be no stopping him once he blew.

His nickname growing up had been 'Savage' and he had it tattooed across his stomach, but with the team as we were, we had already taken the piss and claimed it said 'Sausage'.

I hit the gym hard that night. I needed to release my frustrations so I decided to do some punch bag work at the end of my training session. Rab tagged along and from then on we were training partners and became close friends. The more I got to know him, the more I realised that to the people that mattered, he was a gentle giant. He was a good two thirds of a foot taller than me and about five stone heavier but I insisted on lifting the same weight and told him that he wasn't to go easy on me when we were sparring. I think it was my 'little man syndrome' coming through, and the feeling that I had to prove a point. Still, I gave as well as I received.

Joe avoided us for a while after that and didn't bother to place any mission requests. That suited the team just fine and the longer it lasted, the better. No one was in a hurry to see what the next adventure would have in store for us. We ran a couple of missions in and out of the city as usual and even the odd one to Erbil.

The Corp of Engineers had a small contingency in the Ankawa area of Erbil, close to where I had been living on my last contract. We would drop a couple of clients off for a meeting then two of our vehicles would go out, under the pretext of getting some lunch for the team. In reality, we were normally stopping at the local booze shops and replenishing our supplies. The clients would never be aware of this and we would go to great lengths to hide it from them.

Sometimes we were even given shopping lists from other people on the FOB for their favourite booze. Naturally, we wouldn't do this for just anyone. They would need to be the likes of mechanics, armourers and medics. These people could help us and so we would help them.

Most people on the base didn't go out beyond the wire and would spend the whole of their tour of duty in the camp. With the Americans not being allowed to drink and us travelling to places where we came into contact with alcohol, we would occasionally let it slip while talking to them, if we felt safe enough, to see their reaction. If it was a good one, then a deal could be made and we would pick them up some 'loud mouth soup' in return for something they could do for us.

Unfortunately, it had to be this way. Even though the American Army was supposed to equip and supply us with what we needed, they often didn't have what we requested or it would be easier and quicker to strike a deal instead.

Sean walked into the office one day with a box of about twenty stun grenades he had swapped with the armourer for a bottle of Jack Daniels. Contrary to popular belief, anything can be obtained in Iraq, especially in the north. They have off-licences in Erbil where you can buy pretty much any kind of booze you can think of, and all genuine brands.

Very often we would come back from Suli or Erbil and the men in the gun trucks would be sitting on crates of beer and cases of vodka. One day we brought in an order that was so big, we had cases of whisky in the client vehicle, covered with a camouflaged sheet just beside where they were sitting, and they never knew a thing.

We organised yet another barbeque down in the garage and, as usual, the booze was flowing and we were enjoying ourselves. Another newcomer to the team was a big Welsh lad named Cach. That was his nickname of course, and we found out that 'Cach' was a Welsh word meaning 'shit'.

It was given to him when he was a young boy. On a family camping holiday one year, he had an accident in his trousers, and the name had stuck. Even now, in his early thirties, he introduced himself as Cach.

He turned up to our first barbeque carrying a plastic bag with his favourite drink inside and wearing a pirate's hat. The guy was 6'4" and built like a shire horse, yet here he was, looking more like a down and out swashbuckler of the sea.

By now it was midsummer of 2006 and I'd been on the circuit for a year and a half. During that time, I had noticed a marked difference in the people working in Iraq. At the beginning, it was mainly anyone who had even the most basic experience and skills, but once the word had spread and experienced manpower became readily available, the companies had become more choosey about the people they employed. Some companies wanted mainly ex Special Forces and other companies just preferred employees to have a set minimum amount of years of army service.

The company I was working for was the latter sort. Most of the men on the teams were experienced and well trained, but there was often a plonker that would slip through. Having them in management and out of the way was one thing, but putting them on the ground where they could cause harm to others was a different matter.

Luckily, our team never experienced this sort of level of incompetence but we heard one or two horror stories from other teams and within the circuit as a whole.

A year earlier a call sign from a low profile company had been hit on the BIAP and, due to the lack of skills and training within the team, three men were killed. I won't divulge the full details of the contact or drag anyone's names through the dirt, but the report that came out afterwards clearly showed the lack of experience within the team. Two of them had no military background at all and had only worked as police officers.

The twenty men working on our team all had extensive military experience and had served in numerous conflicts and operations worldwide. I don't necessarily mean that you needed to be ex military to work in Iraq, but serving in the army gives you a set of base skills that are a good starting point.

Anyone who has served in the forces will know that, once your weapon handling skills are up to a good standard on one weapon system, it becomes much easier to learn different weapons systems, from small arms to heavy machineguns as you are already in that mindset. A general starting point in skills and drills would always hold someone in good stead when joining the circuit as averse to someone who had no or very little tactical training and weapon skills. Unfortunately, this was sometimes overlooked when a guy in management had a friend who wanted to get onto the circuit.

Our training days always consisted of drills, either with the vehicles or with weapons, and Dave teaching us medical. Sometimes, when conditions allowed, we would combine everything in scenarios and live firing on the ranges. These were the times we needed to be extra careful to avoid injury.

When we were on the back road of the FOB practicing our vehicle contact drills without using live firing, we didn't expect any accidents. That was until during one scenario in which the second vehicle in the team was to act as though it had been hit with an IED and was immobilized.

"Contact right, vehicle two is down." Dave reported over the radio.

This was to inform us of the particular direction of the contact so that we knew the way to dismount, which would be out of the left hand side, keeping the armour of the vehicle between ourselves and the enemy. I was acting as the commander in the third truck, sitting in the passenger seat.

In this scenario, the gun trucks would go static and return fire as the third vehicle, which I was in, pulled up on the opposite side from the contact of the damaged second vehicle and allow the clients and team members to quickly cross deck into our undamaged vehicle and away we would go, leaving the killing zone as quickly as possible.

The drill went smoothly. During the cross decking I was leaning back from the passenger seat into the rear seating area, holding the door and making sure it didn't close before the clients and team were safely inside. If it had, it would've cost vital seconds while someone from the outside had to pull it open again. Vital seconds that we couldn't spare because we needed to move away from the contact as quickly as possible.

Within seconds, everyone was in and we were away. Quick and easy, the drill went well.

The team members in the back, once the drill was called to an end, jumped out to return to their vehicle. I leant over again to ensure the door stayed open and didn't close on them as they debussed. Omar was the last to get out and at that moment, I was speaking on the radio to Dave getting ready for the next scenario when, Omar slammed the door shut with my fingers safely on the inside, but my thumb in the hinge of the door, so to all intensive purposes I was inside the vehicle and my thumb was outside.

I felt the force of the door and at the exact same time my eyes grew wide, my face changed colour and I dropped the hand mic in my lap. I knew what had happened and for what seemed an eternity, I looked straight ahead as if waiting for the pain to hit.

I screamed like a little girl.

Unable to release my arm from the door, I banged on the window, screaming for Omar to open it. With armoured glass and doors, very little sound escapes and so, he continued toward his vehicle with his back to me and completely unaware and unable to hear my cries for help or my thumps against the glass.

I felt helpless and there was nothing I could do to help myself. I couldn't reach the handle and I couldn't exactly get out and open it while leaving my hand inside.

Looking back, it was hilarious, with me slapping the window like a child watching their parents walk away after leaving them at the nursery for the first time and crying their eyes out. The image of Omar and his nonchalant, not a care in the world walk, as he made his way back to his position in the second vehicle, is still firmly embedded in my mind.

I can almost hear him whistling as he did so.

It was only as he got into his truck and about to close the door that, he looked up and must've seen the most pathetic sight ever. By now I was the colour of paper with my face pressed against the window. He stopped while closing his door and looked directly at me. I could see the confusion in his face and then, with his eyes, he followed the length of my arm and then the penny dropped. His eyes bulged then quickly popped back in his head and he rushed across to open the door.

It had seemed like hours to me but in reality, it had only been a few seconds.

As the door released my thumb, I crumpled into my seat pulling my hand in close to my chest. I could feel the sweat dripping down my forehead and didn't want to look at the area where I was sure my thumb had once been. Having a door that weighs a third of a ton slammed on my hand, I was sure that the digit was now at the foot of the door, having been severed.

With one eye shut tight, partly from pain and partly from fear, I slowly raised my hand from my chest to view the damage with the eye that was still, slightly, open. My thumb was still there but it was twice the size of the one I was used to seeing.

Dave opened my door and he expected to see me minus a thumb also and looked pretty shocked to see it still attached. I climbed out and did the usual running around in little circles dance that people believe will somehow relieve the pain, and I quickly followed it with every curse I could think of, while leaning my head against the side of the hood of the vehicle and growling through my teeth.

It's amazing to see the different stages of this sort of incident in effect and the way a man deals with it. The first is a split second of confusion before the pain hits and wondering if it has really happened. Then, it's the pain itself and the screaming and shouting. That's followed by the dance, mixed with the anger and growling, followed by the shock and whimpering as you check for the extent of the damage.

Women scream and curse during child birth, but if it was a man and he had the means, he would nuke entire continents, swearing that no one had ever felt the same pain before.

No two ways about it, my thumb was broken. But at least it was still there. I could've played on the injury and got myself sent home and allowed the company insurance package to give me paid leave while it healed but, I wasn't willing to take it that far. Looking back, I could've been sitting very pretty if the door had actually severed it because the payout would've been substantial.

I know of a guy who to this day is still being paid a small fortune each month while sitting at home. He had been working for another company and deliberately damaged himself in order to get paid for it. The last I heard, he was undergoing extensive surgery to repair it and he was in negotiations over the amount he should receive from the insurance.

I could still work my weapons and equipment and so, I cracked on. Not because I'm hard as nails or some super trooper but mainly, because I didn't want the fuss and the way I saw it, I had a contract and I was earning good money, so why should I take the risk between getting a good payout or a crap one?

I strapped it up and was careful not to knock it about for a while. I've always been one to heal quickly and within a couple of weeks, it was just a sore thumb. Naturally, I had the piss taken out of me over the whole thing and even Omar ripped into me. You never get any sympathy from the blokes.

I was back in the rear gun truck and a side shooter again. I enjoyed this position and the men I was working closely with were a well oiled unit. The whole gun truck was one entity and everyone could anticipate one another.

It was also around that time, that we received a report on an incident involving terrorists disguised as a PSD. As I mentioned earlier, I had come to the conclusion that with a bit of balls and brass, it could be done and a group had done exactly that.

They had got hold of a few dark coloured SUVs, stuck a siren and some red and blue lights to the front and dressed themselves in similar kit to what we would wear. They headed to a small police station where they knew there were three American soldiers instructing local recruits.

As they approached, they hit the red and blue flashing lights and gave it full on the sirens. The sentry on the gate had assumed they were a western security team and opened the barriers and never even considered to stop and check their paperwork or identification. The three vehicles pulled up in the centre of the compound and went straight into an attack.

They debussed and opened up on everyone they saw. The guards and local police still had their weapons slung over their shoulders and so it was easy pickings for the bad guys. The three American soldiers, as it was later reported, were taken prisoner and one died shortly after from wounds sustained during the attack. The other two were executed by being shot in the head and dumped at the roadside some miles away.

It was a huge PR coup for the terrorists and naturally, every base in the country was on high alert and the camp security was doubled in order to stop anyone else from cashing in on the idea.

In the report from the American intelligence cell, we were told that the terrorists wore U.S uniforms, spoke perfect English with American accents, had fake ID and even carried American issued weapons. Also, each of them had been specially trained for the job in other countries sympathetic to the cause and had been picked for their particular western look.

We were sceptical about the report and we read between the lines. The American military were now flapping and decided to ladle on the extent of the attack and enemy preparation in order to make people more vigilant about camp security and to also minimize the damage done to their own security image.

In our opinion, the terrorists had more than likely just made themselves look as similar to a PSD as possible with what tools they had. They wouldn't have gone to the extent of fake ID's and uniforms and weapons because they wouldn't have had the equipment in abundance, and as soon as anyone took more than a cursory glance at them, they would've realised who and what they were anyway.

But seeing three dark SUVs approaching from the distance and with flashing lights and blazing sirens they knew, there was a chance they would get through and then all they needed was a couple of seconds of shock effect on the guards. They had also most likely watched the camp for a while and studied the routine of the guards and noticed that they never checked PSD and military call signs and just allowed them straight through with a wave.

Unfortunately for us, some American commanders took the report as gospel and believed that Al-Qaeda were now training special units and supplying them with everything they needed to infiltrate bases.

We were tasked to take three clients to a small FOB just to the north west of Tuz. Just getting there was a risky job and took us through a number of dangerous areas where IEDs and ambushes on convoys were regular.

Once we got to the outer gate, we were looking forward to an hour or two to relax while the clients conducted their meeting before we headed back through the gauntlet in order to get to home base.

Just a short word on the clients we were escorting; all three were American citizens and officers in the U.S Army. Two were Majors and pale skinned and the other was of South American descent and a Captain. The three of them wore American issue uniforms and equipment and carried all the relevant documentation and ID you would expect an American soldier to carry. Also, they travelled in four armoured Ford Excursions fitted with U.S communications equipment and tracking systems and occupied by white British men who also carried U.S equipment and weapons and funnily enough, had English, Scottish, Irish and Welsh accents and carried the same kind of ID the American clients did.

If it looks like a duck and it quacks, then it's probably due to the fact that it's a duck.

The guard on the gate was taking no chances and asked us to wait while he spoke to his commander. With this, we had no problem but when a fat colonel approached us thirty minutes later wearing no body armour or helmet and unarmed except for the young soldier with him carrying an M16, we felt insulted.

This guy was coming to check us over and if we turned out to be terrorists after he had checked our fake ID, with us patiently waiting while he scrutinized them, what was he going to do? Tell us he had caught us out and that we should leave?

Dave spoke to him and explained who we were. The colonel didn't seem at all interested and instead, asked where we had got our equipment.

Again, Dave told him that we were a PSD working for the U.S Corp of Engineers and showed him his ID and paper work. The colonel took the documents in his hand and checked both the face and back of the card.

"You can get copies made like this anywhere. They mean nothing."

Dave was doing his best to reason with him, "We are British and we're escorting American clients who are in the American Army. You're commander's are even expecting us here for a meeting."

"How do I know you're really British? You could've been trained to seem that way." The colonel was testing the patience of the whole team now. "I need to check your vehicles and your clients."

"No problem. Check away and you can even speak to our clients too if it clears things up."

How Dave hadn't lost his cool yet I don't know because my own feelings and the looks on the faces of other members of the team told me someone was going to get a smack in the teeth soon. Rab looked as though he wanted to eat him and Toad was keeping his opinions out in the open for all to hear. He clearly didn't like the man.

I and a few of the other team members, including Guy and Cach, stood watching the whole scene in disbelief as the fat colonel walked around, checking the vehicles to ensure they were real and peering inside to view the equipment we used.

Cach was chuckling to himself and couldn't understand that, if the colonel really thought we were terrorists, then why would he be walking amongst our vehicles unarmed?

"What a dick." He said out loud, as he carried on drinking from his water bottle.

"I've never seen anything like it mate." Guy grumbled shaking his head. "He's just on a power trip and has probably just received a "Dear John" letter from his chick back home."

After speaking with the three clients, the colonel returned to the gate where Dave followed, expecting everything to have been put right and we would be allowed to enter.

The colonel turned and said, "I don't believe you are who you say you are."

Dave looked shocked and I even saw a slight smile spread across his face, but I knew it was from disbelief and sheer anger and not, amusement.

"Our clients are American, didn't you notice that?"

"You can get these uniforms from anywhere and I didn't like the look of the dark haired one with the moustache," the colonel replied standing his ground and determined to be the biggest dick head in the country.

"He's a fucking Mexican." Dave stated in frustration.

The team was starting to snap and I could feel a lynching brewing. The argument between Dave and the colonel was becoming very heated and Brian had to step in before Dave hit the colonel.

So Brian, with the diplomatic skills of a cave man, looked at the colonel and spoke, "You're a fucking cock aren't you. You can clearly see who and what we are but you're just being a wanker. If we were terrorists, I think we would've either shot or kidnapped you and that spotty little prick over there by now." He shouted, pointing towards the young soldier carrying the M16, who was starting to look extremely nervous.

The colonel looked shocked at Brian's tirade and didn't reply. Even Dave had stopped in his tracks from walking away to cool off and was now returning to save the colonel from Brian.

The clients had had enough. They got out of their vehicle and informed us that they were scrapping the mission and we should return to base. The colonel immediately changed his tune and told us we were allowed in but, the clients had lost interest and mounted up for the return trip.

"Stuff it up your fucking arse you cock. We don't wanna come into your camp anyway. It's shit." Brian told the colonel as our parting gift of wisdom to him.

We raced off and Smudge gave the colonel the two fingered salute we British are famous for from the rear gunner position.

It had been a severe lesson in the level of stupidity that some people could reach. I'm not saying that the American's are the only ones capable of it because I'd experienced all sorts of idiotic beaurocratic incidents in the British army too.

A report was sent in from our clients regarding the matter, and I'd like to think that the colonel was soon washing dishes somewhere, having been busted to private soldier but, more than likely, he got a slap on the wrist.

The guy was a moron, and clearly had a power trip that day. That was the last time we went to that FOB and from then on, our clients insisted that they come to us for the meetings.

That suited us just fine because it was them now running the gauntlet and not us.

Rocket Man and, Nose Bleeds and Ice Baths

<hr />

By late summer we had gained a few more new comers to the group. Having moved from a three to four vehicle SET, we now required more men to cover guys going on leave.

Den was the first to arrive. He was much older than the rest of us and obviously, with more experience than the whole team put together. He had been on the circuit for years since leaving the army and at the age of fifty six, there wasn't much that he didn't know or hadn't seen. He was a very deep thinker and considerate to the point of selfless. Den always put the concerns of others and how things would affect the team before any other consideration, virtues that we valued in him a few months later when he would take over as our Team Leader.

Den took over from Brian as the team 2ic, second in command, and set to work with helping plan and prepare the tasks ahead with Dave as the commander. Brian continued to shadow Den to help out while he was finding his feet in his new role and to offer advice with the planning. Brian had been the 2ic for a long time and was in need of a break and so, as soon as Den turned up, he stood down.

Den had a million and one stories to tell and not only would he vocally describe them, but he would also act them out. He had been in the SAS for many years and served throughout the world in numerous conflicts and campaigns. When telling a tale, he would lose himself, and it was as though he was reliving the events as he told them. Even one time when he was telling us of a funeral, though tragic in itself because it was a personal friend of his, the story was hilarious because the coffin party had got themselves mixed up and half were facing one way and the rest were facing the other. He also had the appearance of everyone's favourite

Granddad with a hairless head and bushy eyebrows, but he was sharp as a knife and noticed everything.

Lee and Andy came to us from the Tikrit team. Lee had been in the Royal Marines and had served in the first Gulf war in 1991. Before working in Iraq, he had been a taxi driver in Manchester and it was only by luck he bumped into an old mate who offered him work as a PSD for the same company he was with. He always made a joke about one minute driving a cab in Manchester and the next, getting shot at and blown up in Iraq.

His high pitched Manchester accent and his natural ability to tell a funny story made him a much liked member of the team from the start. Whether you wanted to or not, you had to listen to him because he was so loud and his voice could never be mistaken.

The first time I had met him had been a couple of months earlier, when the Kirkuk and Tikrit teams had conducted a joint tasking together in Suli. When we got there, we found out that there wasn't enough accommodation for us all, so the security team had had to spend the night under the stars. Luckily, it was midsummer and warm, and everybody made the best 0f the situation and settled down for the night. But Lee insisted on voicing his thoughts.

"I'm fucking thirty five and I'm camping out, I feel like Ray Mears," was all we could hear for most of the night.

He had become good friends with Liam when they were on the Mosul team together and Liam had nicknamed him 'Chubbs'. It wasn't that he was fat, far from it. He was a fit guy and in the gym every day, but for some reason, he gave off the impression that he *should* be fat. The name stuck and he would even introduce himself as 'Chubbs'.

Andy was from Northern Ireland and an ex Guardsman. Tall, good looking and the spitting image of Patrick Swayze, but his dress sense was none existent. Even when he went home on leave, he would wear the clothes that we were issued by the company.

A guy we knew told us he walked into a pub one day and saw Andy stood at the bar, wearing a company shirt with his jeans.

He lived a life of extremes and one week, he would be eating junk food and smoking like a Russian and the next, he would be eating salads and running every day. His body must never have known whether it was coming or going, but he always seemed to be in good shape and he was naturally strong for a guy who wasn't particularly largely built.

Chubbs and Andy had been close friends since they had first met and the Tikrit team's loss, was our gain when they both came to Kirkuk. The atmosphere in the team was on a permanent high from then on.

It was around this time that we began to have trouble with one of the locals. We had received incoming rockets and mortars in the past from the surrounding city and built up areas and it had become more of an annoyance than an actual problem.

Most Indirect Fire, IDF tended to be randomly timed and even more randomly placed. The FOB was a big place, about the size of a small town and the artillery shells and rockets tended to land in open ground and would be ineffective. Now and then though, they would pull their finger out and get some pretty accurate shots in on us. From time to time they would get a sustained rate going and would even manage to adjust their fall of shot and inflict casualties within the base.

Mostly though, it was usually one or two random rounds and the sirens would go off telling us to move to the shelters and take cover. There were concrete bunkers throughout the base and you were never more than a couple of hundred metres from one wherever you were.

When the wail of the alarms sounded, that was our nod to move to the bunkers and it would be a while before the all clear was given so, being British, we would make sure we took our cups for a brew.

We would be sat in the shelter, chatting amongst ourselves when we would hear the distinct low thump as a high explosive shell hit somewhere in the FOB. Sometimes, we would hear the unmistakable whoosh as a round came in close and the sudden shaking impact of an accurately placed shell. It would vibrate through the ground and pop your ear drums leaving you momentarily disorientated if it landed close enough.

The insurgents had been known to fire a few rounds into a base, watch where the rounds landed and then adjust their mortar tubes to get them onto the target they wanted then they would wait. Once that was completed they sometimes went quiet, knowing the 'all clear' sirens would sound soon enough and people would start making their way back out of the shelters, believing the threat to be over. That's when they would hit again, with a few more shells with better accuracy and causing multiple casualties. They did this one evening on our base and hit a few buildings on the far side of the camp, causing a few deaths amongst the American soldiers.

Rocket Man was a fanatic. He was also a man of routine and we could even set our watch by him. Every evening, at around six o'clock, he would fire three or four rockets into the FOB, causing us great annoyance at having to leave our rooms and make our way to the shelters and end up sitting there for an hour or so before we were given the all clear.

He was a shit shot though and his rounds went all over the place and it seemed he was just firing in the hope of hitting something and not actually aiming. To us, it was a pain in the arse because we would normally have something much better to be doing than sitting in a concrete bunker in the evening listening to clients remarking about how scary it was and that they're going to tell their family friends back home all about it.

After a while, a few of us adopted the drill of locking our doors as soon as the alarm went off to avoid people telling us we had to go to the shelter and just sitting tight in our rooms. It may seem as though we were careless with our lives and taking unnecessary risks but the bunkers couldn't stand up to a direct hit anyway, so our rooms, encased in layers of sand bags was just as good a place as any to sit it out. Our rooms couldn't withstand a direct hit, but neither could the bunker, so it made no difference where we got whacked. The rounds being so randomly placed meant that we could run the risk of getting a shell on our heads anywhere in the base, so why not our rooms?

Also, the fact that Chubbs had brought his Playstation 2 with him and a few of us had gotten into an ongoing football tournament on it that we took more serious than Rocket Man, had a hand in it too. Every evening, when the rockets came in and the head count at the shelter was conducted, I, Chubbs, Cach and Rab were missing. We would be sat in my room listening to the sirens, rockets, explosions and shudders of the panes of glass in the windows in my room from the impacts as we competed for who was the best football team.

A couple of days later, we were informed that the Tikrit team would be coming to Kirkuk and will be staying overnight so as not to be running the same route twice in one day. They were bringing a few clients up who had important meetings and one of them was the commanding officer of the Corp of Engineers in the northern sector.

Whenever the Tikrit team came to us, we always made sure they felt welcome and naturally, they would do the same for us when the shoe was on the other foot. So we planned a get together and a barbeque for them and Smudge and Toad took over on chef duty. They could knock up a scoff out of a scabby rat and it would taste great.

The route that the Tikrit boys would be travelling was, to put it lightly, a little on the cheeky side. They had to cross four road bridges on the way out of the city and very often, they would be mined or an IED placed to hit them or the American call signs' as they crossed.

Next, they had long open stretches of road with virtually no turn offs' and so, they could be watched from a distance and it was obvious where they were heading. It would be easy for someone to call ahead and have an ambush set up miles up the road in ground suiting the enemy.

They say a good commander always picks his battles and the ground they will be fought on, but doing PSD in Iraq, it wasn't the case. To a degree, we could choose our routes and timings and so on but at the end of the day, we had to travel the roads and the insurgents knew that there was always a western call sign going to come along at some point, whether it was military or private security, it didn't matter to them. So it was the enemy that decided when and where the fight would be. It was the least we could do to make sure we were prepared and ready for all eventualities.

Travelling the routes between Kirkuk and Tikrit was always a risk, no matter what direction you were travelling, so when we knew that they were on the way and passed a certain point, our team would be kitted up and ready to move to give them support if necessary. They would do the same for us if we were travelling to their neck of the woods. If they were hit and suffered casualties, we would scramble out, regardless of orders, and get them the extra fire and medical support they needed.

As they approached Kirkuk, we could hear them talking over their radios and listened to their progress as they came nearer. Once they were at the gates of the base, we could relax and dump our kit, knowing they were safe.

As they pulled into our compound and debussed, I couldn't help but laugh. I wasn't laughing at the Tikrit team, I was actually laughing at us. The Tikrit lads were all giants and built like rugby players. Our team looked more like a bunch of runts. We weren't the best looking gang in the world and by no means were we giants. The tallest was Cach but he was an exception. If there had been a model PSD team, it would've been the Tikrit lot. Just by our appearance, we lived up to my own impression of us as the rag tag bunch of rogues compared to other teams.

They settled in for the night and we got the food and drink out to show our hospitality. They were due to head back the next day, so an all night party was out of the question but we at least made them feel welcome and as always, there were plenty of laughs.

Swanny was a big Geordie bloke and as loud as he was huge. Being from Newcastle, he was the life and soul sort and always quick to laugh. Everybody piled into my room and Swanny took over my laptop and started to act as the DJ in between showing us funny videos he had found on the internet. During conversation, we found out that we were both ex 1 Para and had many friends in common, though he had left a couple of years before I had joined, nevertheless, the bonds of being Para Reg and the shared hardships are something that always brings out familiarity, regardless of whether you're talking to a WWII veteran or a new recruit today. It's known as the Airborne Brotherhood. As it turns out, Swanny also knew someone else that I knew very well.

"Aye, you look like a bloke I worked with in Baghdad a couple of years ago. I think he was from your neck of the woods too like."

I raised an eyebrow, knowing already who he meant but I played dumb.

"Really, what's his name?"

"Martin." He replied.

"Yup I know him. He's my brother."

He spent the next twenty minutes hugging me and raving about how much of a great guy my brother was. Again, it's a small world.

When Swanny had worked for the same company as my brother, he had been known as a 'Mong Magnet'. For some reason, certain types tended to gravitate toward him, be it the physically or mentally challenged. A mutual friend once told me a story:

A football match had been organised between Swanny and his team against a bunch of local lads in their company compound in Baghdad. During the picking of the teams and nominating who would play what position, Swanny was asked by an Iraqi team member if it was okay for his brother to play too.

Flustered with trying to organise things, Swanny just gave a wave of his hand, "Yeah, fuck it, he can play in goal."

He didn't even bother to take a look at the potential goal keeper and never noticed the perplexed look on the face of the Iraqi who had asked him if his brother could join in.

Swanny was clearly busy, so no questions were asked.

Once the teams had been picked and kick off was imminent, Swanny glanced around at his team, making sure everyone was in position and ready to go. He looked back at his own goal line, the goal keeper stood between the posts poised and ready.

Swanny looked again, realising that something was wrong. Their goal keeper had no arms. He had lost both his arms a couple of years earlier in an IED.

"What the fuck?" Swanny exclaimed. "You'd better be good at catching the ball with your ears and not let any goals past you."

With roughly fifteen people in my room, it wasn't long before it was trashed. Cans were spilled and piled up in every possible nook and ashtrays were over flowing with cigarette butts. You couldn't see from one end of my room to the other with the thickness of the smoke, but even the people who didn't smoke didn't complain.

It was good to have a bunch of lads we all knew come to visit and if it meant them having a good night, I didn't mind having to clean up the next day. I planned on roping Brian in to help anyway.

Danny and JT were another two from the Tikrit team I got on well with. Even to this day, we keep in touch and bump in to one another now and then. Danny was ex 3 Para and I had known him in Baghdad with the last company I had been with. He was a good boxer in his time and always after a few beers in him, he would sing the Jonny Cash song 'A Boy named Sue'. He knew it word for word and said he used to play it before a fight to help gear himself up.

I also bumped into Matt who I had travelled in with when the Americans had sent us on a tour of Iraq via Kirkutche. We had a quick catch up and still blamed each other for the communication breakdown between us and the pilots with him being from the south and me being a northerner.

JT was from Northern Ireland and had been in the Royal Irish in his military service. During the troubles, and even these days, this isn't an easy thing for a man with a young family, but JT took everything on the chin and nothing ever seemed to faze him. He had been on the circuit a while and had seen more than his share of IEDs and ambushes, but he always insisted on coming back out to his team, and Chubbs later nicknamed him 'Bull's-Eye'.

They left the next afternoon and as always, we were on standby to crash out and help them out if they were hit within our area. They made it as far as the bridges on the outskirts of Tikrit and by that time they were too far away for us to be able to support them.

As the team crossed a large road bridge, an IED was detonated; hitting the rear gun truck and the blast was large enough to throw the vehicle into the barrier.

Half of the truck was hanging in mid air over the sheer drop beneath the bridge, teetering on the edge. We heard the reports as they came in from their Op's Room but we were helpless to do anything because of the distance involved. It would've taken a few hours to get there and by then, everything would've been over. All we could do was hope that they all made it through alive.

As it turned out, the gun truck was pretty much scrapped. It had been hit point blank but to its detriment, its armour had withstood the full blast and most of the shrapnel had been soaked up without piercing the shell.

That doesn't mean that there weren't casualties.

JT had received shrapnel wounds to his arm through the open firing port for the rear gunner and there were a few cuts, bumps and bruises among the rest of the gun truck team.

Danny had had a lucky escape and if it wasn't for his radio being attached to the chest area of his assault vest, he would've took a lump of metal through his heart and lungs. Luckily, the radio took the brunt of it and Danny was able to count his lucky stars and live to sing 'A Boy named Sue' another day. Thankfully, there were no fatalities and the team managed to limp back to their home base.

JT had to be evacuated due to his wounds and was sent home to recuperate. He had suffered nerve damage and even today he still doesn't have the full feeling in his arm yet. But JT being JT, he grew bored of sitting at home and being paid and had himself signed off and back out to Iraq so he could be with the lads again.

The Tikrit team was out of action for a short while due to the loss in manpower and the damaged vehicles and so they were going nowhere for the moment. Brian received an email from them requesting an immediate resupply on 'Essential Items'.

By this, we knew that they meant booze.

Being based in Kirkuk, it was much easier for us to get our hands on alcohol than it was for the teams further south. The only problem we had was how to get it to them? We couldn't justify driving there and risking our lives for the sake of the lads having a bit of grog so, an alternative method was needed.

The ideal opportunity was presented to us a couple of days later when, the commander of the Corp of Engineers for the northern region came to visit our clients by helicopter and was scheduled to return to Tikrit later the same day.

It was the perfect crime.

Brian and Chubbs brain stormed the idea and with close coordination with the Tikrit team via email and phone calls, they worked out the execution and details of the operation.

The colonel would be arriving by helicopter and leaving by the same method. Sometimes, baggage would be checked but we gambled that, with him being a colonel, the Military Police may think twice about checking him so we packed the booze into a black foot locker about four feet long and one and a half deep. It was filled with vodka, whisky, schnapps and a couple of crates of beer. The thing weighed a ton. To be on the safe side, we stuffed sheets and foam in between the bottles to stop the bottles rattling against each other, then padlocked it.

We told the colonel that it was ammunition for the Tikrit team. That would explain the weight. Andy came up with the idea of a second safety precaution; writing the colonel's personal details on the box including name, rank and number so that he could take the fall if it was discovered. He had no idea he was carrying a cargo of contraband with his name on it.

The drop off went perfect and no one was any the wiser. The helicopter picked up our package along with the colonel and it was met at the other end by the lads of the Tikrit team and taken away before anyone could ask any questions. It was like an operation from one of the Columbian drug cartels, only the currier was a ranking officer in the American Army and the drug/booze baron was a bunch of British guys getting one over on him.

Parts of our projects were also the building of schools in the areas as well as the clinics and the rebuilding of the hospitals. Some of these had been going on for a couple of years and they were part of the plan of building public relations with the Iraqi people, rather than turning them against the western powers.

The Corps of Engineers had a number of schools to build in the northern regions and two of them were in Kirkuk. As a PR stunt, the plan was that once they were completed, the people responsible for the project would turn up and conduct a ribbon cutting ceremony. Naturally, the top brass would want to be there, hugging the children and shaking hands with the head teacher for the photographers. It was our job to take them there.

The intended school was literally a few hundred metres from our eastern gate, so in theory, it was a case of driving out and practically being on top of the objective.

As the security team, we had the problem of it being a publicised event and it was planned. Everyone knew we were coming and at what time, from the teachers and pupils to the parents and local terrorist cells. It was a security nightmare but all the same, it had to be done as part of the Hearts and Minds.

Our clients and the team mounted up as usual and again, I was back in the side shooter seat of the rear gun truck. I enjoyed being in the rear truck because I was used to the guys that I worked with and we all knew each other well. Even Chubbs and Andy who were relatively new to the team, slotted in easily due to their experience. As always, I was the right hand side gunner and I now had Andy to my back as the left gunner and Chubbs as the rear gunner. Toad and Brian were up front as driver and commander respectively.

We stormed out of the base aggressively and headed toward the main road with sirens blazing and lights flashing and the usual hollering and shouting of events and possible threats on our intended route through our radios. Every man was geared up and ready for a fight as was the usual atmosphere on every mission we went on.

Knowing that each time we left the base, could be our last, was enough to get our adrenalin pumping and it always helped to focus us on the task ahead. We all knew we were literally a few hundred metres away from safety once we got to our objective but, a few hundred metres is a hell of a long way during a battle.

We reached the main road and swung right toward the centre of town. Every vehicle on the road was going static and getting out of our way as we thundered past at top speed. Just a few hundred metres from the safety of the base, and we could see the grey concrete building of the newly built school. It was on the right, ahead of us, and set back roughly fifty metres from the road. It was surrounded by low buildings and houses and already we could see there was quite a large crowd gathering for the big event. On the left hand side of the road was more of the same, a maze of doorways, roof tops and parked cars to hide behind and take a shot at us.

"That's vehicle one approaching objective." Dave announced over the net.

"Vehicle four roger that." Brian replied.

I unbuckled my seat harness, ready to jump out with Andy and conduct a sweep of the school and the immediate area before allowing the clients to move in. During this time, the rest of the team would be static, waiting for the "all clear" over the radio from either me or Andy. I would take the outer wall of the school and quickly check the perimeter and Andy would clear the building itself.

Den was relaying our every movement back to our Operation's Room. Geoff knew exactly where we were and where we would be going next.

As we approached our objective, our truck pushed forward into the large open area in front of the school and Toad positioned it where it could cover the school, road and the team all at the same time as we conducted our mission.

My truck, with Brian, Toad, and Chubbs went static as far to the back of the project as possible. Chubbs insisted on debussing to find a better firing position with his belt fed gun and Brian pushed out to make sure the whole area was covered.

Andy and I moved toward the school as the rest of our vehicles positioned themselves at the front, with the two client vehicles parking up close to the entrance so that once they debussed, the clients themselves would be exposed for the minimum amount of time before they were in the cover of the building.

Our lead gun truck posted itself at the entrance to the road, preventing anymore vehicles from entering into our security perimeter.

Andy moved into the building and I walked the outside walls making sure there weren't any surprises for us. Once I was happy, and I had received the thumbs up from Andy, I headed back toward the rest of the team and at the same time, giving Dave the "all clear" over the radio.

"Roger that mate, that's the clients debussing now."

At that same moment, I heard the distinct crack of rounds flying over head. It sounded like a short burst from small arms like an AK47 and too high to be affective.

"Shots fired, shots fired." Someone called over the radio.

I carried on moving back toward my gun truck after completion of my sweep. Brian was crouched behind the wheel arch of our gun truck with his weapon pointing at the houses across the road, I headed toward him.

Still in the open and about twenty metres from the safety of the armoured vehicle I continued walking as I shouted, "Brian, are they firing at us or are we firing at them?"

Brian spun to look at me with an expression of sheer horror on his face, "Fucking hell Luke, get into cover, they're firing at us you daft twat."

"Ah right, any idea where they are then?"

I moved into a crouch at the side of him so he could give me any fire indications if he had any and he started to chuckle. It was one of them moments when you should be keyed up and focussed, but the sight of me strolling along as rounds were coming in and asking such a bone question without a care in the world, set Brian off into fits of giggles.

"You're such a tit." He told me.

I peered over the hood of the truck at the road and the houses beyond. There was no sign of a gunman and it didn't seem to come from any of the parked vehicles. The only thing I could think of was they had done a drive by shoot in the hope of hitting one of us.

I looked to the rest of the team and everyone was still covering the direction in which the shots had come. No one knew for sure where the firing point was and with no more incoming, we weren't about to start firing into suspected positions and possibly causing innocent casualties. The best option was to keep in cover.

Dave had been in the process of opening the doors for the clients when the shots had come in and immediately slammed the door shut, keeping them in the safety of the vehicle.

"Anyone see where they came from?"

"Haven't a clue mate, can't see anything." Den replied.

"Right lads, keep in cover and mount up, we're bugging out back to base."

Suddenly, Chubbs opened up from my right with his SAW. He was firing long bursts in to the houses across the street.

"Contact, one hundred, houses at my twelve o'clock, red door, shooter on the rooftop," he screamed out his target indication and continued to fire.

I peered over the bonnet and saw the barrel of a gun pointing over the edge of the roof as it blazed away in our direction. Chubbs was firing accurately and I could see the lip of the roof disintegrating around the firing point as the 5.56mm rounds smashed in to it.

The shooter didn't seem deterred by the fact that he had been pinpointed and now, a large weight of fire was pouring down on him. He continued to fire on us. The loud cracks as his rounds passed over and by us, coupled with the noise from Chubbs' gun, was deafening.

The shooter on the roof fired indiscriminately, his rounds thumped in to the ground and walls all around. The people who had come for the ribbon cutting ceremony were diving for cover and I could hear the children screaming in panic as they run to get away from the danger area.

Everyone that was able to and had a line of sight on the firing point, opened up on him. The weight of fire that we put down was enough to destroy the upper portion of the brickwork around the house. Masonry and plaster was flying in all directions with clouds of dust spouting from the impacts as our rounds hit their mark.

The enemy fire ceased.

"Mount up, mount up," I heard Dave shouting from his position from behind the client vehicle.

I covered Brian as he climbed back into the vehicle commander's seat and Andy did the same for Chubbs. Once the whole team were ready to move, we pushed out having not completed the ribbon cutting ceremony and given the clients the chance to win some local support.

We raced out of the area. We didn't know whether or not we had killed the attacker, but it didn't matter. We had suppressed him enough to give us the vital few seconds it took to get away. We could've had a suicide bomber or rockets next, so we had to move fast.

We headed back the way we had come at top speed and before we knew it, we were passing through the gate, into the safety of the FOB.

A few days later we went back to the school and the clients were able to cut the ribbon but this time, it was a low key event with fewer people there to meet and greet us as we arrived. Because of the last time, we made sure that the clients knew to keep it to a minimum time on the ground in order to give the insurgents less time to mount an attack.

They cut the ribbon and got the pictures in the relevant papers so they were happy enough in the end, and they appreciated our efforts to see that the mission was completed.

Andy decided that he was out of shape and he had been smoking too much and eating excess junk food lately. He left his cigarettes in my room and asked me to ration them to him and he threw himself into his fitness training and healthy eating regime.

Not one to do things by halves, he set out doing eight to ten mile runs in the blazing midday heat, including repetitions up and down a small but steep hill just outside our compound. Most people would start off lightly, with a couple of miles, and build up but Andy only stopped running when his nose started to bleed. He trotted back into our compound looking like he had just been in a brawl.

Chubbs burst into my room later laughing, "Luke come and have a look at Andy."

I followed him across from my hut towards Andy's room and up the short steps to the door. When he opened it, the first thing I noticed was a large green wheelie bin in the corner by his bed.

Andy popped his head out from the lid like Oscar from Sesame Street and announced in his Northern Irish accent, "I'm having an ice bath Luke, you should try it."

I couldn't work out what I was actually looking at and why, but he had got the bin from somewhere, washed it out and filled it with water and crushed ice, swearing that it makes you feel great and it is really healthy for you. I had no doubt about this but I passed up on the offer. Andy seemed happy as a pig in shit though as he sat there in his ice bath, eating a hand full of pumpkin seeds with a bloody nose, getting healthier by the minute while the rest of us normal people just went to the gym.

A couple of days later and we were back out on the road for a task to the east side of the city on a hospital visit. I never liked the hospital jobs for a number of reasons. As well as the amount of people coming and going and the fact that we couldn't control access to the hospital, there was also the health hazard.

As I've already pointed out, the levels of sanitation and hygiene in these places were more than below par. They were none existent. I had horrible visions of something happening while we were in the hospital and me putting my hand on a discarded sharp or a bloody dressing. Luckily, this time, I was part of the outer security and would be staying close to the vehicles and not having to walk through the Bio-Hazard they call the Emergency Room.

As usual, we cut a path through the city with our vehicles as we raced to our objective. We took the direct route which included crossing over the bridges and into the hard line Arab area before we reached the more placid Kurdish district of Kirkuk.

Travelling through this part of town, we always used maximum aggression but without overreacting. Rather than pass through with guns blazing like some companies would have done, we would instead, ensure that our presence was known and that we appeared too strong to be taken on in a snap attack that's been hastily organised. Normally, it worked and before anyone knew we were there, we were gone from the area.

We didn't always use sirens either. Sometimes it would just be a case of using the lights when we thought it better. Still, now and then, we would have to fire a warning shot into a car engine to stop him from getting too close. This would normally immobilise the vehicle and that would be the end of it.

Chubbs being the rear gunner of the rear gun truck, he had the full responsibility of covering our six o'clock position and making sure no one came at us from the rear. Like all our trucks, we had the warning sign attached to our tail gate, telling everyone to stay back at least one hundred metres. Anyone breaking this rule would either be a suicide bomber or a complete fool, which in my eyes are both one and the same.

Still, some people thought the warning didn't refer to them and would try to approach. Chubbs would give them the usual warnings of flashing lights, waving hands, waving marker panels and if they still didn't back off then, he would put a burst into either their tyres or their engine.

Hearing Chubbs shouting to someone approaching followed by, "standby," and a burst of automatic fire, became a regular occurrence in our truck. Chubbs took no chances and neither would any of us in his position as the rear gunner. The signs and warnings were clear for all to see and by the 'Rules for the Use of Force' we were well within the law to protect ourselves and the clients from anyone deemed a threat.

This included dick heads screaming towards us from the rear.

When we reached the hospital, we pushed to the rear of the car park into an open area and set the vehicles in a line ready for a fast move out if things went pear shaped. In an emergency, the team outside would quickly get in the vehicles and head to the hospital entrance while the guys inside the building, would be bringing the clients out and into the safety of the armour protection. The only problem was, we were in an area with no cover from the elements and so we had to make do with what little shade we could find from the blazing midday sun, if any, while we kept a security cordon on the outside around the vehicles.

Thankfully, the clients were quick in their visit and fifteen minutes later we were getting ready to move. Out they came and once they were in the vehicles, the rest of the team mounted up and headed toward the car park exit, leading onto the main road outside. Our gun truck pushed forward from the rear to cover the road and hold traffic as the rest of the vehicles came out and then we would tag on behind them. Instead of stopping, Toad slowed us to a crawl so that the engine was still in gear and we could accelerate away if needed.

When a huge black SUV pulls out in front of you, with guns sticking out and pointing in your direction, most people would slow down. We had used the sirens and lights to warn the traffic outside that we were coming out and to keep their distance and instead of racing out, we came out slowly so that the traffic could clear and hold off from us.

A large truck was coming straight at us from the right hand side and naturally, he was in my arcs of fire. With no sign of slowing and him only around fifty metres away; I had no choice but to fire at him.

I didn't want to aim at the driver and I didn't want to aim at the engine because there were a lot of people on foot in the area and close to the road and there was always a chance of ricochets. So I aimed into the passenger area that looked empty.

"Stand by, this twat isn't stopping." I warned.

I fired three rounds into the window. I felt the weapon thump into my shoulder from the recoil and the cocking handle fly forward, chambering the next round.

Immediately, I heard the screech of breaks and I saw that, before the truck had even stopped, the driver bailed out into the road, leaving the vehicle heading straight towards us. I aimed at the wheels and the engine this time and fired again while at the same time, Toad was accelerating and turning left onto the main drag.

During all this, the client vehicles had managed to clear the turn and we were able to tag on to the back of the call sign before the rogue truck smashed into us. We raced away from the scene and Chubbs informed us that we were clear.

Everyone seemed to be a little confused by the whole incident. Was he trying to ram us and that's why he bailed, so that he didn't injure himself? Or did he just flap when the rounds thumped into his passenger seat and jumped out thinking he was going to get it next? We never found out the whole story and it was just yet another one of them crazy things that happen in Iraq on a daily basis.

Throughout the weeks, Rocket Man never let up. Every night, without fail, he would launch his high explosives into the base and every night, we would hear the sirens blaring, followed by, "ALARM RED, ALARM RED, seek shelter immediately," over the speaker system.

It never made sense to us why he hadn't been stopped by now. As I said, it was pretty much the same time every night and no doubt, if he was using the same timings, then he was probably using the same firing point, probably the roof of his own house. It wouldn't have taken much for the American Intelligence to find him with a little common sense and surveillance, followed by a quick operation to either snatch him or kill him.

One evening, me Chubbs and Cach were sat in my room drinking tea and watching a movie when the alarms started.

"Bollocks. Lock the door and let's finish our brew." Cach suggested, so we did just that.

We heard a couple of thumps in the distance but they were nothing to get concerned about, so we ignored them.

Then, the thumps got louder and more regular. The vibrations below our feet were more noticeable and the crash of the explosions seemed to blur in to one long, loud roar.

Rocket Man really had his shit together that night and it seemed he had brought up extra ammunition for a more sustained attack on us.

The room was shaking and rattling. My personal effects were dancing about on the desk tops and the mirror in my bathroom shattered when a rocket landed close enough to make the room feel like it had suddenly dropped a few feet.

With each explosion, we winced, trying to sink our heads in to our chest cavity. I was clenching my jaw in fear of a close hit causing my teeth to shatter and every muscle in my body was contracted and ready to spring me forward, to where, I had no idea.

I glanced at Cach, "Maybe we should've gone to the shelter this time?" I shouted over the noise of the bombardment.

He shrugged, "We either get it here, or we get it there mate. Either way, I'm having a brew first."

I stared after him in wonder as he casually walked over to the kettle and flicked it on.

The bombardment slowly eased.

At one point, I began to worry that maybe Rocket Man had a spotter within the base, relaying the adjustments needed to him. It seemed he was steadily creeping the fall of shot closer to my room as he corrected his aim. I had to wonder, 'why me?'

After a half hour, the all clear was given and people could carry on about their business and we carried on with our movie. The rocket attack was soon forgotten about and it just became a normal evening in the FOB for us until, a short while later, there was a loud thumping at my door.

I looked at Cach and Chubbs with concern because the sound of the knock wasn't the usual courteous sort before someone entered for one reason or another. It was more of a frantic, aggressive banging. I'd forgotten to unlock the door after the 'all clear' alarm had sounded.

"Hang on," I shouted as I got up and walked to the door, "who is it?" I was expecting it to be someone coming to give us a telling off for not going to the shelter when the voice over the speaker had told us to.

"It's me, Andy. Open the door mate, I'm fucked."

I glanced back at Cach and Chubbs then, opened up.

In front of me stood a strange and pathetic sight, it could only happen to Andy. He was covered from head to toe in mud and I could see that his hands, knees and elbows were grazed and bleeding. He staggered past me and leaned against my computer desk, puffing and panting and generally looking like he was about to collapse. Chubbs and Cach watched him, perplexed and silent. I felt the same myself.

Chubbs piped up, and the hint of amusement in his voice was unmistakable, "What happened to you Andy?"

Andy carried on puffing for air and moved to sit on my bed. He sprawled out and began, "Well, I was out for a run around the camp and I was at the far end, by the fence line. I heard the alarms going off and then, a fucking rocket landed about twenty metres away from me. It blew me into the ditch at the side of the road and I stayed there because more rockets were coming in around me. So I thought 'fuck it', I'd better get crawling then."

Cach Chubbs and I had already started to laugh.

"It's not fucking funny you bunch of bastards, I was crawling for a few hundred metres."

Our laughs got louder the more he told us.

"Then I had to make my way back here and I couldn't find anyone to give me a lift. All the American soldiers just kept driving past me, beeping their horns and laughing at me."

"You'd better go and have an ice bath and some pumpkin seeds to make you feel better mate," suggested Chubbs.

"Fuck that, Luke give me a fag. Who fancies a pizza tonight?" And that was Andy off his fitness regime for the time being.

A week later and they still hadn't nailed Rocket Man. Chubbs and Brian were both standing near our vehicles outside our office one day. Chubbs had just bought a new GPS, Global Positioning System, and Brian was helping him with the ins and outs of it.

As they stood leaning against the gun truck, they heard the whoosh of the rocket and the explosion knocked them flat. It had literally passed just over their heads on its downward trajectory and hit the utility shed on the outer edge of our parking area, just fifteen metres from where they were stood.

No one was injured but the shed was trashed.

Rocket Man had actually done us all a favour though. The utility shed was where the Quartermaster for the Corp of Engineers kept his goodies under lock and key. Getting light bulbs from him was like asking for a kidney, so when we realised the doors had been blown off, it was like Christmas had come early.

While the entire base was taking cover in the shelters, our team were raiding the stores the Quartermaster had stocked in his shed. No one amongst us would now find themselves without toilet paper or air freshener for the rest of our stay in Kirkuk.

Toad, in a frenzy of theft and completely caught up in the moment, decided to break open a few more doors that hadn't been damaged and helped himself to power tools and a vacuum cleaner.

From then on, you would walk into anyone's room and there would be buckets, brushes, mops, and cleaning products along with soap, and even nice duvet covers and rugs on the floor and every colour light bulb you can think of.

When the Quartermaster came to investigate the damage done to his private kingdom, he could only stand there, scratching his head in wonder at how the rocket had managed to blow the locks off every door in his building and disintegrate nearly every piece of equipment he had in there, including his dirty movie collection that I had found in his desk drawer, yet the shed was in one piece still.

The weather was starting to turn and autumn had set in. I had been in Kirkuk for going on four months and I really couldn't wait to get home for a break. I decided that, for a holiday, I would go to Antigua to soak up the sun and Rum.

I had missed my daughter's birthday during the summer and I fully intended on making it up to her as soon as I was home. I hated being away from her and every time I came on leave Leah would ask me, "Are you staying home now dad and not going back to Iraq?"

She knew the dangers and it was heartbreaking having to explain to her that I would be going back after four weeks at home. Even now, she still asks me the same question.

To get home from Kirkuk we were expected to use the military system and fly from the base to Kuwait and then onto a civilian flight from there. It sounds easy enough on paper, but it was a nightmare in practice.

Once we got to Kuwait, we needed to get visas, even though we were just passing through. Although this could easily be done in a few hours, the American logistics company who had a monopoly on the whole Kuwait visa system, decided that everyone travelling through would need to wait twenty four hours for their visa.

The only reason behind this was that they only wanted to do one run a day to the visa office rather than getting them done as they come through and so we had to wait.

After staying in what we called 'Tent City' for the night, we were less than impressed and couldn't wait to get away from the American slow and beaurocratic system. Even the transfer buses didn't travel faster than 10mph on the roads. It was torture for those of us who had better things to do like, get home to our wives, girlfriends, dogs and cats.

After nearly three days travelling, I finally got home. As I had promised, I made it up to Leah and she received a second birthday that year, with a no holds barred spoiling trip to all the toy shops I could think of.

Winter and Christmas in Kirkuk

Most people take the smallest things for granted. It always takes me a week or two to adjust to normal life when I return from Iraq and it was the same during my army days when I had been on operations and long exercises overseas. I remember coming home from the Iraq war in 2003 after spending six months living under the stars, eating army rations and relishing being able to sleep at night without suffering from the super heated wind. I was even fascinated with taps that had clean running water pouring from them.

As private contractors on the security circuit, we had life much easier and more comfortable than we had done as soldiers, yet civilian life still takes some getting used to. For a start, when I'm home, I don't have to carry weapons and wear body armour when I'm travelling from A to B, and I'm not likely to get shot at or blown up when I'm on my way to Tesco.

But it's something that you can't switch off in an instant. It takes time and familiarity with your environment. Even on my way home from the airport, I would notice myself studying the road and searching for possible threats as we drove along the motorway.

On a number of occasions, I had to stop myself from calling to the taxi driver, that there was a vehicle moving up at speed on the right hand side. Craning my neck as I approached overpasses and bridges, in order to see what could be planted on the underside, the people and cars on top, or the patches of ground to the left and right of the road underneath the feature, shaded from the light.

Also, crowds are something I cannot deal with easily at first. Large crowds in Iraq, normally mean trouble. My first night at home normally consists of a quiet night in with drinks and food, or maybe even a restaurant if I'm feeling adventurous.

But to go to a packed bar would freak me out. My eyes would be on stalks and I would have whiplash from my head swivelling as I watched the people around me. Of course, I would be fully aware of my surroundings and know that there's no real threat, but I couldn't just switch it all off.

I'm not talking about the Vietnam style flash backs, with me running out of a pub screaming, "Charlie's in the light," or "we got zips in the wire." It's just an automated action that comes from having to be vigilant 24/7 in a hostile environment, and not easily dropped because I've switched time zones.

Sleep was always a problem to start with. I would wake up during the night in a dark room in what seemed to be a strange bed. I would feel confused about where I was. It would normally take a while for my senses to adjust and realise that I wasn't in my hut in Iraq anymore, and that I was tucked up safely in my own bed at home.

One night, I went as far as getting out of my bed and walking over to the wall and pissing in my drawers. In my room in Kirkuk, that is where my bathroom and toilet would've been. The fact that I had a few beers and Jack Daniels before bed time also helped with the confusion and I spent the next day washing my piss soaked socks and t-shirts.

When we are in Iraq, we make the best of what we have and even though there are laughs and barbeques with swimming pools and gyms, what we don't have is our complete freedom. We are still surrounded by walls and fences and at any moment, we can be given a short sharp reminder of where we are, in the form of an IED explosion or a rocket attack.

The worst wake up calls come in the form of people you know of being killed or hurt. All too often I have heard, "Hey did you hear about such and such a company? They got hit yesterday and lost four lads in one attack." Or, "five blokes have been kidnapped in Baghdad," only to find out that some of the people involved, are personal friends.

We are thousands of miles from our loved ones and friends. Trying to have a relationship when you are apart for three months at a time is going to be a struggle by anyone's standards and yet, many people get through it. I always miss home and the people I have left behind. Lisa and I spent more time communicating through email than we did face to face.

Each time I get leave, my daughter seems to have become more of a young woman than she was before. Yet our bond never seems to be any less than the last time we had seen each other. If anything, it's stronger because we know that to a degree, we're on borrowed time.

Always when on leave, I would enjoy even the most simple of things. I discovered a great fondness for green fields and trees. I could never understand why people would up sticks and move to the likes of Dubai. To me, places like Dubai are nothing more than dust and rock, with featureless arid open desert. You can give me all the skyscrapers and shopping malls you want, but I would rather have the green and lush landscape of home, even if it *is* wetter than Malaysia during the rainy season.

Returning to Iraq was always easier on the senses. Because of the extreme heat and the hostile environment, you adjusted quicker as though it was forced upon you. The lads always made a point of meeting us at the flight line when we landed on the airfield at the Kirkuk airbase.

As we would be walking off the plane, five other guys from our team would be getting on it, to go on leave. The turnaround was so tight that if one man failed to return from leave, for whatever reason, then someone who was stood waiting to get on the plane would have to stay behind.

Normally it would be decided by the flick of a coin between the five lads waiting to board the flight. On a couple of occasions, I've seen tantrums as someone has either lost the flick or had 'Mong Flick' declared on him, because he dropped the coin. Rules are rules and mong flicks are pretty much gospel in our circles.

All five of us returned to Iraq on this occasion, so there was no need for the coins and as we stepped off the rear ramp of the American C130 Hercules, we passed the other lads as they boarded. There was always a quick few words swapped as we crossed paths.

"Good leave?" Someone would ask.

The reply was always the same, "Yeah mate, fucking mega leave thanks. Shit to be back here though."

Naturally there would also be a slagging or two.

"Fuck me Luke, you been eating people while you've been at home? You look like Danny DeVito you tubby little shit. Get back in that gym."

"Shit and fall in it, cause I'm gonna brake into your room and piss on your TV while you're away."

The banter would continue until the noise of the aircraft engines drowned out our voices, then it would be conducted by hand gestures.

The first person to greet us was Rab. He stood there, larger than life, with the world's biggest beard and wearing a bandanna.

Company policy was that our hair had to be short and we were to be clean shaven. Rab always had to be different and with his new look, along with his white vest and camouflaged trousers, he looked like a Serbian mercenary. He loved the new nickname I bestowed upon him and from then on, he was known as 'Random Rab, the Serb Merc' cut to 'Rabski' for short. He even still signs his emails with it.

Brian and Andy were also there and it was big group hugs and welcome backs all around. Cach had been on leave along with me and the little reunion on the airfield was a nice way to be welcomed back to Iraq.

I saw Geoff, who was about to board the flight to go on leave back to the U.S and shook his hand, wishing him a good trip and an even better leave.

He didn't exactly look too keen and he told me, "To be honest Luke, I'm not really all that fussed on going home and, I won't be coming back anyway."

"How come, you had a better offer of work?"

"Nah, I'm having trouble with the wife and she's taking me to the cleaners over it. Don't think you'll see me again Luke." And with that, he shook my hand and walked toward the plane.

I couldn't think of anything to say to him really and his whole demeanour seemed almost on the edge of despair.

"I'm sure it'll all be sorted out Geoff and you'll be back here in four weeks time so enjoy it while you can." I called to him as he walked away.

With that, the leaving lads boarded and we lucky ones, who had just arrived, made our way back to our huts to sort ourselves out and settle in.

Cach, Brian and Andy all piled into my room. I sorted my kit and broke open my fresh box of Yorkshire Tea while they gave me a heads up on what had been happening.

Nothing much had been going on. A big guy named Martin had come on to the team while I had been away and he was my new next door neighbour. Other than that, it was the usual run of the mill, problem clients and shootings, IEDs at the gates and of course, Rocket Man.

As before I had left, he had continued to pound the base every night at the same time. From what the lads knew, he had also managed to score a few good hits within the FOB and even cause a number of dead and wounded. Enough was enough and the American Army had decided on doing something that the British Army would've done from the moment he fired his first rockets.

Surveillance had been put out into the areas suspected to be where he was firing from and after a while, they had pinpointed the exact location. An operation was then planned by the Special Forces on the base and during the raid on his house; Rocket Man was killed before he could cause anymore damage. No doubt, he is now sat in Paradise as a martyr enjoying his seventy two virgins, or at least that's what he would've believed before he was filled with 5.56mm sized holes.

It was now early December and the temperature was dropping steadily. Contrary to what people tend to think, Iraq isn't warm all year round, especially in the north around Erbil, Suli and Kirkuk. During the height of winter, it often drops below freezing and sometimes as low as minus ten in certain areas. Head in to the mountains north of Erbil, and you're looking at minus twenty.

I had known it was going to be cold and so, I made sure I brought back plenty of warm weather gear from leave. I also knew that I would be spending Christmas away from my loved ones.

The year before, I had arrived home on Christmas Day and had to race up the M6 in a hire car from Heathrow because there were no connecting flights to Manchester. At least my mother had saved me some Christmas dinner.

This year, my Christmas dinner would be spent with the bunch of rogues I called my friends. Still, we would make the best of it and even the clients wanted to celebrate the day as best they could and so they made sure there were to be no tasks for that day.

Everyone in the team knew cold weather and had experienced it each year for their whole life. All accept one.

Guy was from Brisbane on the East coast of Australia and it never drops below t-shirt weather there. Already, he was in the habit of wearing multiple layers and thick jackets and looking bigger than he normally did as a result. Everyone else would just add a jacket or jumper to their usual clothing, but Guy, would be wearing enough clothes to make an Eskimo sweat.

One of our first missions was a visit to the forts in the mountains, far off to the east on the border between Iraq and Iran. After the Iran/Iraq war, neither side had completely ceased hostilities, and even during the coalition led invasion in 2003 there were reports of skirmishes between Iraqi and Iranian troops in the border areas. Iran obviously seeing their opportunity to grab a bit of land from the already hard pressed Iraqis.

Naturally, when the war had finished and the U.S government started to rebuild the country, they also realised that it was in their best interest to maintain the border defences, especially with Iran. So the border forts that were already in place were reinforced, and other positions were also built to support the forts already constructed. The Corp of Engineers was in charge of the construction and even though they were built by local contractors, now and then they needed to be inspected and checked over by the Americans.

It would be a long journey for us, taking roughly four hours to get there and the higher up we went into the mountains, the colder it would get. This wouldn't be a problem for the men and clients in the sealed vehicles but for us in the gun trucks, it would mean extra layers and ensuring the heaters in the vehicles were working perfectly. With the side windows removed to make open firing ports, and the rear door nothing but an open void except for a tail gate for the rear gunner, it meant the inside was open to the elements, and so were we.

Chubbs had gone on leave and Guy had taken over from him as our rear gunner. On the day of the mission, Guy turned up wearing his entire wardrobe. He looked like the Michelin Man and must have been wearing enough arctic kit to supply an expedition to the North Pole.

He climbed into the back of our truck and then produced a sleeping bag that he slotted his legs into while he sat with the machinegun, covering our rear. For sure, Guy wasn't going to allow himself to freeze during this trip, and fare play to him. For Guy, just a couple of degrees above freezing, was like minus ten to us. The last thing we needed was for our rear gunner to switch off due to him suffering from the cold.

Andy was the left hand gunner in our truck and typical of him, he turned up in just a long sleeved shirt covering a vest and wearing a woolly hat. To anyone else, you could be forgiven for thinking he was just trying to make a point of how tough he was but, Andy being Andy, it was more likely that he just didn't feel the cold as much as the rest of us.

Rab also turned up in very little, just a t-shirt and even though it provided no insulation whatsoever, his bandanna. He insisted that his thick beard would keep him warm enough, but it was more than likely to do with the fact he would be sat in the front of the lead gun truck as the driver and would have the heaters on full.

To get to our objective, we had to travel through two major cities; Kirkuk first and then Sulimania. We took the longer and safer route out of Kirkuk around the northern edge through the Kurdish area. There had been reports of a number of Suicide Vehicle Born Improvised Explosive Devices, SVBIEDs, positioned within the city, waiting for a good target to detonate on.

Normally, an SVBIED would be packed with artillery shells and mines and they would be rigged to either detonate on impact with the bumper, via a pressure switch or, remotely by the driver himself. You only have to look on the internet to see the sheer scale of damage a car packed with explosives can cause in a crowded area or even against an armoured vehicle.

On the open road, the cold wind bit into us in the gun truck now that the speed could be increased away from the city. I was glad to be wearing my layers and even Guy seemed comfortable enough. There wasn't even the slightest complaint of the cold from Andy, even though Brian was from his neck of the woods in Northern Ireland and he regularly voiced his thoughts on the temperature.

"It's fucking freezing in here. Turn the heating up Toad."

"It's on full mate, but any heat the engine's giving off is going straight out the open windows. I brought a flask with me though."

If he wasn't so ugly, and I wasn't so shallow, I would've kissed Toad for his forethought with the flask.

"Toad you're a star."

"You're just a big girl Brian," Andy remarked, "and you shouldn't even be in this gun truck because you're a puff."

As always, once we were clear of the cities and on the open road, we could afford to relax a little and that's when the hustle and bustle would ease off and the slagging would start.

Often though, the conversation would be of everyday things like, what we did on leave and what we planned for the next one or, the Filipino guy on the base that worked in the food court, and was currently undergoing a sex change.

We had first noticed him in the cook house and even though he was clearly a man, he seemed very feminine and even camp. He minced rather than walked and it soon became obvious that he was taking hormone treatment. We had all been on the team for roughly six months now and as far as we could tell, he was becoming more of a woman by the week.

"Have you seen his tits?" Toad asked no one in particular, "they're definitely growing like."

Brian was always slightly homophobic and was clearly uncomfortable with the conversation, which just encouraged Toad, along with the rest of us, to speak about the lady-boy all the more.

It even got to the point when, if he walked into the canteen while we were there and Brian saw him, he wouldn't be able to finish his meal. I could never understand it myself, so I constantly teased Brian about it, claiming he had feelings for the base transsexual.

"Yeah they weren't that big before I went on leave," I added, "I wonder how big it's gonna have them?"

Andy burst into laughter, "*It?*"

"Well, yeah, *it*. You can't exactly call it a man or a woman at the moment so, what the fuck *should* we call it then?"

"I'm gonna find out *its* name. In fact I'm gonna invite *it* to our next barbeque as the guest of honour." Toad said.

"Yeah nice one, we can even make *it* a tiara to wear."

By now, Brian was squirming in his seat. "You're all sick fucking bastards." He growled.

"Come on Brian, they all need loving." Guy shouted from his gun position at the rear.

An hour later, we were at the American base on the outskirts of Suli and we stopped for a leg stretch and a hot drink. The clients went into the offices to talk shop and so, I took the opportunity to visit Liam.

As always he made a big deal of me and offered me a brew while telling me how great it was to see me. The feeling was genuinely mutual. With Liam, it was all or nothing and if you were a friend of his, then you meant the world to him.

As usual, his initial talk was of his little boys and how great they were and how much they were growing. Unfortunately, he and Lyndsey had split up and after trying to make things work they had gone their separate ways. I knew he was gutted but he did his best not to show it.

After half an hour I said good bye to Liam and we hit the road again. Guy had felt the cold, regardless of his sleeping bag and multiple layers and wasn't looking forward to the next three hours of driving.

Toad had topped up his flask though and to that end, we had plenty of hot tea to thaw him out if need be.

"It'll get colder the closer we get to the border Guy." Toad said to him. "There'll even be snow up there."

"Actually, I've never seen snow. Well I've seen it on TV and that, but never in the flesh."

Guy was in for a treat because as we cleared the eastern edge of Suli, we started on to the mountain roads and we were travelling up hill. Suli was at least three to five degrees colder than Kirkuk so we were now in the minus band and the difference could be felt, even by Andy who now had a blue nose but still, claimed he was okay and he probably was.

The roads were narrow and the cliffs and drops either side were sheer and steep. The speed was reduced and the drivers had to be extra careful in case of black ice. With the speed down though, it meant less wind chill, so the journey wouldn't be as uncomfortable as it would've been on straight open roads but it would be much longer. After a couple of hours winding our way through valleys and over peaks, we started to see patches of snow here and there.

"Snow over to your left Guy." Brian shouted.

"Yeah cheers. Ah look at that." He exclaimed. Guy was clearly in awe of something we took for granted.

The further into the passes we travelled, the more rugged the terrain became. Small villages were scattered here and there, made entirely of mud huts and thatched roofs, and of course, many had satellite dishes erected above them.

We could tell that life was hard and most of the men who grew up and stayed in the village would make their money from goat farming while the women, would make clothing to sell on the market in the city. Surrounded by hills and roads, that were nothing more than gravel in the best places and mud in most areas, they were not much further advanced from the dark ages, with the exception of Sky Movies and the Nat Geo channel.

As we approached the border fort we were to visit, we came onto a steep metalled road leading up to it. The government were willing to tarmac the last five hundred metres to the position but not the couple of hundred miles to the nearest city. We approached the main gate and for the first time I saw what, to me, looked like a small terracotta castle or, even the sort of defensive fort you would see in the old black and white films, with the Spanish fighting the Texans. It even had turrets and was clearly just for show.

A real defensive position would be subterranean and reinforced concrete, with trenches leading off and depth positions for further defence and support. This was a token gesture to tell the Iranians that Iraq was guarding her boarders.

A platoon, roughly thirty men, of Peshmerga manned the fort. They took their duty very seriously and as we entered, they even snapped to attention and presented arms for a salute. They must've thought we were Iraqi Army top brass and trying to impress us. When a bunch of western blokes stumbled out of the vehicles, honking on about the cold and their stiff joints they must have been very disappointed, but they never showed it.

The building was surrounded by a nine foot wall and while Dave, Brian and Den escorted the clients around the interior, the rest of us relaxed and had a nosey about the area. Guy made a beeline for the nearest patch of snow and crouched down to pick some up in his bare hands.

He stood looking at it, studying it and then informed us, "It's really cold isn't it."

"What do you expect Guy? It's frigging frozen water." Toad replied.

"Yeah but, I didn't think it would be this cold though."

His face had an almost confused expression on it, as though it was impossible for such a thing to be formed outside of a fridge freezer.

While Guy studied his hand full of snow, we carried on with drinking tea and shaking the cold out of our bones. Even Andy had conceded and was now sat in the warm passenger seat of the client vehicle.

The clients had a lot of meeting and greeting to do with the men at the fort. The local commander had even put in an appearance to show the visitors around the structure, and allow them to inspect the defences he had put in place. He even informed them that every now and then, they would have a shoot out with the Iranian border towers that were in range across the hills. He claimed it was because they were trying to infiltrate and kidnap people on the Iraqi side, but no doubt, it was just to relieve boredom, and a fire fight now and then gave them something to think about because from what I could tell, there wasn't a bowling alley or cinema nearby.

Once the visit was complete, we mounted up and set out on the long journey back. The temperature became painful and by the time we got back to the outskirts of Kirkuk my fingers, face and feet were numb.

Thankfully, most of the insurgents are fare weather terrorists, in a literal sense, and wouldn't want to play when the weather was either too hot or too cold. Our plan was to get ourselves through the town and into the FOB as quickly as possible and so, we took the direct route through the centre and across the main bridge. It seemed as though the whole town didn't want to play out either and we had a free run of it. And, because there was so little to get worked up about, it was almost to the point of boring, compared to the normal adrenalin fuelled race through the built up area.

In the base, we unloaded our weapons and sorted our kit within the vehicle. Then it was time to stagger back to our rooms and thaw out. We had travelled from the border, all the way to Kirkuk, without a stop off at Suli like we had on the way. Hopefully, we wouldn't be heading into the mountains too often but if we did, then next time I would take my sleeping bag too. Guy had sat in his but still he waddled off to his room like a cardboard cut out because his joints were frozen solid.

It was around this time that a young guy named Pete came to the team. He was an ex Guardsman and at the age of twenty three, the youngest out of all of us. Pete was a typical rogue from Liverpool. He had a plan for everything and it was never above board. Even if doing it the legitimate way was easier, he would take things the dodgy and more adventurous route.

He turned up in Scouse (indigenous people of Liverpool) uniform, which consisted of a tracksuit top and bottoms and a pair of white training shoes. His appearance raised a few eyebrows and people began taking the piss because he looked like he had just come from football training. Pete took it in his stride and before long he was accepted as another member of the team, even if he did look like a drug dealer.

Things began to slacken on the run up to Christmas and less mission requests were received from the clients. This didn't stop the like of Joe, the problem child, from putting a request in on the morning of the day he wished us to take him out. It was policy that, all missions, should be requested at least forty eight hours in advance and so, Dave and Den took great delight in telling him to, 'fuck off'. Any other client, we would always try to accommodate for but because Joe was such a pain in the arse, favours toward him were never considered.

We were due to go out on a task one morning and as usual, we met at the office by the vehicles forty five minutes before we were to roll out. First thing we would do is grab a brew and sit down for the QBO's to listen in for any changes. Dave would give us a quick rundown of the mission and away we would go.

"Lads, I've some bad news."

We looked at each other, wondering what it could be. It actually crossed my mind that maybe the contract had been finished and we were all out of work. Someone's death didn't even occur to me for some reason, even though the look on Dave's face should've made it obvious.

"We got an email from HQ just a few minutes ago. Geoff's dead. He killed himself at home while on leave."

I was taken aback by what I had heard and now, I knew what it was that had bothered me when I had last spoke to Geoff. Looking back in hind sight, it was clear that he had given up and had every intention of ending his life if his last ditch attempt at resolving his marital problems failed. They had, and so he had taken his own life at home in the U.S. The team was quiet for a while and everyone was deep in thought over the news of our Op's Manager being dead.

"I've got first dibs on his Playstation then," Brian declared.

Martin spun on him and growled through gritted teeth, "Anyone touches his kit and Ill cut their fucking fingers off."

We all knew he meant it.

Martin was a big Scottish man with a squashed nose and a rough tough look about him and he was as every bit as hard as he looked. In spite of his appearance though, he was a very considerate and thoughtful person and because he lived next door to me, we spent a lot of time chatting general shit together. Now and then he would have an angry moment and I would hear him crashing about in his room. It often sounded as though he was about to come through the wall and into my room.

What Brian had said was typical British squaddie black humour. We dealt with most things with humour. It was never meant to be disrespectful or to make fun of the death of another. It was how we came to terms with loss. Knowing that it can happen to any one of us, at anytime, we tend to approach death in a different way from how civilians do. We had all lost friends and we mourned them in our own way.

In a room full of men about to go out beyond the wire on a mission, Brian had decided to break the ice to snap us out of our thoughts and back to the job in hand. He knew the job still needed to be done so we would have the chance to mourn Geoff later.

After we returned, Dave collected messages of condolence from each of us and they were sent to his wife in a card with a bouquet of flowers from the team, offering her our deepest sympathies.

Geoff had a couple of daughters and most of the guys felt for them and how they would cope with their dad committing suicide. Being killed on the job was one thing, but taking your own life at home was something I couldn't understand. Regardless of the situation you are in, there is always another option.

Geoff was a good guy and I had gotten on well with him. His death was a sad event but it wasn't something I was going to dwell on or even get upset over. He had made his own choices. That night, we drank to Geoff and that was that.

Our job didn't change. We continued to conduct missions in and around the city and visits to other cities, like Erbil and Suli, were regular. And with Christmas around the corner, we knew we would need to stock up on certain supplies. None of us who were left behind in Kirkuk fancied the idea of not being able to celebrate Christmas in our traditional way; by getting shit faced.

Sitting in my room on Christmas Eve without a drink and thinking of home, knowing that everyone would be at parties and with family and friends, would've been more than miserable for me. So our next priority would be, to stock up on party equipment.

As always, we didn't do things by halves. On a trip to Erbil we loaded up a whole gun truck with booze and on the return journey, the gun crew were sitting on boxes of whisky and beer. If we had been ambushed, there would've been a great deal of upset if the booze was destroyed.

I remembered a story of another team in a similar situation. They had been returning from a mission and while they were out, they had had the chance to restock their supplies. On the way back to their base, they were hit by an IED that took out the truck loaded with booze. It was blown clean off the road and the vehicle was a complete write off, I saw the pictures and it looked like a steel cabbage. How they survived, I have no idea.

The rest of the team had gone static and rushed to help the injured. Two had fractured skulls and, I'm glad to say, eventually made a full recovery. One guy was lying on the ground screaming with what appeared to be a few minor wounds.

"I'm bleeding out, I'm bleeding out." He was screaming.

With the dust and debris in his eyes and the disorientation from the blast, he was unable to see his wounds and assumed that the warm liquid he felt soaking through his trousers, was blood escaping from his severed femoral artery. With the artery in your leg cut, you can die from loss of blood within a couple of minutes and so, he was in a flap.

When the medic got to him, he realised what it was and told him, "Shut up you dick head, it's just beer. The crate has been hit by shrapnel and a few cans have burst."

Everybody got into the festive spirit as best they could and people even began decorating their rooms. A couple of barbeques were organised and people from all over the base were invited, including pilots and medics. These were the people whose friendship we valued most.

Pilots gave us air support and very often, offered us assistance and cover when they could've told us, "No, it's not part of our mission."

And the medics of course, they would be the people to patch us up if the worst came to the worst. So it was important to keep them onside.

I phoned Leah and told her I love her and wished her Happy Christmas. I was gutted I wouldn't be there to see her open her presents, but I had made sure that she had everything she wanted waiting for her when I returned home and she would then have a second Christmas.

For our party, we took over one of the empty accommodation huts. Naturally, everybody had a good drink and the room needed a good clean up the next day before anybody noticed it and reported us.

The clients knew that we were smuggling drink into the camp, but unless we made it blatantly obvious, they would turn a blind eye and leave us be. We could always do our job and no one ever turned up with alcohol fresh in their system because we would never drink the night before a mission.

On Christmas Day, we all sat together in the canteen and celebrated; American style. Compared to a British Christmas dinner, what we were served was more like a microwave meal, but it was better than nothing and the efforts the American Army had put into making the day as enjoyable as possible for their soldiers and ourselves, was greatly appreciated. We even sat wearing silly hats and pulling crackers, while sipping non alcoholic beer and listening to Christmas Carols played over the speakers. Still, I would've preferred to be home.

The Americans don't celebrate Boxing Day, or so I'm told and so the day after Christmas, we were once again, out on a task. We drove to a small town named Dibis just an hour's drive from the base to inspect the water treatment plants being constructed there and returned straight back to Kirkuk to watch the 'Muppets Christmas Carol'.

As New Year approached, the clients decided they had no mission requests to hand in and once again, we organised a do. Rab's room was full to bursting point with around twenty people crammed into it. We had chosen his room for our get together because it was decorated the most prettiest and the barbeque was closer to it.

He was a great host and saw to our every need, keeping the music playing and the drinks cold, even when I had to pull him away from beating up the mechanic because he thought he had grabbed his arse.

By eight o'clock the party was in full swing and by midnight, I was pretty much an empty wetsuit. I don't remember the clocks hitting midnight and I don't remember getting back to my room.

I woke up the next morning needing fluid and once my throat was moist again, I decided to jump in the shower to freshen up. Feeling human once more, I thought I would go and visit the rest of the lads and see how everyone got on for the night.

I reached out to turn the handle of my door and it wouldn't budge. It wasn't locked so I couldn't understand why it wouldn't open. I barged my shoulder into it and still, it didn't move. I realised I had been stitched up and someone had piled something against my door as a practical joke.

After half an hour of pushing my way through, I managed to get out of my room and saw that someone had gone to great care and effort to remove a few dozen sand bags from around my hut, and stacked them against the door, wedging me inside.

I knew right away it was Andy and maybe Brian had a hand in it too. It took Andy five days before he finally admitted it and even then, he blamed his alter ego who he claimed only made an appearance after a drink.

The insurgents during Christmas time never let us forget where we were. Mortars and rockets were still a regular feature of everyday life on the FOB and outside the wire, IEDs and suicide bombers continued to hit teams and military call signs alike; no doubt, the fact that it was Christmas and knowing that it's an important time of year for westerners, they probably wanted to have some sort of physiological impact on us as well. It never occurred to them that, regardless of the time of year, it made no difference whether they managed to kill some of us now or at any other time. The loss would still be felt all the same.

In early January, the mission requests had started to come in thick and fast and we were also snowed under with stupid emails from our HQ. Our head shed during Christmas, as always, had been sure to take care of themselves and many of them had swindled it so that they would be home for the festivities, leaving just a skeleton crew of administration staff behind to deal with the running of the company.

What bothered us most was that, when they returned, they got straight back in to sending out bone emails to everyone in the company. From advice on how to spend our money and how much we should have saved up in case *THEY* fuck up and don't pay us on time, to silly messages about how important it was to stay professional and keep the contract going.

It never failed to piss us off. To be lectured by a bunch of people who were sat in cushy offices in Baghdad and having the best of everything, while talking to us as if we were a bunch of kids.

On a few occasions our money wasn't paid into our banks on time, which was supposed to be at the end of every month. Naturally, the men on the ground wouldn't be happy and would want to know why it's not gone in and when they can expect it to go in.

Sometimes we would receive replies saying that we have no right to email them directly about such issues and we would then be threatened with disciplinary actions because we hadn't used the chain of command. For instance; I should report my grievance to the Op's Manager, who would then get in touch with the Regional Manager and he would get in touch with Baghdad on my behalf.

"Bollocks, it's my money and I'm not here for any other reason than to make money." I said to the Op's Manager.

None of us were there to make a difference for Iraq, or fight the 'War on Terror'. So not being paid on time was worse than missing out on leave.

On other occasions, when everyone had been paid late, we would receive emails from management, lecturing us on the fact that we should all have sufficient savings in our banks to cover the delay, which to us, was like a red rag to a bull.

It was none of their business what money we had saved or didn't. It was their job to pay us on time and not our responsibility to aim off for their incompetence.

If a guy was paid on the 28th of the month and on the 29th, he decided to blow his entire wages in a casino, then that was his prerogative. Everybody nevertheless had savings and could cover it, but it was always the principal of it all.

A lot of lads had scores to settle with many of the management, especially in the Administration Department. These were people, who sat protected behind their desks and felt a certain amount of power in writing threatening emails to the men who crossed the wire every day. The blokes on the teams were the people who won the contracts, by putting in the hard work and making sure that the tasks and missions were complete. Every day, they risked injury and even their lives and many men were killed while the management and administration staff sat safe behind their desks, talking tough via email.

You can have corporate management who can waffle till they're blue in the face about how great their company is, but without the guys on the ground risking life and limb, they could never win a contract. This fact was something that many people higher up tended to forget, especially the ones who had never been out of the Green Zone.

Brian, Andy, Cach, Marty and Rab as the rear gun truck crew

Andy

Brian

Guy

Cach as rear gunner

Low profile in 2005

Marty, Toad and Guy in the mountains

The author and Guy

Pete and his SAW

Pistol training in Kirkuk

Kirkuk team with Kiawah support helicopter

Toad and Chubbs

View from my gun port during a mission

Typical equipment carried by each team member

Close air support from Kiawah

A close call

Interior of a destroyed gun truck after IED attack

Destroyed gun truck

An effective IED hit

Liam Carmichael, RIP

ROADSIDE BOMBS AND SHRAPNEL

By now, Chubbs was back from leave and as soon as he arrived, the atmosphere within the team got louder. He brought me a fresh supply of teabags and little bits and bobs for Brian, Cach and Andy. Once he was settled, one of the first things he did was to play a new practical joke he had thought up on Andy.

Forever stitching each other up, there was a continual war going on between them. Before he had left, on the drive back from the canteen one day, Chubbs had tipped a plastic container full of yogurt over Andy's head and Andy, immediately counter attacked by throwing the contents of his take away box from the canteen all over Chubbs. The problem was; there were four of us in the vehicle with him so we all got covered in it.

Chubbs sat at the wheel, in shock at the speed and extent of Andy's retaliation, covered in mayonnaise and beans while Andy jumped out and ran off laughing, out of reach from Chubbs.

Chubbs had now thought up a new one. The day after he had arrived back, he knocked at my door. He had Brian and Cach with him.

"Luke, come and watch this."

He walked towards Andy's hut, which was across from me, and I noticed that the wooden steps leading up to his door were missing.

All our huts were built three feet off the ground and to get in them, everyone had a set of purpose built steps, with hand rail and all leading up to the door. Chubbs had gone to a lot of trouble to move them without Andy hearing and I suspected that Cach was involved too.

Chubbs banged frantically on Andy's door, screaming that we had been crashed out to an emergency and that he was to get his kit on.

In his panic, Andy rushed to the door, threw it open and barged out at top speed to see what was going on. He ran in to mid air like the coyote does in the cartoons while at the same time, half way through asking what had happened.

He crashed down, in bare feet, with all his weight on to the small pebbles. I winced as I saw his feet curl in on themselves and the look on Andy's face as the pain hit him. He froze on the spot, with a look of absolute terror and shock in his eyes, before collapsing to his knees and screaming.

Anyone who has been to a pebble beach knows how much they hurt under bare feet and Andy had landed on them with the full momentum of his run and the gravity of fourteen stone as he dropped from the step.

We that were watching were creased up. Chubbs was blowing snot bubbles and Brian and Cach could hardly breathe. I even had tears in my eyes as I stood leaning against my door to balance myself. We stood, laughing and pointing, as we watched Andy crawl around trying to lift himself back up onto his step and into his room.

"You fucking bastards, I can't walk." He shouted.

His Irish accent could be heard from a distance and other people popped their heads out of their doors to see what the commotion was and what we were laughing at.

I still owed Andy from the time he had barricaded me in my room on New Year's Day, so I considered my laughing and pointing at him as justified.

Later in the canteen, Andy got himself an ice cream in a cone and sat eating it at the table with us. As he dipped his head to taste it, I hit the bottom of his hand, forcing the ice cream into his face and smearing it all over his nose and top lip.

"Is it 'pick on Andy day' or summat?" He asked from behind a face full of ice cream as it dripped from his nose and chin.

"Nah mate, I still hadn't got you back from the sand bags thing on New Year, oh and also, for shooting at me at Drumcree."

In 1999, 1 Para had been sent over to Northern Ireland on an emergency tour to cover the marches at Drumcree. The Orange Order intended to march down the Garvaghy Road and we were tasked with building barricades and ditches to stop them. The government had deemed that it would cause too much trouble between the catholic residents and the protestant marchers. So we were to stand between them.

As soon as we got there, we set about digging ditches and erecting barbed wire obstacles and barricades. It began to take on a feel of the First

World War at one point. There were deep trenches, surrounded by mud that had been churned up by the thousands of feet trampling around them and barbed wire. Row upon row of it was strung out across our front.

Riots soon kicked off and at times, on the barricades, we were fighting hand to hand with our riot shields and batons as the rioters tried to storm us with ladders while throwing house bricks and petrol bombs.

It was like a Theme Park from a movie. On one side you could experience war in the trenches and on the other; you could be a medieval knight, swashbuckling on a castle battlement.

Covering the ditches was the same, only it was more open and easier to use the baton guns, firing plastic bullets. The riots never ceased and during the night, pipe bombs were thrown at us and a few of our lads were injured in the blasts.

I saw an RUC, Royal Ulster Constabulary, officer standing next to me lose his front teeth from a ball bearing fired at us from a sling. The speeding little steel ball punched through his helmet visor, through his lips, and smashed out his top and bottom incisors.

A few days later during another riot, we heard shots fired and because it was coming from the crowd, we couldn't see who was shooting. There were far too many people, thousands of them and although they were rioting and throwing stones, petrol bombs and even dog shit, by the 'Rules of Engagement', which was written by some desk jockey in Whitehall who more than likely, had never got his boots dirty, we couldn't fire unless we had a definite identified target with the weapon. All we could do was take cover behind the vehicles and fire plastic bullets at anyone who came close. I fired fifteen baton rounds on the first night and altogether, our company exhausted our non-lethal ammunition supply. However, the shooters were never found and they just melted away into the crowd, only to pop up in a different position and shoot at us again.

Later, we got a report that members from the Royal Irish Regiment of the British Army had been arrested in connection with the shootings and rioting. Weapons had also been found in their possession. We couldn't believe what we were hearing, British soldiers firing at British soldiers because they weren't happy that we couldn't allow them to march through the area?

When I had first met Andy and he found out what regiment I was from, he admitted to being at Drumcree on the opposite side and he had thoroughly enjoyed the riots. At one point, we may have even clashed swords (him with a stick and me with a hard rubber baton) on the battlements.

"I told you Luke, I never shot at anyone, especially you lot, at Drumcree. I just got stuck into the riots. They were a laugh though weren't they?"

We were tasked to go to Mosul with a couple of clients who had been transferred there. We were to drop them off with all their baggage. As soon as Den, who had taken over as the Team Leader while Dave went on leave, informed us of the mission, there was a sigh in the room.

Travelling through Mosul in a high profile convoy was going to attract more attention from the locals than we had when I was with my previous company. We were a big target and in that area, they never passed up an opportunity to hit us when they could.

It was back to planning the mission and researching the areas and recent activity. Mosul was never a run of the mill kind of job and a lot had to be considered. Routes, areas, insurgent activity, coalition activity, support; including air cover and, even the weather.

It was now the beginning of February and the rains had started again now that the temperature had raised a couple of degrees. With the rain came mud and insurgents were less likely to lie in wait on the open road areas with IEDs and ambushes. So if we were to get hit, it would more than likely be in the city itself.

We had a number of options on routes to get there. We could go the direct route, which would bring us out on a road called Tampa for the last leg. Or we could use the longer route, through Erbil. We would have to do both anyway because it would be tactically unsound to travel the same roads twice. We opted for the longer route in and the shorter route out. At least that way, we could stop off in Erbil for lunch.

Chubbs Andy and Brian had all worked in Mosul with our current company and none of them thought we had much chance of getting through unscathed. When Chubbs had been there, they had been hit repeatedly during missions in the city and even on one occasion, one of their team had fired at their own guys in the confusion.

Then, Mosul had had two PSD teams working for our company. Travelling north through the city back to their FOB, the team Chubbs was in was hit by an IED and then opened up on with machineguns from an embankment and a bridge over looking their position.

An American, named Jon, in the side gunner seat opposite had no targets to fire at because the contact was on the right and he was facing left. That was until four black SUVs had come racing past on his side. He started firing at them. Chubbs was in the rear gunner seat and while he was engaging the insurgents, he could hear the side gunner firing.

"What you firing at?" He screamed over the noise of the contact as Jon continued to fire.

Later, once they were back in base, they conducted a debriefing. Everyone had to give an account of their actions and what they had seen from their positions.

When they came to Jon he said, "Them insurgents have now got vehicles like ours. They came up on our left and one of them even had a mask on and he looked like Rodney."

"That's because it *was* Rodney you dick head, you shot up the other team."

We loaded up our kit and everyone took extra care to make sure his ammunition was accessible and we were carrying extra. I was to be the communications guy in the lead gun truck while Sean was on leave. That meant I had to call out everything I saw on our journey, giving the team behind a running commentary. I hated the fact that I had no forward firing capability and to that end, we were vulnerable from a head on attack. I just hoped that the insurgents hadn't also realized this.

The drive to Erbil was an uneventful and easy one. We set out at first light through Kirkuk and headed north. We stopped to eat once we got to Erbil and by the late morning, we were ready to head towards Mosul. This is when everyone would be doing his own mental checks. Pulling on straps to make sure everything's tight and secure, checking weapons are loaded and ready to fire; medical kit was easy to reach, spare ammunition and weapons at hand, etc.

Everyone was revved up and on high alert. Even though we were heading into possible trouble, the adrenalin rush and the buzz of possibly being moments away from a contact put us on a high. Anyone who has been in that situation would understand. It's not that we are macho and don't care, it's the fact that you're all in it together as a professional team and ready to take on anything that comes at you. The senses become finely tuned and more acute. In the moments before, you feel more alive. You know that you could die, but it's never dwelled upon.

As we approached the city limits, everyone tuned into their own little world. If you were a gunner, then you were covering your arcs of fire, with your finger running along the side of your trigger guard, ready to fire. If you were a driver, or vehicle commander, your eyeballs were rolling in your head as you scanned every inch of the road surface in front, scrutinised every person you saw and watched with suspicion, every building roof top and window and static car along the route.

We all had our weapons made ready, with a round in the chamber, and the gunners had their safety catches off. The drivers were watching the roads, junctions and other traffic while the vehicle commanders were keeping communications with each other and home base, who would be tracking our route and progress.

I was calling out the road ahead and directing the rest of the team for turnings and directions. Because I had to speak so fast and continuously, I was starting to drool.

The city streets were packed bumper to bumper. Just getting through the outskirts was a feat in itself. However, the sirens and strobe flashers mounted on the front of our gun trucks, helped cut us a path and aggressive driving helped to clear the way. The sirens informed people that we were coming, which was both good and bad. It got people out of the way but also informed everyone that we were there. We had no choice but to use them.

We tore through the city and my commentary got faster. Even on corners and junctions, we hardly slowed and the guys in the gun trucks would be holding on for dear life so as not to get thrown against the interior of the vehicle. Even I, strapped in to the front passenger seat of the lead gun truck, had to hold on to the dash board, to keep myself from banging against the armoured glass at the side of my head.

The buildings were all a dull grey or dirty brown and the people were all the same colour. The winter months in Iraq don't seem to have any other shades in them, especially in the cities. People in the market places and around the buildings were all wearing multiple layers with very little flesh showing in order to protect them from the cold. The buildings were constantly bombarded with dirty rain, sleet and snow, mixed with the exhaust emissions and general pollution that hung in a grey green haze above the city. With the mud and rain, the filth of the city looked like something from an apocalyptic film set.

No one smiled.

We made it through without incident and we were able to breathe a sigh of relief once we were clear of the security barrier to the base. The FOB was named 'Diamond Back' and it was huge. Similar to the one we lived on in Kirkuk, it had an airfield and so it was a vital base in the northern regions of Iraq. The place was full of American soldiers and private contractors like us and it was a beehive of activity; teams coming in and out, helicopters landing and taking off and soldiers pushing out on patrols in large armoured vehicles.

We headed towards the USACE compound to drop the clients off and during that time, the drivers would refuel and the rest of us would grab a brew and a fresh intelligence update from the head shed there.

I knew that a mate of mine was based there, so I planned a surprise visit on him and made my way to his room once I had been pointed in the right direction.

I kicked his door open, "Get the brews on Yung Ting Ping Wang Pong."

Si and I had been through our whole army career together, from day one recruits, all the way through to the time that we left. He was adopted by a British couple when he was still a baby in Hong Kong. His adoptive parents had been based there with the army and he had returned to the UK with them. Obviously, he was of local origin and so, I made up nicknames for him that, I considered, sounded indigenous to where he was born.

He looked shocked to see me, but his mouth agape appearance soon changed to a big grin and manly hug, the sort were only the tops of your shoulders come into contact with each other, which I appreciated because he was in just his underpants.

"What you doing here?" Si asked.

"Dropping a client off, so I thought I'd pop in and say hello."

We chatted for a while and caught up on current events. During the last couple of years, a number of friends had been killed out in Iraq and I was shocked to learn that Dave Vine had been killed in an IED, a good guy from our days in 1 Para.

Whenever we saw someone who we hadn't seen for a while, inevitably there would always be a, 'did you hear about such and such?' moment.

The year before, another old mate of ours who we had gone through depot with as recruits had been killed in Afghanistan while serving with 3 Para.

Brian Budd had posthumously won the Victoria Cross for his actions and it was the first Si had heard about it. It's never that people don't care, it's because in Iraq, you are out of the loop and either people can't get hold of you or you've not been keeping up on current events on the news.

Though when a private contractor like us is killed, it's very rarely news worthy material.

Once we were refuelled and our brews were finished, we all piled into the conference room to have a quick heads up from Brian on the intelligence he had received for us. It didn't look good.

Due to changes in the road system, our route out was going to take us through a few naughty areas where we would be hard pressed to support each other because of the tight road conditions. On top of that, the first couple of miles south would be over looked by high roof tops as we travelled through the streets towards the outskirts of Mosul and onto Route Tampa.

"We're gonna get hit lads and that's basically it. Just be ready for it and keep your feet and heads down."

"That's it? That's your intelligence brief? Fucking hell Brian, you should be working in management or even MI5." Cach threw in.

"Well you know the route, and you know the area too." Brian spread the map out on the table and run a pen along the intended route. "As we're coming through here, it's gonna be ideal for an IED." He indicated a narrow road that bottlenecked. "If not there, then there's this bit just before we hit the main road south," he pointed to the bend that would force us to slow down before we pulled on to the main carriageway. He continued to follow the route with his pointer, "and then there's Tampa itself. You all know that road. It's IED Alley."

Route Tampa is one of the main high ways, running the whole length of the country from south to north. Long and straight, with long distances between turn offs, it was easy for the enemy to plot our course.

The threat now, wasn't just an IED or an attack; it was multiple IEDs and multiple attacks. We could be hit as we left the city and manage to push through, unhurt, only to get hit again a few miles down the road. They could watch us and know where we are going, and put another IED or attack in place further on.

Very much like the Battle of the Atlantic during the Second World War. Groups of German U-Boats known as 'Wolf Packs' would lie in wait for British and American shipping convoys then, attack them en-masse. Once the first line of U-Boats had finished their attacks, they would radio ahead, warning other U-Boats further along of the convoy's speed and direction of travel, and the ships would be attacked again. We were the Allied Convoy and the insurgents; they were the U-Boat Wolf Packs.

It was an anxious time and we wanted it to be over as quickly as possible. So once we were done and ready, we moved out.

"Did you ever tell your kids bedtime stories Brian?" Cach asked over the radio. "I bet you always told them that Goldie Locks was caught and savaged to death after she tried to run from the three bears didn't you?"

"No, I told them that she was arrested for breaking and entering and damage to private property and got addicted to heroin while she was inside."

We thundered out of the gate and turned right, back towards the city centre. Our plan was to keep as close to the base as possible as we skirted the outer edge of Mosul before we came onto Tampa.

In the built up area, the only trouble we had was pot holes and sharp turnings and we were relieved to reach the open road. At least on long stretches like that, we had a chance to see what was coming or waiting for us, though the insurgents had come up with ingenious ways of planting IEDs. From digging up the road, planting the device and putting the tarmac back and even hollowing out crash barriers and concrete blocks and placing the explosives inside. It was never a case of a big round black thing at the side of the road with the word 'BOMB' stencilled across it and with a fizzing fuse in the top. It was a constant battle of wits between them and us.

Once out of Mosul, the road ahead was clear and seemed unending. We opened up the speed and raced south to home base and safety. On some of the junctions, there were Iraqi Police guards and soldiers conducting check points. They would see us coming and clear a path for us so that we could push through without having to slow down too much.

As we reached a junction that we intended to turn left at, the lack of Iraqi Security Forces became apparent and the reason soon followed. As our vehicle rounded the bend, a loud clap, like thunder but shorter, louder and sharper, hit our senses. At the same time, the shockwave caught us and momentarily, lifted the vehicle from the road, throwing us around inside, jolting us against the vehicle interior and each other. A cloud of dust and debris followed and it poured straight in through the open gun ports and rear gun hatch.

We were swaying violently and I thought we would flip onto our side or even the roof. My ears were ringing and my vision blurred as my eyes struggled to focus. Rab, who was driving, was struggling to control the vehicle because he was in the same condition as me and how he kept us on the road, I'll never know.

The force of the blast had thrown us on to two wheels and threatened to topple us as Rab fought with the wheel, half blind and deaf, to keep us on an even keel.

I could hear the engine racing and the vehicle began to steady itself and drive straight. I couldn't see through the front windscreen and I heard Den screaming through my ear piece. "Push through, push through. Luke, keep going."

It sounded like it was being said to me in a dream, low and hollow, but I was fully aware of where I was and what had happened. Our truck had been whacked and somehow, we were still mobile. The dust began to clear and we were able to see the road ahead again.

"Keep going Luke and once we find a good area, we'll go static and assess from there. Is everyone in your truck okay, any casualties?"

I looked to Rab, he seemed fine, and he was even reaching for pack of cigarettes on the dashboard. I looked over my left shoulder at Martin, and though he looked a little dizzy and shocked, he seemed okay. Pete and Cach were in the same condition. We all had ringing ears and blurred vision but for the most part, we were all still good.

"No mate, everyone is alright, dizzy and deaf but we're okay." I replied through the radio.

A few miles further on, we found an open flat area where we could pull over. Everyone debussed and took up fire positions and even though the road was empty, we positioned the vehicles so that we completely blocked our side of the carriageway. Anyone wanting to pass would have to cross to the other side and Kamikaze against the oncoming traffic.

We were taking no chances and at that point we would treat everyone as hostile to us.

We walked around our gun truck to check the damage. The whole of the left side was peppered with shrapnel and holes, as big as snooker balls, had been punched into the metal outer skin of the truck. None seemed to have penetrated the armour. Two tyres needed changing and we checked the engine, suspension and fuel tank for damages.

It was obvious to us that the Iraqi Police and army had had a hand in the IED. At the very least, they knew about it because they were nowhere to be seen at the checkpoint.

Typical, great and British, we got a brew out of Toad's flask and then, we were good to go again. We still had a way to go but we still felt relieved to have survived without a scratch up to that point. We all grew more admiration for our Ford Excursions and the standard to which they had been built. They were strong and steady and their armour plating was second to none. Most other vehicles would've crumbled in the blast or even been blown clear across the road. Ours seemed to shrug it off, like it was more of an annoyance than a clump of steel and explosives designed to kill and destroy us.

Our vehicles got us back safely to Kirkuk and with that, we had survived another attack on our team. How many more until someone was hurt, we could never say, but as long as the vehicles held out and we maintained them and ourselves, then we had a fighting chance.

In the compound where we lived we had adopted a stray cat and named him Woolfy. Most of the men on the team were animal lovers and the cat was quite a character. He would spend each night in a different room and before long; he was completely tame, and fat.

Blokes would be in the canteen, picking up take away boxes from the sandwich counter full of tuna for him. Sean hadn't realised it, but he had automatically been asking for tuna and mayonnaise and before long, Woolfy had started to become tubby and horizontally challenged. Still, we all took care of him and he was treated as our very own mascot for the team.

Often I would walk into someone's room and there would be our team cat, sprawled out on the bed watching TV, as though the place was his own. Woolfy had mates in the local area and before long, we had four cats and each of them would visit and be fed. For us, it was ideal because it kept the rodent population down and we no longer woke up in the mornings to find mouse shit scattered around our rooms and our kit and equipment covered with little chew marks.

One night, Woolfy staggered into Den's room limping and clearly in pain. We lay him on the bed and had a look at him and it was obvious he had a broken leg, and maybe broken ribs from what we could tell. None of us expected him to live through the night because we suspected he had internal bleeding from his damaged ribs, but he fought on and after a day or two, he regained his appetite and began eating again.

He was completely immobile and needed to be nursed back to health. Den kept him in his room and insisted that he would play nurse.

Andy came into my room a few days later, looking angry and annoyed. It turned out, he had found out what had happened to Woolfy. We had local Iraqi men who worked in the laundry room of our camp and one day, they had gotten their hands on the cat, dragged him into their room and given him a good kicking just for the fun of it.

Andy had been told by another local guy who either, had affection for animals or just wanted to see the others in the shit. It didn't matter to Andy what the reason was. He stormed into the laundry room office and grabbed the nearest person he could find. He dragged him across a desk and slammed him against a wall while the others watched in horror. The man's feet were literally off the ground while Andy gripped him by the throat and snarled in to his face.

"Any of you bastards touch my cat again, and I'll kill the fucking lot of you." He hissed through clenched teeth.

To make his point he gripped his throat that little bit tighter, cutting off the flow of oxygen and making him turn purple. He released his grip and dropped him to the floor after a while.

"I fucking mean it you cunts." He glared at the others and then, casually walked out.

It didn't matter whether they spoke English and understood him or not, it was clear for all what he was saying and it needed no translation.

As he told me the story in my room, even I was a little scared, because he retold it and relived it at the same time.

Woolfy made a recovery but not a complete one. Because none of us were a vet and there was none on the base; not for a stray cat at least, we couldn't get him proper treatment. So his leg and ribs healed but they were never set right again and he walked about with a constant limp after that. It never affected his character in the slightest though.

I got my own revenge on the locals in the laundry room a few days later. I pretended I was so grateful for their services that I bought them a pizza for their lunch. I went to the Pizza Hut at the food court and asked for a Super Supreme with extra spicy pork. They loved it and had no idea what was on the pizza. I enjoyed the fact that if there is a God, then Allah wouldn't be letting them into Paradise when they die because they had eaten pig.

In 2003, during the Iraq invasion, our section had been tasked with securing a villa on the banks of the Tigris that would become an outpost to conduct operations from.

We got there and made sure the area was clear. Looters had been there before us and anything of value had been snaffled away. The windows were smashed and the walls knocked through to provide building materials for the locals.

Personally, I would've just taken the building as my own rather than wreck it if I had been an Iraqi, because even though there was a lot of damage, I could still see that it had once been a beautiful villa. In fact, we were later told by the locals that it had belonged to one of Saddam's Generals and he had fled once he knew the war was lost.

We placed a stag (guard) on the gate and went about settling ourselves in because we were told that we could be there for a few days before we were relieved. While we were cracking on with our routine of eating, sleeping, and taking turns on the gate, a crowd had started to gather.

John, our section commander, went to investigate and it turned out that a few of the local Imams and Sheiks had turned up with their entourage and personal security. All in all, there were roughly twenty of them and so as not to insult them, we allowed them in to sit and talk with us over some local tea as per the custom.

Basically, they were weighing us up and used the 'welcome to the neighbourhood' routine to get close to us. At that stage, the insurgency hadn't really taken hold in Iraq and the local population were still very much onside with the coalition forces.

We all sat around a large wooden table and through their own interpreters, we held a long and meaningful conversation that was way above our pay grades.

They spoke of politics and what will happen next now that the war was over and how Iraq should be governed. Being religious and tribal leaders, they had a big hand in the local politics and so meeting with us, they hoped, would give them an idea of how to play the game in the coming months. Little did they know that the highest rank amongst us was a corporal; just two steps up from the bottom of the rank ladder. They probably thought we were officers.

In the British Army, a corporal is considered the backbone of a unit. He is the section commander who makes the snap decisions in the heat of battle. Whether he decides to go left flanking or right, could dictate the outcome of an assault. In most other armies around the world, a corporal is nothing more than pond life and would be given no more responsibility than supervising dishwashing or road sweeping. In the Iraqi Army it was the officers that made all the command decisions.

As we chatted, they had their people bring in large pots and kettles of tea which we drank with them as we discussed the rebuilding of Iraq. We just pretended to know what we were talking about and cracked on. Being infantry soldiers on the ground we had no access to the news and we were only ever told what we needed to know, so even the lowest of the locals knew more than we did of what was happening in the bigger picture. It wouldn't have been a good idea to tell them this because it would've made us look like dick heads, so we made up most of what we were saying. Including that Tony Blair and George Bush were on their way to Baghdad to choose a new president, which they all got excited about.

We were digging a big hole and we needed a way out. Just then, a bunch of the Imam's boys came in with trays and platters full with rice and lamb with local bread and vegetables. It was the best feast we had ever seen, or so it seemed that way after living on army rations for the previous four months.

They saw how delighted we were and encouraged us to tuck in and we all ate together. The conversations changed from politics to a more relaxed and pleasant nature. We began talking of our homes and family and even swapped jokes. Everyone was smiling and laughing as we ate and drank and it was then that John nudged me.

"Luke, what can we give them in return?"

We couldn't let them go empty handed because they were doing the, sampling each other's culture thing as a way of showing friendship.

"Shit, we can't give them any of our rations 'cause that would be an insult." I said, scratching my head.

Army rations aren't the worst food in the world, but compared to the feast they had just laid on for us, it would be like we were just fobbing them off.

Smudge, a young lad in our section came over to us and said, in his Manchester accent, "I got a parcel from home yesterday, so we could give 'em summat outta that."

"Nice one, what you got then?"

He started to dig about in his kit and began pulling out packs of noodles and sweets. We handed the sweets to the nearest of the Imam's bodyguards and he took one and passed them along. As they were circling the table, Smudge continued to delve into the depths of his kit. Out came two large bags of what looked like crisps to me. I took them from him and studied them.

"You dick head, we can't give 'em these."

He looked at me bewildered, "What's wrong with that? I love 'em."

"Yeah, no doubt they're great and even better in your local pub with a pint, but these Imams' are Muslim." The look on his face told me he still didn't understand the problem. "So, they can't eat certain things. It's a big no-no to them. It's like walking into a church at home, and pissing in the Holy Water, but worse."

"Ah right, I'll not pass them out then."

But it was too late. They had seen the bags pulled out and they were expecting them. The bodyguard even stood ready to receive the next gift. I looked down at the bags and realised that it didn't say anything on the packaging about their ingredients, and there were no pictures to arouse suspicions.

So, I handed them over.

Within no time, they were going round the table and everyone was thoroughly enjoying them. I watched as the Imams' nodded their heads in approval and passed them to the people seated next to them. I was cringing at the thought of being found out. We would be lynched for sure.

John leaned over to me. "What you given them?"

I leaned in close to John, trying to look as though we were having a normal conversation and not making it look as though I was telling a dirty little secret. I put my head slightly closer and continued to watch the table, smiling as I did so, pretending to be having a great time.

"Pork Scratchings," I whispered.

As I lay in my room one evening, watching TV, Liam came bursting in, larger than life as always.

"Way hey Frankie, get the brews on you little shit."

I did as I was told. "What are you doing here Fatty?" I asked

"Drop off mate. And we have to wait until he's ready to come back so we're here for a couple of days. I'll be crashing in here if you don't mind because I'm not staying in the transit accommodation, there's no telly or internet connection."

He wasn't really asking me, he was just being polite about telling me he was my roommate until he's gone.

I looked at my bed and then at Liam. "Right, you're on the floor because I'm not waking up with you spooning me and stroking my hair."

"No worries buddy, I've brought my doss bag"

And with that, we became a regular couple. We would wake in the morning and have a brew, then go and do our work for the day. Then come home at night and go to dinner together and on the second night, Brian, Cach, Andy and Chubbs cracked out the vodka and whisky. I knew right away it was going to get messy because Liam was never a 'couple of quiet ones' type of guy. Eventually the majority of the team piled into my room and it became a full on party.

I woke up the next morning with Liam jumping up and down on my bed like a kid on Christmas morning, telling me to come running with him. I really didn't want to but Liam wouldn't take no for an answer.

I dragged on my running shoes and downed a litre of water before falling out of the door. He minced along and breezed through a five mile run that he had dragged me on, while I stumbled and shuffled at his side like a newly born giraffe the whole way, covered in my own snot and vomit.

What seemed like days later, we staggered back into our compound and I collapsed into my chair, guzzling water like my life depended on it, and with the way I felt at the time, it did.

I could hear Liam singing away in the shower and I hoped beyond hope that he would be heading back to Suli that afternoon. If he wasn't, then no doubt it would be another vodka/whisky mission that night.

He stayed.

This time we headed up to what we had started to call 'Toads Bar'. Basically, it was Toads room but he had done it up to look like a bar with pictures on the walls and trinkets from around the world to grab your attention, scattered as ornaments.

As we walked into his room, the bar was set up on the right of the door with stools, seats, cushions and his bed as the seating area on the opposite wall. Half of the team were already in there and Toad greeted us with a mug of his homemade punch, which he ladled from an actual punch bowl. Where he had got it from, we could only guess because Toad kept most of his contacts secret to himself.

I took a sip from the cup and to my reckoning, the punch was two parts whisky, two parts rum, two parts vodka, two parts brandy and two parts cats piss, with maybe a slice of pineapple thrown in it somewhere as the fruit addition. Just a taste was enough to curl your toes and give you a nervous tick.

Next, we were treated to a bowl of his homemade curry. It was hotter than any curry dish I had tasted before and I've always liked Indian and spicy food. I enjoyed it, but it forced me to drink more of the punch to cool my mouth. Naturally, everyone in the room was hammered in no time and the music blasted while we shouted to each other to talk.

In hind sight, I could've quenched with water, but I think it would've been seen as an insult and plus, the punch was pretty good once you got used to it. To anyone walking past, it must've sounded like a regular bar. If anyone opened the door, they would have been hit with a wall of cigarette smoke and noise.

The clients hadn't been too keen on venturing out lately and so, we had more time on our hands. Most of the lads saw this as an opportunity to blow off some steam. We were cooped together for three months at a time and away from our homes and families. Plus, we were all grown men and even though we may have taken things to excess now and then, it never interfered with our jobs and people always stayed sober the night before a task.

The next morning I had to dig my heels in, "Fuck off Liam; I'm not coming for a run."

Returning from a mission, we approached the rear gate of the base. We had been to a small town named Dibis, just an hour's drive away, to the north of Kirkuk.

USACE had a sewage and water treatment plant there that they were overseeing. All had gone well and we had raced back to base and were now on the home stretch of the rough road to the rear of the airbase.

Once off the main road, we were in open country. To our left was farmland with crops and goats and the odd building here and there. To our right was an old Iraqi Army base with high ground beyond. The road itself was a mixture of dirt track and old tarmac, with culverts and small bridges we had to cross now and then.

These choke points were always a concern to us because it was easy to have an IED planted underneath them, and short of stopping and getting out and checking each one, we would never know if they were clear until we had passed over them.

The route was full of pot holes and sharp tight bends and as we passed over a small bridge and climbed the slight rise on the other side, our lead gun truck was hit.

A loud bang that echoed back and forth from the foot hills of the high ground and seemed to linger for an eternity with a long low boom filled our ears. For a second after, all was silent.

From my position in the rear gun truck, as the right hand side gunner, I couldn't see much, but I could hear people screaming what I assumed were contact reports over the net. Next, I heard gun fire from up ahead and I knew that it was the lead truck engaging targets.

I recognised the fast steady crack of the SAW being fired as the belt fed rounds filtered through the feed tray, throwing home the next 5.56mm round in to the chamber to be fired.

From what I could tell, it sounded as though both the rear and side guns were engaging. I still didn't know what side they were engaging from or even, if the convoy was still mobile. All I could do was watch and listen. I was scanning my side of the area when we passed through the debris and dust thrown up by the explosion so I knew that the lead truck was, at least for the time being, still moving.

I snatched a quick glance over my left shoulder and through the front windscreen to get a better idea of what was happening. The two client vehicles had pushed to the centre to keep as much distance as possible from themselves and anymore IEDs on the left or right hand sides of the road and also, to allow Chubbs, the rear gunner in the lead vehicle, a better field of view and arcs for his SAW.

Now I knew that the contact was on the right hand side, my side. My glance had taken a second and I was back to covering my arcs, looking for the firing point from where the terrorists had initiated the charge.

Things were confusing because, as people were firing, they were also giving target indications. It was hard to hear what was being said and with the noise of the vehicles on top of the gun fire, it was impossible to distinguish details.

Then I saw it, from Chubbs' SAW I saw the distinct red glow of the tracer ammunition as it sailed from my left peripheral vision and into the middle distance at the target he was engaging. Still, I couldn't see the terrorists.

More tracer rounds followed and I watched as I saw them hit rocks or other hard objects, causing them to ricochet off into the sky. I aimed my weapon in that direction and watched. Since the contact had started, it had been no more than a few seconds, yet we were still in the killing area of the insurgents and the contact was ongoing.

I saw two figures jump up from the rocky outcrop where Chubb's and Pete's rounds where landing. They begin to run in the direction of the hills. They were roughly one hundred metres away and obviously had thought they safe to engage us with their AK47s from that range and that we wouldn't see them.

As they ran, I sighted just slightly ahead of them to give my rounds time to get there and by then, they would've crossed the distance and my burst would hit home, hopefully in the centre of mass around the middle of the torso.

I started to fire and watched the rounds lighting up in front of them. Then, we turned a bend and they were gone from my sights.

I screamed behind me, in to the rear gun seat where Smudge was sat, "One hundred metres, left side, rag heads in the open heading towards the hills."

Smudge opened up with his SAW and from what I could tell, Chubbs was still able to get rounds on target from his position in the lead truck too.

We were still racing for the rear gate and we had no intention of allowing the insurgents the chance to stop and turn, to put more fire down at us, so we kept up the pressure on them as we bugged out of the area.

I covered my arcs and quickly reloaded my weapon in case we got into a fresh contact further on before reaching safety. It was a drill we all knew from our military days. During a fire fight or battle, as soon as there's a short lull, the first thing you do is, get a fresh magazine on your weapon.

When you're firing, regardless of what you're taught, its nigh on impossible to count your rounds and it's better to just slam in a fresh magazine when you get the chance because then you know it's full and ready for the next spot of bother.

The firing ceased and everyone in the lead vehicle answered up to let us know they were okay and no injuries. Later, when we were back at base, Smudge, Chubbs and Cach had to draw fresh ammunition from the stores to replenish their depleted supply. A lot of rounds had been fired, yet we still weren't sure if we had hit any of them. No one had seen the insurgents drop.

The vehicles needed to be checked over and any damage repaired. Just above the firing port on Martins side, was a chunk of metal imbedded into the armour plating.

"Fuck me, have you seen this?" Martin exclaimed as he pried the lump of shrapnel loose with his knife.

It was half the size of my hand and if it had been a couple of inches lower in its trajectory, then Martin would have lost his head.

During the contact, the gunners had fired four hundred rounds between them. Me, I had fired four and I wasn't best pleased. I cursed the road for having a bend in it at that particular moment. But the lesson of the day had been, when a contact starts communications will go to rat shit due to noise and confusion and so, it's a case of, "watch my tracer."

Seeing Chubbs' tracer rounds hitting the firing points where the enemy took cover was better than anyone screaming directions and distances to me. It had given me an aiming point immediately and all I had had to do was look for movement.

Spring was approaching and with that, so was my leave. I had spent Christmas and New Year in Kirkuk, and the whole of January and February too. I was itching to get home and see my loved ones.

On my wall, I had what we called a 'Chuff Chart' marking the days left in country. I wouldn't be doing that again though because the days seemed to drag more.

Rab and I were hitting the gym harder than ever on the run down to leave and on the way there one time, we came up with a solid plan on how to count our days instead of using a 'Chuff Chart'.

"Right, you don't count the day you're on, so today is crossed off. And you don't count the day you leave, so that's two days down already." I had used this method in the past and called it 'Lukey Logic'. It just painted things a slightly nicer shade of rosy.

Rab considered it with great thought. "Okay, well once it's past a certain time in the evening then you may as well knock off the next day as well, and it's pointless counting the last week either. And say its Thursday today then, you may as well not count the weekend."

I couldn't understand his reasoning but he was happy with it. I managed to shave two days off my time left in country, but according to Rab's method, as soon as he stepped off the plane coming into Iraq, he may as well turn back around and go home with the amount of days and weeks he was hacking off.

Two days before my leave, we were tasked with a job to Tuz. It was the last thing I needed at the end of my twelve week rotation.

Ambush and Fight Through in Tuz

Up ahead, there was an incident of some sort. We didn't know what it was and we had received no updates on any dramas in the area.

There was always something happening in Tuz. The place was a hotbed of insurgent activity. The main route ran directly through the centre of the town, running north to south. Either side of the road was jam packed with makeshift mechanics garages and truck stops.

On any given day, the area to the immediate left and right of the main highway would be crawling with vehicles and people.

Travelling through Tuz was always an eerie moment. Like Mosul, it had a very distinctly hostile atmosphere. The general feeling of the area was that of a town in the Wild West, where strangers, namely westerners, were scrutinised and unwelcome when they passed through.

My heart always stepped up a gear and my adrenalin never failed to begin surging through my veins when driving that stretch of road. Everyone in the team had pretty much the same reaction to missions that involved a visit to Tuz.

As we approached the build up of static vehicles in the centre of the road, the people either side began to take more notice of us. Rarely did they get to see a PSD call sign in detail; due to the speed they would travel through the area, wanting to get clear of the place as quickly as possible.

Their stares and expressions of antipathy and hostility were easy to read as I watched each and every one of them from behind the sights of my weapon. I gripped the M4 tighter in to my shoulder. The safety catch was off and my finger, gently rested along the trigger guard; ready to be snatched in to action.

The people stood and followed us with their eyes as we came level with them. None made any sudden movements, but many of them snorted and spat at their feet. The gesture was clear enough of their feelings toward us.

Guy was covering the left hand side of the vehicle and no doubt, he was seeing the same unwelcoming sneers and glares from the locals as I was.

"Multiple static vehicles up ahead." Sean announced over the radio from the lead gun truck. "Looks like a possible RTA. Push left, we'll see if we can pass on the hard shoulder."

"Roger that." Den replied, "Try and keep some speed up, we wanna get outta here as quickly as we got in."

I agreed whole heartedly with what Den had said, as did the rest of the team. Going static or, even reducing speed in Tuz, was asking for trouble. And the locals, including the Iraqi Police, wouldn't often miss an opportunity to take us on.

All along the outskirts of the town, there were telltale reminders of just what can happen in that place should you give them the chance. IEDs and RPG attacks had always been a regular thing in the area. The charred and wrecked corpses of military and private security vehicles littered the roadsides. Craters and burn marks from IED detonations stood testament to the hospitality of the area.

It wasn't insurgents, coming from foreign countries that were carrying out these attacks; it was the locals and the IP. It was as clear as the nose on my face. Just from the atmospherics of the town, we could deduce that, even the so called security forces there were hostile toward us.

With the Iraqi Police, much of their recruiting is done locally. And although they supposedly come under government control, their loyalty lies more with their tribes and family clans.

If the president was to personally come down and say, "Do not attack anymore Western Security Forces," but the local Sheik countermanded the order, they would obey the Sheik.

The convoy had to push through and stay mobile, avoiding becoming a static target and every man in the team was poised, with our weapons ready for a possible attack. We had all been in attacks, either from roadside bombs, rocket attacks and even small arms. It was new to none of us. But still, we would never take it for granted that we would come off better than the attackers.

Our convoy began to slow and veer to the left to avoid the obstruction in front. Sean was leading us around the mass of static vehicles and wandering pedestrians and IP. As we came level, the crowd turned to glare at us, including the police. Their minds were momentarily distracted from the tangled mass of crashed vehicles in the centre of the road and their complete attention, now rested upon us.

I felt uneasy and for a moment, a shudder ran the length of my spine, closely followed by a trickle of tingling sweat.

We were clear, and we immediately picked up speed and raced for the far end of town and toward the open road leading to Kirkuk. We were trying to put as much distance between ourselves and Tuz as possible, and as quickly as we could. We knew that due to us having to slow down to avoid the accident, we had given them the exact chance they needed. Someone would call ahead and advise anyone who was interested in the juicy target headed their way.

The last checkpoint was in sight and Sean hit the sirens and flashers to clear us an unobstructed path. We barged through; paying no attention whatsoever to the IP guard that manned the checkpoint. If he had stood in our way, he would've been run down and trampled beneath our armoured wheels.

"Road clear ahead, keep centre," I heard Sean call through my earpiece, "rooftops to the far left and right, keep eyes on."

I was scanning the areas he had pointed out, looking for possible firing points.

"People on the rooftops to our left," Brian shouted over his shoulder, struggling to be heard over the noise of the racing engine.

"Roger that, seen," Guy replied as he began scanning for himself in the area that Brian had pointed out.

"Contact right." Sean screamed over the radio.

Quickly, I snapped my head away from my weapon and to the front, looking through the front windscreen in the hope of quickly identifying the threat. From the right, I saw a line of trailing white smoke, streaking across our path and narrowly missing the second vehicle in the team. It was an RPG, and I recognised its signature immediately.

I spun my weapon to aim in the direction of the firing point and began to squeeze the trigger, releasing three to five round bursts in to the suspected area of where the rocket had been fired. I felt the slight jerk as the weapon juddered back in to my shoulder. My tracer, lit red, sailed in the direction of the firing point, but I still hadn't seen a target, just the puff of telltale smoke that marked it as the point where the RPG had been fired. The best I could hope for was to suppress the firer and make him think twice about popping back up to fire again.

"RPG right," Brian screamed from the commander's seat in front.

I caught sight of a flash and a white puff of smoke then, we were thrown from the road. It felt as though an invisible force had gripped our truck, squeezed it tight, and then flung it to the side. The impact was like a giant hammer blow slamming in to the side of us.

My lungs were almost sucked out from my chest as all the air was snatched away in the vacuum of the blast. My head hit the armour plating beside me and the straps that held me in place, strained against my body weight to keep me in my seat. My vision blurred and my eyes seemed to roll around inside my skull as we were tossed violently. The loud bang of the detonating RPG echoed and reverberated around inside my head. Everything else became distant and disconnected as I felt like a separate entity, thrown around within the shell of my own body.

The vehicle lurched and crunched as it skidded from the tarmac and began to career down the embankment to our left. I was forced back in to my seat as no doubt, Guy was forced forward, toward his firing port as the truck tilted and gravity took effect.

I was distantly aware of the sound of scraping and crunching metal as our Ford Excursion slammed in to the desert floor at the bottom of the slope and come to a sudden stop, forcing our bodies to jerk in our seats against the retaining straps.

I could hear people groaning and even shouting, but I was unable to distinguish who it was or what they were saying. I was dazed and completely confused for a moment as the vehicle came to a complete stop. I was unable to force my mind to reconnect with my body. I sat, inactive, for what seemed an eternity, incapable of moving, and staring through my gun port back up the slope we had slid down.

Slowly, my senses gathered themselves in to some form of coherence. I could hear the voices more clearly now and I recognised the panicked voice of Brian to my left, and the frustrated shouts of Chubbs, still strapped in to his rear gunner seat. Also, as well as the sounds within our smashed gun truck, I could hear other noises from the outside.

Machineguns were firing. The sound never let up and took on the resonant quality of ripping cloth and rapidly beaten metal. It was obvious that a fierce gun battle was raging somewhere above us on the road. For the meantime, we were protected by the embankment. Our vehicle lay at the bottom of it and we were safe from enemy fire, giving us the chance to recover.

"Toad, Toad you okay?" Brian was trying to get some kind of proof of life from Toad, shaking him and checking for a pulse.

Toad was still. His head and face were buried in to the steering wheel and blood was splattered over the dashboard and windscreen in front of him. Brian continued to speak to him and began checking the back of his neck for any obvious spinal and head trauma.

Toad raised his head and groaned.

I looked over my shoulder at him, fumbling with my harness to free myself, and I could see that his face was covered in blood. He pulled his head back from the steering wheel that he had smashed in to and snorted and coughed, spraying blood over himself and Brian.

Guy was struggling in his seat behind me and kicking at his door, shouting and growling in frustration. I heard his door swing open with a resounding creek and a clunk then, the sound of Guy freeing himself from the damaged and cluttered interior of the destroyed gun truck.

I burst of fire from behind me jolted me in my seat and I hastened to release myself from the harness, believing that the attackers had began a follow up and were now firing on to our vehicle as we struggled to regroup.

"That's the IP bastards taken care of." Guy shouted from the outside.

As he had climbed out of the vehicle, he could see from his position, that the Iraqi Police checkpoint on the outskirts of Tuz still had line of sight on us. If there is line of sight; there is something to aim weapons at. As far as we were concerned, the police were part of the attack. It had taken place just a hundred metres away from them. If they hadn't been part of it, how could the insurgents set up such a large ambush, right under their noses?

So, Guy neutralised any immediate threat he identified.

The firing from up the slope continued to rage. From our position, we had no idea of how the rest of the team had fared. We could hear the rapid clatter of machinegun fire from further down to our left and we could tell it was from the other gun truck, so at least we knew that some of the team had made it.

I managed to crawl from the vehicle, helping Toad and Brian once I was out, while Guy helped to free Chubbs. Toad was in shit state. His face was completely red from blood and his nose looked more smashed than it normally did. His lips were shredded and his eyes had already begun to swell.

Brian hobbled by his side, holding his leg. He had hurt his knee when the RPG hit the front wheel and the blast had reverberated up through the foot well below his feet.

We quickly checked over ourselves and tried to assess the situation. I had no injuries other than a thumping headache and jelly legs. Next, I checked my weapons and ammunition. I had my rifle in my hands and my pistol was still attached to my hip in its holster. I had remembered to look for my grab bag, full of extra magazines, and found it wedged between mine and Guy's seat as I was climbing out from the wreck.

We huddled behind the damaged hull of the gun truck, using its still intact armour for protection against any sudden attacks from further up the slope.

Brian began trying to gain communications with Den and the rest of the team.

"Den, this is Brian, radio check."

"Strength five Brian, what's your sit-rep, any casualties?" The sound of relief from Den was obvious, even through our earpieces.

"Nothing serious, Toad is hurt and my leg feels pretty fucked. What's happening up there? The vehicle is written off. The RPG took out the wheel and most of the engine, so we're on foot from here."

The sound of gun fire continued. Now and then, we heard the snap of rounds passing overhead as the enemy, or even our own team members, fired in to our general direction. From what I could gather, there were multiple enemy firing positions and the remainder of the team were in a fierce gun battle, pouring huge amounts of rounds in to the enemy, trying to suppress them and win the fire fight.

"Is there any way we can extract towards your position?"

"No Brian," Den replied, "you'll be exposed about fifty metres further along from where you are. We can't get any closer either. They've got the road between us completely cut and they've fired more RPG's since. Anyone trying to move in that area of open ground will be exposed to the other side of the road"

I looked at Guy, and he looked at Brian.

"Fuck it," Chubbs snapped from the rear, shouting over the loud cracks and snaps as more fire sailed overhead. He knelt at the rear of the vehicle where he was covering the road, "we'll have to head back toward the built up area. It's only a hundred metres and then we can take it from there."

I nodded at Brian, "He's right. We can't stay here and Den can't get to us."

Brian shook his head in resignation. He knew it was our only real option. Though we were heavily armed and the position could be defended from an assault coming from the slope to our front, we were vulnerable from our right flank. All it would take is for the attackers to realise it and place men on to the rooftops of the nearest houses on the outskirts of Tuz, and we would be caught in an enfilading cross fire.

"Okay, who has smoke?"

I pulled two smoke grenades from my vest and handed one to him. On the count of three, we would toss them in to the road, and hopefully, obscure our movements as we turned back toward the buildings and in the opposite direction from the rest of the team.

"Toad, you okay to move?" Brian asked over his shoulder.

Toad stood behind him, covering the area to the front of the wrecked gun truck. "Yeah," he spluttered, "My legs are fine; it's just my face that's fucked."

Even in a bad situation like this humour was ever present, to a degree.

I heard Guy chuckle from my right, "That's always been the case anyway Toad you ugly cunt."

Brian relayed the plan to Den and warned him that we would be 'popping smoke', then moving back toward the cover of the town. Once the smoke began to billow in the road above, Den was to increase the rate of fire to pile the pressure on the attackers and to keep their attention away from us. They still hadn't made a move toward us. It was either because of the amount of fire they were under from the other gun truck, or they had assumed that they had written us off with the RPG.

I held the smoke grenade in my hand. I had already removed the pin and I was crouched, looking in the direction we would be running. About seventy five metres along, the desert at the side of the road was raised and became level with the tarmac. That would be twenty five metres of exposed movement to our left on the opposite side of the road, where the attack had come from.

I quickly checked the wind direction and realised that it seemed to be blowing roughly south east. At least the wind was on our side.

I looked back at Brian and nodded. He pulled his arm back and hurled his grenade in to the air and on to the road beside us. I did the same, throwing it as far to the south as I could, hoping to give us a complete smoke screen for the mad dash.

Purple and orange smoke began to billow from our grenades, shrouding the road and obscuring us from view.

"Moving now," Brian told Den across the net.

Immediately, the rate of fire from the other half of the team tripled in intensity. For a moment, the fire from the attackers seemed to falter and it occurred to me, that maybe we should have turned and fought through; charging the enemy positions, with Den and the others acting as our point of fire from our left and firing across our front as we advanced.

It was a fleeting thought and I knew it wouldn't have worked. We didn't know their strengths and dispositions, and if they were strong enough to stop Den from being able to link up with us, then surely, they were able to withstand a direct frontal assault from five men.

We began to move, paralleling the road.

Chubbs and I were in front, with Guy bringing up the rear. Toad and Brian stayed in the middle and we ran at the fastest pace they could manage. Brian was limping badly and I could hear him puffing and panting behind me, but he was covering the ground a lot quicker than I thought he would have done. Toad sprinted at his side, snorting and hacking up blood from his damaged nose and mouth.

A burst of machinegun fire from behind stopped us in our tracks. We all turned as one to face the road to our left, weapons in the shoulder and ready to fire. Guy had dropped to one knee and was pumping bursts of fire from his SAW in to the area at the top of the embankment, within the now thinning smoke. I saw bodies moving toward us from the road and together, Chubbs and I fired long bursts in to their direction.

"They're coming across. They're coming across toward you." I could hear Andy shouting with panic in his voice over the radio to warn us and the rattle of gun fire from the other gun truck.

The attackers had decided to bring the fight to us and began to move from their side of the road in the hope of finishing us off with a frontal assault. They were met with a wall of fire from all five of our guns. I saw bodies topple over as rounds ripped through them and others, dropped to the tarmac, in the hope of getting below our deadly hail of bullets.

"Peel right, peel right." I began to scream as I continued to fire.

Guy was the first to move, as he was on the extreme left. He jumped up from his fire position and ran behind us and placed himself at the far end of the line, on Chubbs' right, taking up the fire again. Now it was the turn of Brian to move, then Toad, then me. We continued this movement, leap frogging behind each other, all the while, at least three men were static and suppressing the enemy while the others moved. We would carry this on until we either broke contact or, we reached the cover of the nearest building.

We were close now and on a level plain with the far side of the road. I could see the other half of the team in the distance further north from us; they were still pouring rounds in to the enemy positions and causing them to split their attention between us.

Across the road, I saw the flash and smoke from numerous machineguns and assault rifles as the insurgents tried to stop our retreat.

We continued to move toward cover. Rounds snapped and hissed in the air around us as the enemy fire tried desperately to stop us. Clouds of dust and shards of rock shot up in to the air all around as inaccurate fire thumped in to the ground at our feet.

Now and then, someone would scream, 'magazine' as his weapon ran dry and he would immediately get up and run, changing magazines on the move. If you weren't firing, then it was pointless staying still.

Chubbs was the first to reach the buildings and he instantly took up a fire position from the cover of a wall and began firing long bursts in to the area of the road to cover the rest of us as we piled in beside him.

Sweat was dripping in to my eyes and I was breathing hard, my chest heaving and my legs shaking. We were ankle deep in the filth and detritus that ran between the houses and as my lungs fought to take in oxygen, I was vaguely aware of the fetid and putrid odours from around our feet that crept in to our nostrils.

I dropped the magazine from my weapon and slammed in a fresh one. Everyone around me was doing the same.

We were leaning against the wall of the house, keeping ourselves tight against the building. Chubbs continued to fire in the direction we had come, while the rest of us made a quick assessment of our situation. No one had thought past this part, and to be honest, I don't think any of us had expected to make it as far as we had.

The wall of the building that we were against led in to the street to our immediate south, the street ran roughly east to west.

"Head for the street, then turn right and we'll see if we can skirt around the far western side of Tuz and link back up with Den." Brian decided.

He sent the same message to Den over his radio, but there was no reply or acknowledgment. They were either too busy or, they were out of range for our small handheld radios. It didn't matter because we had no choice anyway. We had to move.

With a final long burst from Chubbs, we then moved toward the street. There were now buildings between us and our attackers and that gave us, at least a little, breathing space.

We turned the corner and headed west. People, with wide terrified eyes, peered out from behind their doors and garden walls. Children were snatched off the street by worried parents ahead of us and the street was soon empty as we charged along.

Guy was in front, his weapon in the shoulder and his knees bent, ready to spring should a threat appear ahead of us. I was slightly behind him and to his left, covering him as we moved. Chubbs jogged along at the back, his SAW in his arms and protecting our rear.

"Keep going straight. We'll follow this road for as far as possible and hopefully hit the outskirts to the west and turn north." Brian instructed us.

We were travelling fast, but not so fast that should something happen ahead of us, that we would run headlong in to it. We needed to gain some distance but, at the same time, we didn't want to race in to possible trouble that was waiting for us.

Our eyes scanned every window and doorway as we made our way west. In the distance, and to our rear, we could still hear heavy gun fire from the direction of the road. We knew though, that the attackers would've realised that we had retreated back in to the built up area and as far as we were concerned, this was their backyard. They wouldn't want to pass up the chance of trapping us and either killing us, or taking us captive. Either way, we would end up dead.

If they didn't follow us up, or put in a block ahead of us, they would be allowing us to slip away.

Guy's weapon burst to life to my right. The noise of the SAW rattled and echoed around in the tight confined space of the narrow street. I snapped my eyes away from the rooftop I had been scanning as I moved, just in time to see an Iraqi Policeman, crumple to the floor ahead of us. His AK47 clattered as it was dropped from his hands and he curled up, groaning and clutching at his abdomen. Brian fired a burst in to his head as we past him, ensuring there was no threat left behind us.

Around the bend and to our left, an IP pickup truck had gone static and the police were dismounting from inside, their weapons held at the ready. The moment we saw them, Guy, Brian and I all opened up. Toad also stepped forward and began to pump rounds in to the men and their vehicle.

The windows shattered and caved inward, the doors and hood bent and buckled as our weapons reduced the truck to a steaming and smoking perforated mass of twisted metal and men.

Those who had managed to get out of the vehicle were soon lay sprawled, or writhing on the ground as our rounds smashed in to them, the men that remained inside, jerked and screamed as they were shot full of holes.

We pushed on.

My lungs were burning and the muscles in my legs felt like they were being pumped full of syrup, rather than fast flowing oxygenated blood. Brian ripped the helmet he was still wearing from his head and tossed it to the floor. I had lost my helmet in the crash. Rarely did I wear one because they tended to trap heat and leave me feeling like my head was in a pressure cooker. But, for trips in to places like Mosul and Tuz, I always made a point of donning the Kevlar dome.

Our pace was slowing. With Brian and Toad being hurt and the weight of our kit, sustaining a rapid retreat on foot was always going to be unsustainable. I could hear my heart pounding in my ears and the sweat that dripped in to my eyes, blurred my vision. My mouth and throat felt like I had been eating sand, but we had no time to stop. We needed to push on and reach an area where we could gather what strength we had and make our next move.

Brian had his phone in his hand, desperately trying to get through to Den to inform him of our whereabouts, condition and intentions. I heard him shouting down the phone, struggling to be heard over the sound of gunfire on the other end, and his own heavy breathing.

"Den, Den we're moving west. Yes, west. Once we hit the outskirts, we'll turn north. Try and find a track that can meet us somewhere to the west of your position." He paused for a moment while Den gave his reply.

He raised his hand to us, telling us to stop at the corner of a house. We huddled together, panting for breath and wiping the stinging sweat from our eyes, while Brian continued to speak to Den. Chubbs and Guy covered the approaches with their machineguns, while I began digging around in the pack on Brian's back, looking for water.

I took a long gulp and immediately felt the fluid quench my parched throat and mouth. It was the best thing I had ever tasted. I held the bottle to Chubbs' lips as he glugged the water and then did the same for Guy. I moved toward Brian to do the same again and Toad reached out for the bottle.

"Fuck off Toad. You're going last on it. Look at the state of your mouth. You might have AIDS for all we know, and I'm not drinking from a bottle you've bled in to." I winked at him and he did his best to grin back at me, blood and snot drooling from his nose and lips.

"Right," Brian turned to us as he tucked his phone back in to his pocket, "Den says the Kiawah's are inbound. They've already left the FOB and should be here pretty soon. Also, a ground call sign is en-route to help. We're gonna push along and turn north. Den is gonna try and link up with us along the way."

Even though we were far from being clear of the woods, I felt relieved that we weren't left to our own devices and expected to pull ourselves out of the shit situation we were in. Just the knowledge of Kiawah helicopters coming to our aid was a comfort. As soon as they appeared, we could call them in close to our position to give us immediate air support.

Guy stepped out and continued to lead us north. We had travelled roughly a kilometre through the northern outskirts of the town and we knew that we would soon hit open country again, leaving us exposed in all directions.

We reached the outskirts. The buildings had steadily changed from being hard smooth walled houses, to bare breeze block shacks and then, mud huts on the far reaches. Beyond them there were fields and open desert, crisscrossed with narrow dirt roads and tracks.

Brian stopped us in the cover of a rickety looking shack that someone was using as a house. Though the locals must have been aware of what was happening on the road further to the east, they couldn't have not heard our gunfire as we cut through the town toward them, they didn't seem to be as concerned for their safety as the rest of the indigenous population was. They were curious about us, and even braved standing in their doorways and peering around corners at us. The adults whispered amongst themselves and the children smiled and even waved.

"Head for the road Guy, according to my GPS, there should be a track about four hundred metres up, running north east. I'll try and get Den to meet us on that."

Brian pointed in the direction we needed to head as he looked down to his GPS. I squinted, and in the distance, I saw what looked like it could be a raised road. It seemed a long way and I didn't fancy the idea of having to fight our way towards it. But we had little choice.

Brian made a final phone call to Den, informing him of what we could see ahead of us and that he was to try and find a way on to the track to give us support and also, lift us out.

We all got water down us, glugging as if our lives depended on it, and our lives *did*. We were all suffering from dehydration, exhaustion and shock and we still had a ways to go.

We pushed out and headed in the direction of the track, away from the last of the mud huts on the outskirts of town. We travelled in an extended line, side by side, already prepared to turn and face the enemy should they follow us up.

We tried to follow the natural folds and dips in the ground as best we could to use them as some degree of cover, but we were still severely exposed from all around. We were now, pretty much, doubling back on ourselves, running parallel to the road that was roughly a kilometre to our right. As I looked across, I could just about make out the area where our wrecked gun truck must have been. There was smoke all around the road and I assumed that the vehicle had caught fire.

We continued to push ahead. I was becoming weaker. The adrenalin in my blood was starting to run short and I was now on my reserves. We had been fighting a running battle for what seemed like hours and there had been no let up. We were constantly moving and trying to get away from the threat. But, it seemed, they were always there, close on our heels.

The road was becoming more visible and recognisable now. At least once we made it there, we could use the rise of its embankment as cover while we could turn east on the other side, keeping us out of view and effective enemy fire.

A row of loud cracks made me spin on my heel, "Contact rear," I screamed and at the same time, I brought my M4 up in to the aim.

The other four had done the exact same thing and we were now returning fire in to the buildings behind us. Everyone was getting as much fire down as they could in the direction of the enemy.

The idea is to return fire immediately, even if you haven't identified the exact location of the firing point. As long as you can put rounds in to their general direction, you can at least make the firer duck, giving you the vital split second it takes to drop in to cover then pinpoint his location.

That's the theory anyway.

What actually happened was, we all remained standing, in a line and poured all of the firepower we had in to the enemy. If I had been on the receiving end, I would've been digging in with my eyelids. We held our ground and continued to fire.

My weapon stopped.

"Magazine," I yelled and dropped to one knee as I ejected it and replaced it with a full one.

I was back up within a second and firing once again. With the noise from the weight of fire we were putting down, I couldn't tell if we were still being fired at. We were just focused on suppressing them to the extent that they would become demoralized and think twice about showing their faces in the light of day again, never mind returning fire.

"Luke, move." Brian shouted to me from the right.

"Moving," I hollered back and turned to run in the direction of the road and away from the town.

Brian, Toad and I ran for a few metres then, stopped and turned to face the threat again. It was our turn to fire.

"Move," the three of us shouted in unison to Guy and Chubbs.

As we fired, they moved back in to line with us. Again, we were leap frogging and covering each other as we moved. Chubbs and Guy fired rapidly while the rest of us bounded back and we did the same for them. There was always 'one foot on the ground', meaning that no one was moving without fire support.

We were close to the road now and still firing and manoeuvring. Getting over the embankment would mean being exposed and sky lined as perfect targets. As we closed in on the rise, I realised that we were, in fact, still taking enemy fire. Their rounds were pounding in to the embankment, sending clouds of dust and sand in to the air around us. But with the weight of fire we returned on them, we couldn't hear the report of their weapons or, the snap of their rounds as they passed by.

There was obviously more than one enemy firing point throwing rounds at us, and now we had a dilemma. How would we cross the road? To do so, we had to climb the embankment and we couldn't do that without sustaining casualties. But we had to move.

Guy and Chubbs were still firing as the rest of us steeled ourselves for the 'over the top' manoeuvre. I was crouched and ready to spring up for the mad dash when, our problem was solved for us.

From the east, and further along the track, we heard the rapid thumping of machineguns. At first I thought we had been flanked and were pretty much fucked. Then I looked and saw the dark silhouette of a Ford Excursion, headed in our direction.

Sean and his gun truck had made it up the track and they were now hammering away at the attackers from their vantage point overlooking the area. Andy, Martin and Cach weren't sparing their ammunition and they fired in long bursts, stitching the whole area with their deadly concentrated fire.

"Move, get over the road." Brian screamed to Chubbs and Guy.

They turned and followed us across as we scaled the high ground. Enemy fire still cracked above our heads and slammed in to the embankment behind us, but they were obviously less enthusiastic about keeping up the pressure since the other gun truck had arrived.

Now they were faltering.

The five of us hit the other side and were down in cover from the enemy. We turned east and trundled, at the fastest pace we could manage, toward the rest of the team.

Once we came level, I looked up and saw Martin's face looking out from the left side door, waving us in and calling to us. It didn't matter what he was saying; he could have been calling us all the names under the sun for all I cared. As far as I was concerned, on that day, his face was that of an angel in my eyes.

We piled, as best we could, in to the cramped space of the interior of the gun truck. Cach and Andy were still giving it to the insurgents in a big way from their belt fed machineguns while the engine roared and sprung us forward.

"Den is still static on the road," Sean called over his shoulder, "they're still under fire but it's sporadic. I think most of the rag heads followed you in to the built up area."

My ears were ringing and my heart pounded against my chest wall. It felt like 'ALIEN' was in there, trying to smash its way out and through my body armour.

I caught a glimpse of Chubbs, who looked back at me and raised his eyebrows twice in quick succession. I knew exactly what he was saying, "*Fuck me.*"

"Top cover far left." Sean announced, meaning that he had caught sight of the Kiawah's coming from the north.

It would've been nice to have stayed and watched the fireworks display as the helicopters made short work of the insurgents on the ground, but we needed to link up with Den and the others to become a complete call sign again.

Sean spoke to the pilots through his radio and directed them in to the area they needed, while at the same time, identifying us as the black SUV racing to the east along the track.

It was good thinking from Sean because, in their haste to join battle, the chopper pilots could've mistook us as insurgents fleeing from the area and an anti-armour rocket in the side, would've ruined our good fortune.

Once we were complete again, Den ordered our vehicles to push further north along the road to get out of reach of any enemy fire. The Kiawah's were doing a grand job. We could hear their guns firing and the sounds of explosions as they smashed what remained of the enemy.

We pulled in to the side and did a quick reshuffle of the team. The survivors of the destroyed truck would be split between the two client vehicles.

On the way to my vehicle, I had to stop. I leaned against the side of the Excursion and threw my guts up. It was pouring from my nose as well as my mouth. I couldn't stop it.

With the adrenalin, dehydration, exhaustion and most of all, fear, all mixed together, my body succumbed to them once we were clear of the danger. My legs were weak and I had to hold on to the side of the client vehicle as I made my way along, still dry heaving and trying my best to compose myself.

I climbed in to the vehicle and I found myself sitting beside a wide eyed and terrified looking client. I smiled at him and nodded, sick and snot still dripping from my nose.

Den sent a radio check to all the remaining vehicles. Everyone answered up, "okay."

We pushed on for home base.

Part Timers and Brothers in Arms

Spring was well underway by the time I returned from leave. The first days were always the hardest because you knew you had twelve weeks ahead of you before the next leave. I always made the most of my time off and so, it was always a sad occasion saying goodbye to my family.

With the start of spring, came the rain and with the rain, came the mud. Travelling about on sites was always a pain in the arse because each time you lifted your foot; you had an acre of land on the bottom of each boot. It was a workout in itself just walking about with the clients because of the lead boot effect the thick sucking mud had on us. Worse yet, was the fact that on my leave, I had invested in a new pair of fancy desert boots and I was well chuffed with them. Well, at least until our first site visit.

"Fuck sake." I grunted as I stepped from the vehicle when we pulled into the site. Id stepped out and gone ankle deep in a mixture of sticky clay and wet mud. My new shoes didn't look all that GUCCI anymore, and I wasn't impressed.

While I was away, we had received a new commander on the client side. The colonel had taken over as the USACE boss for the Kirkuk area. No one had any information on him and so, no one knew if he was a decent guy or not. We did know that he was in the American National Guard, which is the part time army you always hear the President order to be mobilised in the movies, "Call in the National Guard" or "Mobilise the National Guard."

They would do a tour and then, return to their towns and civilian jobs as war heroes.

The colonel's appearance was that of an American Sit-Com type dad; barrel chest and a beer belly. He also had a moustache and thinning grey hair. He walked around the site, looking very uninterested in what he was supposed to be looking at, while Joe pretended to know what he was talking about, and spent the entire visit, trying to impress the new boss. The colonel just stumbled from project to project and I had the impression that he wasn't exactly best pleased about being there and wanted to get back to base.

Once we were back, I set about cleaning my new boots. Just a few missions later and I completely give up on them for the rainy period and admitted defeat. They stayed a shitty brown colour until the weather dried up.

The war between Andy and Chubbs had continued while I was gone and the latest story was:

One day, the team had been having lunch in the canteen together. Once they were finished, Andy stood to leave holding his tray in both hands, piled with empty plates and cups. As he turned to walk towards the tray collection point, Chubbs ran up behind him and gave a downwards tug on the jogging bottoms Andy was wearing.

Down they came, and as it turned out, Andy had gone Commando that day and wasn't wearing any underpants. With everything on display, he stood looking about with a look of utter shock and complete helplessness on his face. He was incapable of doing anything about it because he had his hands full and he didn't want to drop the tray.

He turned and snarled at Chubbs, who sat laughing and pointing at him with the rest of the team, "You fucking little shit, pull 'em back up."

No one came to his aid and Chubbs and the rest of the lads continued to sit and ridicule him. More and more people were noticing the event and slowly but surely, a hushed silence fell upon the immediate area around him. Soldiers and civilians alike sat and gawped at the spectacle that was Andy. Frozen to the spot, he looked around at the hundreds of eyes that stared at him, mouths agape.

He still didn't want to drop the tray.

Andy started to shuffle, ever so slowly, toward the nearest table with the intent of placing his tray down and correcting his state of dress. The people seated at the table began to shuffle away in the opposite direction, as though Andy was radioactive.

An American Sergeant ran up to him with a look of disbelief and horror, "Hey man, you can't do that." He said as he pointed at the bare legs and arse of Andy.

Through gritted teeth and an air of contempt for the stupidity of the Sergeant, Andy replied, "Do you really fucking think I did this to myself? Ask yourself two questions, how and why."

The Sergeant stood slack jawed as Andy then shuffled past him, waddling like a penguin.

The noise from the rest of the team sat at the table was deafening as they rolled up laughing. They all got to their feet to follow Andy to the tray drop off and the American Sergeant was still standing there, not knowing what to do next.

From then on, everyone in the team always made sure they were either, wearing a belt or at the very least, underpants. I always took the belt option for comfort reasons.

The contract was up for renewal in the summer time. At that moment, our company and one other shared the Corp of Engineers contract between them. I'm unsure of how this came about, but both were large companies and the work was pretty much equally split. However, the powers that be announced that the contract, when it was renewed, would be given to only one company and they would take over responsibility for the entire security of the project.

This was both good and bad news for us. If our company won the contract, then it would be at least a few more years work for us and possibly, better pay and equipment because our head shed wouldn't be competing against anyone else to give the client a better price on the security.

If we didn't win the contract, then we would be knackered and out of work.

Around that time, we started to hear rumours about a deal between the two company head sheds'. Apparently, whoever won the contract, they would take on the teams of the other company because they would still need the same amount of men on the ground and it would mean that no one would become unemployed. It sounded like a good deal to us but we knew it wouldn't work that way.

The bone emails started from our HQ. Daily we were reminded about how important it was to keep our professionalism and help win the contract. Why they felt the need to tell us this, we don't know. None of us were exactly rocket scientists but we knew that a lot was riding on our performances on the ground. To us, nothing would change. We would carry on working at the same level and providing the same standard we had from the start. We weren't about to begin sucking up to the clients, hoping they would put in a good word for us because that wasn't in our nature and we knew that the clients we had, were at the bottom of the food chain when it came to making decisions on such matters. We just cracked on as normal.

As the weather warmed up, people began working on their tans during slack days and before long, the pool was open again. Barbeques were often organised around the pool and we Brits' were always invited. The barbeques; with soft drinks and skateboard music and Air Force girls that weren't allowed to wear bikinis due to dress codes and had to walk about in big baggy shorts and t-shirts, weren't really barbeques in our eyes. No matter how fun they tried to make it, it still seemed like a tame and supervised school day out to us from when we were kids.

Our idea of a barbeque was lots of food, lots of alcohol, then making human pyramids at the poolside and drowning one another. So, out of politeness, we would turn up, grab a burger and make our excuses and leave soon after. We never wanted to turn down the offer outright because we wanted to keep good relations with them for scrounging reasons.

While sitting around the pool, we started to notice that the colonel was there quite often too. One thing we did know about him was, he was married back in the U.S but here he was, frolicking in the pool with a female client who worked in his department.

It was none of our business so we paid no more attention. That is, until a few days later when we received a complaint that the colonel wasn't happy that we had time to spend at the pool. In his view, we should've been either training or preparing for missions.

There's only so much training you can do before the lack of time to yourself shortens tempers and people lose interest. We trained often and our drills were slick. At least three once a week, we would be down the ranges conducting live firing drills, three times a week conducting dry (without firing) vehicle drills and we couldn't prepare for missions if we had none to prepare for. All our kit was ready and the vehicles were squared away and maintained to the highest standard we could, so we had time on our hands, and why not relax by a pool?

It was obvious this new client boss was going to be a pain in the arse.

During our army days, we had all experienced the training for the sake of training. Officers could never stand the sight of soldiers sitting around idle. I think it was a mixture of thinking that, having time on our hands would cause us to get into trouble and also that they were trying to impress the higher ranking officers. Most of the time, the training was bollocks and normally consisted of some knocked together, half hearted lesson.

But with the colonel's complaint, we suspected it was more to do with the fact that he wanted to be away from prying eyes so he could continue his little love affair. Naturally, his demand for us to be doing more training was ignored and more of the team began to turn up at the pool just to piss him off. He had no power over us anyway. We weren't military and when it came to operations and training, our managers and Team Leaders were in charge. This became a problem when he had to be put into his place while out on site one day.

We had travelled into the heart of Kirkuk to visit a clinic under construction. Because of the position of the site and the area it was in, we couldn't allow more than twenty minutes for the clients to do what they needed. Then we would have to bug out.

On that day, we happened to be escorting the new colonel's secret lover too. We entered the site and the team pushed out to cover the approaches and the flats that over looked it. Everyone was on high alert and Den and Brian stayed close to the clients as they escorted them around the building, while Sean and I acted as the outer security within the building.

Even though the building wasn't fully complete, it was now considered a functioning clinic and so, they were open for business. This fact made our jobs harder because of the amount of people on the location.

After twenty minutes, Den informed the clients that it was time to go and asked if they were ready. They weren't ready, and they were less than happy with Den telling them that it was time to go. They had been fully briefed and told that, due to the area and the threat situation, we couldn't afford to give them more than twenty minutes and even that was pushing it.

Again, we encountered the problem of clients seeing us as nothing more than a taxi service with guns and no brains. Now and then, we would have a client who believed they had authority on the ground and they were always brought down to earth with a bump, normally in the form of, "Get in the fucking vehicle now. We are leaving."

As the female client began arguing the toss, through our ear pieces we heard, "Shots fired, shots fired," from someone on the outer cordon.

I didn't hear the shots but, I was later told, that a car had driven past the site on the main road, which was about thirty metres away, and took a couple of shots in our general direction. Then they were gone from sight.

Brian and Den grabbed the clients as Sean began cutting a path through the building and towards the exit. I brought up the rear as we stormed through the foyer and out into the open. The client vehicle was already on the steps with the rear doors open and Brian and Den pretty much threw the clients in, probably being a little rougher than they needed to be, just to make their point of who was in control, and we mounted up.

Omar told me later, that the female client had been kicking off big style in the back of the vehicle, going on about how they had the say in how long we visit a site for and when we leave.

"With all due respect Ma'am, read the contract, and you'll see that you're very much wrong." Omar replied to shut her up.

We bugged out back to our base and Den debriefed the clients, apologising to them about the sudden hustle and bustle and that it was for their own safety. It was just Den covering his own arse, making sure he had it on record that he had explained that he was looking after their wellbeing. Obviously it made no difference because the colonel kicked off over it anyway and even emailed our bosses in Baghdad. He was told by them though that we, the team, have complete authority on the ground and we make all the tactical decisions, regardless of him being an officer in the army. He couldn't come back with anything after that, so it knocked the wind out of his sails for a while and we went back to making him feel uncomfortable in the pool.

On the 29th of May 2007 we were having a little get together, as usual, in my room in the evening. It wasn't a party as such, just a few drinks and a laugh.

Toad came bounding through the door, looking flustered, "Has anyone got any mates working for Kroll?" He asked.

Kroll was another security company working in Iraq. They worked mainly low profile and a lot of the guys were either ex Para Reg or Special Forces. Toad had worked for them for a while in Baghdad and knew a lot of them.

I answered, "Yeah, I've a few mates working for them. Why?"

Other lads in the room also had friends in Kroll.

"Five of them have just been lifted in Baghdad. No one knows where they are or who has them, but they suspect they've been taken into Sadr City." Toad replied.

Sadr City was a Shia Muslim area and a suburb district of Baghdad. Until the invasion, it had been named Saddam City and when he was toppled from power it was then, unofficially, called Sadr City after a dead Shiite leader.

Sadr City was never a good place to be, even in armoured vehicles with air support. It was like a rabbit warren, with a maze of streets and alleyways all linked and easily used to move about by insurgents on foot carrying Rocket Propelled Grenades or small arms.

The Kroll guys had been escorting a client to the Iraqi Finance Ministry in Baghdad when, the building was surrounded and stormed by what was claimed as, forty insurgents dressed in Iraqi Police uniforms driving stolen police vehicles. They were taken outside, bundled into the vehicles and driven away towards Sadr City.

It was obvious to me who it was that had taken them.

You don't get forty insurgents, dressed in forty stolen Iraqi Police uniforms, with stolen police vehicles. You get forty Iraqi Police, dressed in their own uniforms, and driving their own vehicles.

Time and time again, we had experienced the corruption of the Iraqi Police in both the north, and the south of the country. If they saw the opportunity of making money from you, then they would take it, even if it meant kidnapping you and selling you to the highest bidder. Everyone was in agreement with this view and yet, we saw the governments and powers that be, pussy footing over the whole thing instead of going directly to the source; the Iraqi Police themselves, and confronting them on the issue.

Since that day there have been a lot of conspiracy theories on what happened and why, and who was really responsible. But it all boils down to the governments, both British and Iraqi, didn't do enough to secure the release of our lads.

They may have been working for a different company but they were doing the same job as us and taking the same risks. They nevertheless, were brothers in arms and it was sickening to imagine what they and their families were going through while the head shed did nothing.

In 2006 they had managed to locate and rescue Norman Kember, a Christian activist who had been kidnapped in Baghdad in November the previous year, so how could they not find five British men?

At the end of December of 2009 Peter Moore, who had been the client, was released from the hostage takers. During his time in captivity, he had been kept separate from the other lads taken with him and he had known nothing of what had happened to them or what condition they were in.

The bodies of Jason Creswell and Jason Swindlehurst were returned to the UK in June 2009 and in September Alec MacLachlan's body was returned. Alan McMenemy is presumed dead, but his body is still unaccounted for.

It's still unsure where the hostages had been held but, there were rumours of them even being in Iran at one point. Regardless of where or why they were held, it was a tragedy that the deal that got Peter Moore released was not made sooner to ensure the release of the others.

The pictures and footage of David Miliband looking pleased and proud with his self, as though he did a great job in securing the release of Peter Moore, is sickening to see. Shame the government didn't pull their finger out sooner.

Our colonel and a couple of his entourage had a meeting with the Kirkuk Police Chief in the north of the city. It was a simple task and just a case of heading out of the gate and bomb bursting in pretty much a straight line, heading north, and then hanging a right turn at the last minute off the main road and driving through the barriers to the station.

We headed out and Sean took up position as the driver of the lead gun truck, with me in the commander's seat giving commentary. Andy was sat directly behind me as the side gunner.

We had made some modifications to the vehicle and added extra armour plating in a few areas, namely the area directly behind my head so that I had some protection from the open gun port behind me.

After the Kroll incident, we all decided that even in a so called secure area like the Police Station, everyone would keep their kit on and travel nowhere alone or unarmed.

As we left the FOB we approached the main road. Sean hit the sirens and flashers and the Iraqi Police check point, immediately outside, began holding traffic left and right to give us a clear run. We screamed out at top speed and Sean swung the vehicle to the left in a wide arc to allow the client vehicles to come through on the inside of us, remaining protected from any possible IEDs in the open ground directly in front of the exit to the base. Once clear of the turning, Sean put his foot down and gunned the engine, picking up speed heading to the junction three hundred metres further on.

It was mid morning and the spring air was already warm. It was more like a good summer's day in the UK. Everyone in the vehicle was calling out possible threats from left and right and I called out what was to the front as well as giving the usual thousand mph commentary over the net to the whole team.

As always, we had no intention of stopping for lights, checkpoints, slow traffic or even potholes. The latter, I hadn't realised we had agreed upon until we turned a bend and hit a rough patch of road at full speed. With the weight of the vehicle, plus the armour, the suspension didn't cushion any of the blows to our arses and we felt every bump. It was like being kicked in both cheeks.

"Slow moving traffic up ahead Den, we're gonna cross over and go Kamikaze." I informed everyone, meaning that we would be travelling on the wrong side of the road against the flow of traffic.

In a manoeuvre like that, we always slowed the pace a little and kept the sirens and lights going to warn everyone to get out of the way ahead of us.

"Roger that Luke, crossing over."

As all four vehicles made their way over the central reservation, we slowed to a crawl to ensure mutual support for each other during the vulnerable time it took to complete the crossover. It may sound like a risky thing to do, but it was better to travel against traffic and keep mobile instead of getting stuck in a jam and being static, while someone comes and lobs grenades or fires RPG's at the big daft black SUVs sat there like sitting ducks.

"That's vehicle four clear the crossover Luke." Brian sent from the rear gun truck. We were all on the same side of the road and ready push on.

"Roger that, increasing speed."

Sean began to build up our momentum and I kept my eyes on the civilian vehicles going static on the left of us as we travelled close to the central reservation.

Now and then, you would get some idiot that didn't notice that all the other traffic was slowing and pulling over onto the side of the road and amazingly, they also wouldn't hear the loud sirens getting louder and coming straight at them, which should be a good indication for them to join the rest of the cars on the hard shoulder because something was coming along that you should get out of the way of. Maybe some people just thought that it was everybody else being good eggs and letting them past?

As we travelled along, the traffic up ahead made a big point of getting out of our way as far as they could, some even mounted the curb. I had the hand mic in my hand, giving my commentary, informing the rest of the team that we would be crossing back over to the other side of the road in about one hundred metres time.

Up ahead, a white saloon car pulled out from the line of traffic on the hard shoulder with the intent of over taking them. Unfortunately, it was a two lane carriage way and one lane was taken up with static and slow moving civilian vehicles travelling south toward the centre of the city, and the other lane, was occupied by four large armoured SUVs, driven by western lunatics travelling north. He had pulled out at speed and I saw him right away.

We had nowhere to go. By now, the central reservation was all crash barriers, and the left hand lane was static vehicles. I thought the worst; SVBIED. I had visions of us being blown up in an ideal opportunity for a suicide bomber coming straight at us. If I had a gun port facing to the front through the windscreen, I would've given him a long burst from my weapon in a heartbeat.

Our speed meant that we couldn't stop in time and reverse as he was also travelling at a rapid rate of knots. No matter what we did, he was going to hit us.

In a split second before impact, I lifted my legs and forced my head and neck back into my seat. I can't remember what I did with my hands, maybe I was peeping from behind them.

Sean slammed on the brakes and I screamed a quick warning so that everyone in our vehicle knew there were dramas inbound, "Shit, shit, shit," or words to that effect.

I had no time to say anything else and I don't think my mouth would've formed any other words more complex than 'shit' anyway.

We were still travelling at a good thirty mph and he seemed to be doing the same. I saw his eyeballs grow in his head as he slammed on his brakes, causing smoke to billow from his wheels. The look of horror on his face was complete by the time we hit and I watched as he travelled from the front seat, into the windscreen and then into the back seat and half out the rear passenger door. His car bounced off the solid steel bumper of our truck and into, and through, the crash barrier of the central reservation. It must've been like hitting a wall for him.

On the moment of impact, I heard a loud dull metallic thud as Andy's head bounced off the armour plating behind me.

"Ooof," I heard from him as his head impacted with the plating.

Luckily he was wearing his helmet. Sean had kept hold of the wheel up until the very last second and then let go just before impact, to save having his arms ripped off if the wheel spun.

The crash had stopped us dead in our tracks and for a moment, we didn't know what to do.

"Give us a minute here Den, we've just been spanked," I said over the radio.

From within a haze, I looked into the central reservation to our two o'clock position and saw, what could only be described as, a 'fucked washing machine'. It looked nothing like a car anymore, just a twisted lump of white metal. The driver was half in and half out of one of the rear doors and slowly dragging himself out of the vehicle.

"Roger that Luke, any injuries? Are you still mobile?"

I was convinced that the truck must be written off. I looked at Sean who looked back at me.

"Well, we still good to go or what then?" I asked him.

"Yeah I think so, the engine is still running and I don't think any serious damage is done."

Everyone in the gun truck was dazed and confused and it was like trying to work out some kind of puzzle the minute you wake up in the morning.

Sean stepped on the accelerator and we began to move again.

"Yeah Den, I think we're good to go mate."

I looked over to the 'fucked washing machine' and the driver was now standing and holding a cloth to what must've been a cut on his head. Blood covered his face and his shirt was torn and hanging from him. He was swaying and holding on to what was left of his car to support himself. I half expected to see him keel over.

"Okay Luke, the driver looks alright, so let's push on." Den reported from the second vehicle.

We carried on as the guy on the hard shoulder watched us move away. He looked confused and began shouting something to us, but we couldn't spend any more time static than we already had done. It was actually only about ten seconds all in all, but it seemed like hours. As we carried on, we approached our turning.

"Is everyone okay in here?" I asked, looking around at the lads.

I got the thumbs up from everyone, including Andy, who had smashed his head into the armour plating. Even with a helmet on, it could've caused some serious damage to his skull and neck.

"Fuck me, did you see him bounce? He went from the front to the back in the blink of an eye." Sean exclaimed.

Everyone began to giggle. We were like a bunch of kids who had just got away with something that would've got them in the shit big time, and feeling the relief afterwards. Before we knew it the whole truck was howling laughing and we couldn't stop. It was just a release and the more we thought about it, the more we laughed.

I tried sending, "Turning right towards the police station," over the radio, but because I was laughing so much and trying to control it, it must've sounded like a baby had gotten hold of the radio and was sat gurgling and drooling into it.

We got into the Police Station and once the initial clearance was done, the clients were escorted in and we took stock of our vehicle and ourselves. I walked to the front, expecting to see a tangle of grill, engine and bumper, all mixed together. What I actually saw was exactly the same as what we had set out with, except for the small dent in the middle of the bumper.

I couldn't believe it and nor could anyone else. Two vehicles had hit each other head on at speed and one of them weighed the same as a small planet with the amount of armour bolted to it and the other, had been crumpled beyond recognition, like tinfoil, while we had a few minor scratches.

We loved our trucks.

The driver of the 'fucked washing machine' wasn't neglected and he was later compensated for the damages. His hospital bills were also paid for by the U.S Government. Basically, the clients threw him a few thousand dollars and he was as happy as a pig in shit.

Rumours were rife about the contract. Everybody knew someone who claimed to know something about the contract and how it was looking for us. Our main worry was keeping hold of our jobs. If the contract went to another company, then we didn't mind as long as we were taken onto their books. At that moment though, the duty rumour was saying that our company were the favourites to win.

We came in from a task and Fifi, who had taken over as our Op's Manager after Geoff, walked out of the office with a grave look on his face. He called us all in to give us a briefing. We all took our seats and grabbed a brew, completely unaware of what could be up.

"The Diwaniyah team got hit this morning lads. A gun truck was hit and three of them are dead and one badly injured," Fifi informed us.

PSD teams from all over the country were getting hit on a daily basis and people were getting hurt and even killed, but for one of our teams to get whacked and a whole gun truck taken out, was a shock to us.

In most gun trucks, there are normally five men; a driver, a commander, two side shooters and a rear gunner. However, the Diwaniyah team were travelling with four. Most of us knew people on the Diwaniyah team and everybody began asking questions and wanting information on who was dead and injured.

I had a close friend on that team myself. Bryn had been in 1 Para with me and even lived in the next town along to me in the UK. He was a passionate Rugby League player and fan, and we had even played for the battalion team together.

"I'm only just getting this info myself lads and as soon as I know more, I'll give you all a heads up," answered Fifi. "Tonight there's gonna be a conference call from the management in Baghdad and all teams across the country will be listening in. I'm not sure what it's about but obviously, it's summat to do with today's events."

Everyone returned to their rooms to dump their kit, all of us, deep in thought. Even the guys who didn't have friends on that team still felt the loss because they were British and they were the same company. I feared the worst for Bryn, as everyone else feared the worst for their friends on that team.

I got to my room and began emailing about to try and get some information on what had happened and who was hurt. No one seemed to know much and what I was getting back was very sketchy. Mainly rumour or third hand information from someone who had heard a rumour in the first place.

I was getting frustrated and annoyed, so I headed back up to the office. It seemed that everyone else in the team had had the same idea and they were hovering about, smoking and drinking brews and talking amongst themselves while they waited for information. HQ was giving nothing away and there was an Information Blackout.

Toad, who you could always rely on to find a way either, through or around the system, came into the office with a list in his hand.

"Lads, I've just spoke to a mate on the phone that's based down in Diwaniyah, and he's give me a heads up on the casualty list."

The three dead were Noah Stephenson, Fraser Burnett and Carl Ladden. Bryn was the only survivor.

They had been hit with a shaped charge IED, known as an EFP or, Explosive Formed Projectile, as they travelled to a task. It was specifically designed for armour penetration using a shaped charge to punch through armour plating.

The vehicle had been blown off the road and into the marshy area at the side and onto its roof. Bryn had come to in the commander's seat and realised that he needed to get out as quickly as possible. He drew his knife and cut himself loose of his harness, then crawled from the vehicle, through the mud and sewage and to the side of the road.

When he got to safety, he looked back to see if anyone had followed him, they hadn't and it was then that he noticed his legs. Both were badly damaged and he was losing a lot of blood. What remained of his right foot was held on by just a thread of skin and muscle and his left leg was badly peppered with shrapnel. He also had severe wounds to his abdomen and it was a miracle he had managed to make his way to the road.

The conference call was scheduled for seven o'clock that night and we all turned up, ready to be given a full brief on what had happened and how, and what the company was going to do about it.

Two of the head shed from Baghdad came over the speaker and asked all of the teams to answer up to let them know that everyone was there. That was the only point in which the conference call was actually two way. Once it was established that the teams were in attendance, the switches were flicked at the management end and it became a one way conversation, the head shed talking to us.

They started off briefly mentioning the events of the day, like a passing comment to something that had happened long ago and to someone else. They gave no details and they failed to confirm the list of casualties to us.

All we got was, "But the best we can do is to crack on in a professional manner and win the contract."

There were a number of thuds in the room as jaws hit the floor. Our ears were surely playing tricks on us. Here we were, having lost four of our boys and now these dick heads begin lecturing us on our standards and how we can still win the contract?

"What a bunch of fucking wankers." Chubbs shouted at the phone. His face was bright red and his eyes burned with anger.

The rest of the team were getting just as worked up and one or two even stormed out, kicking doors and punching walls as they went.

"This is a fucking joke. We've just lost four good blokes and all these cunts can think about is the fucking contract. Well I hope we fucking lose the contract if this is how much they think of us who are on the ground." Chubbs was clearly upset as were the rest of us.

The head shed continued to spout their verbal diarrhoea over the speaker and it seemed, apart from their initial fleeting reference the Diwaniyah team and what had happened, they had completely forgotten them.

They began talking about meetings that were currently ongoing between management and clients in Dubai and how great it's going to be once the contract is awarded solely to us.

The speech went on for roughly fifteen minutes, and even though my blood was boiling and Chubbs was hurling cups by now while Rab and Cach punched holes in the ply wood walls, I couldn't turn away. I guess it was in the vain hope that on the other end of the phone line, they would realise their fuck up and speak more about what mattered to us at that time but, they didn't. It was like watching a car crash, I couldn't help but look on, and it got worse.

Their final words were, "We all need to pull together on this and keep our great levels of professionalism up. The fight is still on and it could go either way, Elvis has not yet left the building."

And that was it.

I had to walk away before I lost my cool and went to my room where Brian was waiting for me with a large glass of whisky and coke. I necked it in one go and began pouring another. Cach, Andy, Chubbs and Rab were soon in my room and it became a ranting session as we banged the world, and our company management, to rights.

If the send capability had been left on during the conference call, then the head shed would've had new arseholes torn verbally. They would've been lynched if they had been there in the room.

"These shit heads aren't worth the contract." Cach decided. "I hope they fucking lose it to be honest."

Everyone was in agreement.

After he was evacuated, Bryn was flown to Germany and underwent some extensive surgery on both his legs and abdomen. His right leg was amputated and his left leg almost followed, but it was saved in the end.

Afterward, and during his long recovery, Bryn slipped down hill. The realisation of not being able to do the things he loved anymore hit him hard. He suffered from depression and frustration.

Paul, another ex 1 Para lad and I dragged him out on the piss for old time's sake to Airborne Forces Day in Catterick. True to form, he received no sympathy and asked for none. We took the piss out of him for being too lazy to go to the bar, even though he had a prosthetic leg by that time and was even driving again.

He's active and mobile again now, though not completely recovered, and I often see him and we always get together when I'm home on leave. The last time was on Remembrance Day, when I got so drunk I pissed my suit.

Summer was now in full swing and leave, for me, was fast approaching but not fast enough. The last month always seemed to drag for me and the closer I got, the slower it went. Dave had come back from his leave and soon after, he had resigned to move onto something else, leaving Den as the Team Leader full time. Brian slotted back into the position of the 2ic and we carried on as normal from there.

The colonel continued to be a thorn in our sides and now and then, he would throw a track for one reason or another. Mostly, it was just him walking about with his chest puffed out trying to be the main man in front of his bit of fluff. We learned that the more polite and professional we acted towards him, the more it pissed him off. I was never the sort to put on false Ayres and Graces, so I avoided him completely.

During a period when there were no tasks to be getting on with, Brian the Techno Wizard, had managed to find a large amount of internet cable, Toad had helped him source it, so no doubt, half the base was now without cabling.

Brian decided that it would be better if we all had our laptops hard wired in our rooms to the internet and he set about running the cables from the main router in the office, down to our accommodation, which was about a hundred metres.

To stop the place from looking like a gypsy camp, with wires and poles hanging everywhere, we all got to work on digging trenches to run the wires through which we then filled in and replaced the shingle over the top. That way, the wires couldn't be seen or damaged and everyone was a winner.

In a few areas, the cables needed to be run up the side of buildings and along the roof. Brian saw to it that the wires wouldn't be seen and they were all taped or fastened down securely. It took a week before it was complete and after all the hard work of digging, climbing on and off roofs, the job was done. It was worth it too.

We now had a better and more secure internet connection in our rooms and everyone was happy.

That was until the colonel walked into the office and confronted Den and Fifi, telling them that he wasn't happy about the guys having internet access in their rooms. Den couldn't understand the problem and asked why.

"I just don't want them to have it is all." The colonel stated.

"Yes, we understand that colonel, but is there a specific reason? It's causing no harm and it's not interfering with anything you need to do." Den reasoned.

"I'm in command of this compound and I don't want them to have it in their rooms." The colonel stormed from the office.

To keep him quiet, the colonel was told that the connection had been switched off. Everyone carried on as usual and used the internet to their hearts content. Now and then, no matter how good the set up was, the internet would go down. Normally it just required the system to reboot itself and five minutes later, it would be up and running again. One night, I was half way through an email and without any warning, the signal went.

I sat patiently, waiting for it to start back up but after ten minutes, I went to investigate. The other lads were having the same trouble, which confirmed for me that it wasn't my computer suffering from AIDS or anything.

Rab smelled a rat and went to check the wires. Rab and Brian followed the route of the exposed parts along the buildings and after twenty minutes, the complete team was called into Den's room.

"The wire has been cut." Brian informed us. "Not only has it been cut, but it's got a whole four foot section missing out of it, so we can't splice them back together." It was obviously sabotage and we knew right away who.

The lads went nuts.

This may seem a petty and trivial matter, but the internet was our main lifeline back to the real world and our loved ones. Without it, it was like living in the dark ages.

Some of the lads wanted to go and drag the colonel out of his room and give him a kicking. Rab even went as far as wanting to chop him up and dump him in the waste ground for the stray dogs. At the time, I thought this the best approach, but Den and Brian kept their cool.

"The best thing we can do," Den began, "is to not react at all. Don't even acknowledge it. When you see him tomorrow, just be pleasant and professional, without making it obvious that you hope he gets his balls pulled off in an accident."

Brian added, "If we start kicking off now, then he's won. He wants us to go round there and smash his face in, so let's not give him the satisfaction of getting us all sacked and black listed from working in Iraq. It'll fuck him up, believe me."

We did exactly that and no one reacted, even in so much as a snarl towards him. Even I managed to walk past him a couple of days later and wish him good morning. I headed straight to my room afterwards, dizzy from a sudden blood flow to the head and feeling dirty and used.

A few days after the cutting of the wires, while Den and Brian sat in the office, planning our next mission, in stormed the colonel. He was visibly upset and annoyed and his fat cheeks glowed red as the beads of sweat dripped from his brow. He had probably spent the whole day working his self up for the confrontation.

"It was me that cut your internet wires." He announced to Den and Brian.

Den looked up from the maps sprawled on his desk. He carefully lowered his reading glasses and calmly folded his hands in his lap as he leaned back into his chair.

"Yes sir, we know it was you."

The colonel was flustered and taken aback at Den's calm, unflinching manner. "Uh, do you? How did you know it was me?"

"Because, there's no one else it could've been. We're not the bunch of morons you think we are colonel, and we are very capable of thinking for ourselves."

"Well I cut the wires because I wanted to get a reaction from you."

225

Den looked to Brian, who shrugged his shoulders and continued to look on, amused but without showing it.

"A reaction sir, what sort? Were you hoping that we would all be up in arms and come looking for you?"

The colonel was grunting and flustered and obviously uncomfortable with the way things were going. He had obviously hoped for a different style of confrontation.

Den continued in his extra mild manner, like a Headmaster speaking with a problem child. "What you fail to realise colonel, is that every man on this team is a professional soldier. We have all served a minimum of ten years in the *regular* British Army unlike you, in the National Guard, playing war in your local woods one weekend out of every month as a part time soldier back home in America." Den was in his element. "Our professionalism could never be put into question by you, and no matter how hard you try, you will never get the reaction you want. Now if you'll excuse us sir, Brian and I have to get on with planning this mission, *for you.*"

Without another word, the colonel turned on his heels and stormed from the office, looking as though he was about to burst.

Brian came straight to my room and told me and Chubbs the whole story. We loved it and we pictured the colonel sobbing with frustration in his office.

What the colonel didn't realise was that there were two lots of wires running to our accommodation. One lot was red and the other, grey.

In the American Army, red wires are considered as important and not to be tampered with and anyone caught interfering with them could find themselves facing disciplinary action. He assumed that *our* red wire wasn't *ours*, and that it led to somewhere else on the compound and he left it alone.

The red wire actually ran straight to our rooms and was the main internet cable from then on after Brian changed the cables in the router.

That night, we celebrated our victory.

MOSUL

Getting home had been a pain in the arse but I had made it eventually. Due to a possible SAM, Surface to Air Missile, threat in the Kirkuk area, all flights in and out of the airbase had been suspended.

Every day, we would go to the flight line with all our baggage and wait patiently, hoping for the best, only to be told a few hours later that our flight had been cancelled, again. To say it was frustrating is an understatement. After twelve weeks in country, the only thing we could think of was getting home.

I was a few days into my leave and enjoying the freedom, when I got a call from Chubbs, who was still in Kirkuk with the rest of the team. Chubbs was never the sort to call for a social chat and getting replies to emails, was like getting shit from a rocking horse. As soon as I saw his number flash up, I had a sinking feeling in my gut.

I answered, "Hello mate, what's the beef?"

Chubbs sounded quiet and unsure of what to say, "Got some bad news mate," I held my breath, "Swanny is dead."

It hit me like a fist. "Fuck. What happened?"

"He was shot in Tikrit by a sniper." His voice quivered a little.

I was standing at the time and I remember having to sit down as I felt my stomach churn. I had last seen Swanny just a few days before I'd come on leave when the Tikrit team had stayed overnight again. As usual, he had taken over my laptop as the guest DJ while the rest of us had a roaring party.

"Have you got the full details, or is it all still up in the air?" I asked.

"Dunno exactly what happened mate because it was only a couple of hours ago. We've not had a full heads up on the incident, but I thought I'd better let you know all the same."

"Cheers Chubbs." I hung up and sat, deep in thought for a while. I'm not ashamed to say that tears were shed that afternoon. Yet another good guy had gone.

The Tikrit team had been tasked with a visit to the government building in the city and once they were there, the clients had gone into a meeting while the team provided the outer cordon of security. During missions like that, there were always team members guarding the main entrance to the venue, with others on the doors leading to the meeting rooms. Whenever possible, we would always try to get somebody on the roof to give an over watch and feed us information on what was happening in the immediate area.

That day, Swanny had been on the roof in a guard tower. During the visit, the team had come under small arms fire. Someone had opened up on them from beyond the compound of the government building with what they believed to be an AK47, or a similar weapon. The rest of the team had reacted to the threat and returned fire and after a short gun fight, the insurgents withdrew.

As per the SOP, the Team Leader made sure that the clients were secure and asked for everyone to check in over their radios and let him know there were no casualties. Everyone answered up, except Swanny.

At first, they didn't rule out the possibility of a faulty radio or dead battery, so the request was sent again for Swanny to answer up, still nothing. It was obvious something was wrong.

He was found on the roof, lying in a pool of blood with a gunshot wound to the neck. He had died while the rest of the team were in contact.

As it turned out, the contact had been nothing more than a diversion to grab the attention of the team and at that point, the sniper was able to pick his target. Swanny had been the easiest choice for him.

The reports we received on the incident was that it was a father and son insurgent sniper team and that they had worked in the same manner in many other areas. While the son drew the fire and the attention of the team, the father lay in wait for the opportune moment to fire.

Swanny was a big Geordie lad from Newcastle and his funeral was a testament to the kind of man he was. Hundreds turned up. His wife, friends and family were overwhelmed with the amount of people that attended to pay their respects to Robert Swann.

The Parachute Regiment Association was there, as well as still serving soldiers and bodyguards he had worked with in Iraq, all to give the final salute. There were so many people, there wasn't enough room in the church for everyone and the street outside was lined with people wanting to say a last goodbye to him as his coffin was brought out.

Afterwards, in true Geordie fashion, everybody got together and got absolutely hammered and swapped stories and told tales of Swanny and his antics.

To anyone who met him, he will never be forgotten, and to those who knew him, he will always be loved.

My leave had taken a sombre turn and although I was with family and friends, I wanted to be back with the lads. It may seem strange but, because we all share the same risks and dangers, we had that special bond that's always needed during shit times of loss. I knew the blokes would be ripping the place up and saying goodbye to Swanny in the way they knew best and I felt like I should've been with them.

I returned to Kirkuk three weeks later and as always, we had a welcome party on the tarmac of the flight line. The usual suspects were there to greet us and rub our faces in the fact that we have twelve long weeks to push till we next went home.

We cracked straight on with work and in no time, I was back into my routine of training, working and taking the piss out of everyone else on the team.

Pete had become a big character and his rogue side was ever present. He had never been the gambling sort but, during a conversation with another team member, he soon realised that he could make some money in the online betting game. If I had suggested prostitution to him and painted it in a good light with big profits, he would've jumped at the idea, disregarding the cons' for the pros'.

In true style, he did nothing by halves. He began to spend more time in his room and became a somewhat less sociable creature than usual. Normally, he would come for a brew and a chat at least once a day, so I decided to call in on him and see what was happening. For the past week, I had only seen him on days when we had missions and I hadn't noticed him in the gym lately.

"What you up to Pete?" I asked as I walked into his room.

Pete was sat at his table with his head glued to his laptop and the reply was nothing more than a mumble.

"Oi you ignorant twat, get the brews on and tell me what you're up to." I shouted, trying to pry him away from his virtual reality.

He managed to drag himself away from his computer long enough to look in my direction, "Have a look at this Luke."

What I saw was nothing short of a big bowl of Greek Salad to me, but it obviously made a lot of sense to Pete.

One thing I did recognise was the name of the site and I could tell it was something to do with online gambling.

"Fuck sake mate, you're not getting into that are you?"

Myself, I'd never been the gambling sort. I'd played Black Jack and Poker for small amounts and did the lottery, that was about it. I never allowed it to get its claws into me.

Pete, however, looked engrossed.

He then went into the details of the sites he was using and explained to me what to look for and how to bet. It was still Greek to me and I intended for it to stay that way. He had been given tips and advice on what to do and how to do it and, over the past week, he had found his own way around the risky world of online betting.

"Well, I started off by putting a couple of grand into my betting account and carried it on from there. I don't always win, but I'm learning and I'm getting to grips with it."

I looked at him, "So how much have you actually lost then?"

"A couple of grand," he replied sheepishly.

"Thought as much, you gonna carry on with it or cut your losses and become an alcoholic instead?"

"Nah mate, like I said, I'm just starting out and I could spare it anyway. I've made lots of bets over the last few days and I've had some good runs, but made a few silly mistakes. Now I know what I'm doing, I'll have no probs."

"Righto," I said, "Well, when you're a millionaire, will you pay my mortgage?"

A couple of days later and Pete was still the recluse, but the whole gambling thing had attracted the attention of Brian and Chubbs who kept themselves informed of his progress. I knocked on Pete's door one day and when I walked in, Brian, Martin and Chubbs were already in there, looking really excited, while Pete sat at his laptop.

"Luke, you'll never believe this, I'm up fourteen grand." Pete beamed at me from his desk.

"How you managed that then? Sounds like you've really got to grips with it now."

Pete was clearly over the moon and with fourteen thousand pounds in a couple of days, who wouldn't be?

"I've just been really careful mate and kept the bets sensible. I'm gonna do a few more bets to round it off, then bank it and start all over again with a couple of grand."

Pete really had been doing well. Initially, he had lost a couple of grand while he found his way around the game and by natural flare for the gambling or sheer luck, he had come out as a winner. His idea of starting from scratch with his big winnings safely banked was his best idea yet.

The next day, we all met at the office for a briefing and Pete turned up looking well and truly pissed off over something. For those of us who knew about the gambling, we had an idea what had happened.

He had got carried away with himself and became overconfident and instead of banking the money he had won, he wanted to get it up to twenty thousand first.

"Because it's a more rounded number," he said.

In his haste, he had got bolder with the bets and before he knew it, he was betting a few grand at a time on ridiculous odds. His lucky streak was over, and he lost the lot. True to form though, he was smiling and laughing about it the next day. It made no difference to us though because he received a constant slagging for a week afterward whether he was suicidal or not.

There was a meeting in Erbil for the Corp of Engineers from Kirkuk and Mosul. Erbil had its own USACE office and the plan was for both teams, the Mosul team and the Kirkuk team, to meet there, drop the clients off and when the meeting was over we would go our separate ways and head back to our respective FOBs.

Travelling to Erbil was never a problem for us. Getting through Kirkuk was always the hardest part. We planned on leaving in the early morning, before the town got busy and while the traffic was light. I was in the right hand gunner position of the lead gun truck, with Sean in the commander's seat and Chubbs as the rear gunner.

Summer was drawing to a close, but the weather was still hot and the days were long. We were hoping to resupply our booze stocks while the clients were at their meeting before heading back and maybe, get a little shopping done in the supermarket there. I was after a big tin of Quality Streets.

Travelling north in the early morning, the low rolling countryside of northern Iraq was scenic to say the least. Men were out washing their cars in the rivers and farmers tended to their crops, while herds of goats crisscrossed the landscape. Even now, I would still sometimes squint, causing my vision to blur slightly, and I would picture myself being back in Britain with green fields and hills in the distance. It was a habit I had picked up a couple of years before, when I had been surprised at the greenery in the northern regions, but mud huts and burnt out cars would always destroy my little daydreams.

When we reached Erbil, we followed the flow of traffic to the north of the city, to where the meeting point was. I was looking forward to a brew and catching up with Si, who was still with the Mosul team. When we reached the compound, the Peshmerga guards allowed us in and we saw that the others were already there.

The clients were escorted in while the rest of us went about checking vehicles and stretching our legs before we were given a heads up.

The other team had been there a few hours by now, having set out at first light to get ahead of any dramas that could be laying in wait for them as they drove through the city of Mosul.

I caught sight of Si with a brew in his hand, "Hey up mate how's tricks?" I asked.

"Not bad, but we're having dramas with one of our gun trucks, its broke down and it can't be fixed here."

With one of their gun trucks knackered, that meant that they were down to two client vehicles and one gun truck. They had fifteen men and three clients and so, there wasn't enough room in their vehicles now for everyone. On top of that, they couldn't travel through Mosul with only one gun truck. They needed all the fire power they had to be brought to bear should they need it.

I knew right away it was going to be a shit day.

Den pulled us all to one side, "Right lads, one of the Mosul team's gun trucks is fucked as most of you probably already know. I've spoken to their TL and he reckons he can take one of our gun trucks and we can crack on with just the one, back to Kirkuk."

We had to wait for an answer from the head shed first before we could make a decision on the matter. They may be happy with our suggestion or they may not. They weren't.

The decision was made that; we would escort the Mosul team back to their base and then head to Kirkuk from there. That meant a seven vehicle convoy heading through a major city, where insurgency was rife and a target like ours would not be missed, but at least we had three gun trucks now.

Everybody began checking and double checking their kit and equipment, as well as the vehicles themselves. We had a couple of hours yet before we would be heading out, so we had time to sort ourselves out and plan what we had to do.

I checked my ammunition and medical kit and began checking through what was in the vehicle trauma packs. All that was done on a weekly basis anyway, but I wanted peace of mind, knowing that if someone was bleeding out, then I knew exactly where to look for a tourniquet and blood replacement fluids.

My magazines were securely in their pouches around my assault vest and I double checked that they slid out easily when I reached for them. I always carried a grab bag with me, loaded with additional magazines and medical kit and I made sure that it too, was easily accessible. I placed it by my left foot and wedged it in to stop it from rolling about. That way, I would just have to reach my left hand down to my grab bag and pull out the extra ammunition, saving the magazines in my vest in case we had to debus and fight on foot.

I was happy with my set up and I realised, everyone else in my truck was doing the same. Chubbs had linked ammunition for his SAW in boxes all around him and he carried more on his body. Sean was going over all his little gadgets in his 'Buzz Light Year' outfit and no doubt, he was playing about with something that generated a force field around him.

We had decided that, the three vehicles left from the Mosul team, would be taking the lead through the city. Being the lead gun truck of our team, we would be slap bang in the middle of the convoy with the rest of our vehicles from Kirkuk following. That meant there was a gun truck at the front, centre and rear of the whole seven vehicle convoy.

Firepower wasn't going to be a problem.

A couple of hours later and we were set to go. The clients were finished and briefed on what was happening and we had still even managed to stock up on booze while all that was going on. The priorities were never thrown out of the window, regardless of what was happening.

We had a final brew, and a set of QBO's was given by the Mosul team leader, going over the route and actions on. We all knew Mosul, but they knew it that little better than we did and having passed through it just that morning, they had already covered the ground and so it made sense for them to lead us in.

That way, we weren't going to take any wrong turns or turn down roads that were now blocked since last time we had been through the area.

We pushed out and headed west towards the city limits of Erbil and onto the road linking us to Mosul. It was the same road I had travelled many times in the past, where Alexander had fought all those years ago. Being the history buff that I am, I would always picture the scene of thousands and thousands of men and horses battling in the scorching heat of the day.

I was feeling uncomfortable in my body armour and assault vest along with my helmet on top. It was almost like a pressure cooker with the amount of heat that was trapped. With the hot air blowing in through the open firing port, I found myself constantly squirming in my seat as I felt yet another flood of sweat, rush down my back between my skin and body armour. I had my thin leather gloves on to stop my weapon from slipping in my hand and also, to protect myself from the hot metal.

On a few occasions, I have picked up a rifle without thinking and instantly, dropped it back down because the sun had been shining on it and made it so hot; it could actually cause blisters or melt the skin.

When we reached the halfway mark, we began to receive live updates from HQ on what had been going on in the city. We were informed of friendly forces in the area and what insurgent activity had been going on. At that moment, things didn't seem too bad. Still, no one was about to get complaisant or let their guard down. If we made it into Mosul, then we still had to get out again and back to Kirkuk.

It was a double gauntlet run for us.

The usual signs of the friendliness of Mosul began to show as we approached the outskirts from the east. The route I knew well. I knew that we would pass through security check points with high walls and search bays, covered by heavy machineguns and I knew, beyond that, we would travel through the outer suburbs with villas and mud huts and the usual signs of terrorist activity in the form of burnt out vehicles and bomb craters.

We gave a blast of the sirens as we approached the check points and the guards waved us through. I looked to my front and I noticed that the burnt out truck that Jules had been blown up in a couple of years earlier was no longer there, yet all the other scrap metal and craters were.

"Roof tops left and right," Sean said over his radio, warning us of possible threats and firing points.

We knew they were there, but it was Sean's job to make sure we kept them in mind as well as everything else he was pointing out.

"Debris on the immediate left of us, people out on foot in the middle distance to our right."

We always kept as much distance as possible between ourselves and anything left at the side of the road. Even if it was just a pile of rags, we would give it a wide birth because we never knew what was under it.

When it comes to booby traps and IEDs, all you need is a good imagination and at the very least, a sick sense of humour. Soldiers have been killed by picking up the simplest of things; from apparently dropped magazines or water bottles, to women's knickers. The same stood for IEDs. What people would think is nothing more than a carcass at the road side, would actually be a hollowed out dead donkey and packed with explosives.

Even the most innocent looking things, like a man on a push bike, they didn't always have to hit you from a car. You can strap a hell of a lot of explosives to a person and send him on his way to meet his maker, though it didn't always go according to plan.

My brother told me a story of a Sunni Muslim in Baghdad who, strapped himself up in a suicide vest in his local Mosque, climbed on his bicycle and set out to peddle down the street into the Shia Mosque, just a couple of hundred metres away. He planned to detonate himself once he got there, taking lots of Shia Muslims with him.

As he reached the gate of his own mosque and started to turn onto the street, he lost his balance and the bike slipped, causing him to fall. Normally this would mean a grazed elbow or knee to most people, but the dick head had his detonator in his hand and he blew himself up as well as a bit of his own Mosque.

"We're gonna get hit, we're gonna get hit boys," I was saying in the back jokingly.

"Don't be fucking wishing it on us." Chubbs snapped.

"It's Mosul Chubbs, and there's seven big juicy targets bouncing along so, we're gonna get hit."

It was going to be difficult getting through the built up areas with such a large call sign, so it took a lot of coordination between both teams to make sure we stuck together. Each time the lead vehicles turned a corner, they would slow down once they were clear so that no large gaps appeared between us. Mutual support was important to us and we all relied on each other.

We were making good progress through the city and we were approaching the main road, running south along the east side of the river that ran through the centre of the city. We got onto the slip road which filtered round to the left and down onto level ground with a tree line on the right hand side of us.

"Watch that tree line Luke," Chubbs shouted over the noise of the engine and radio chatter, "we always get hit from there."

"Roger that mate, I've got it covered."

I kept my eyes on the area that he had pointed out to me, which was now directly to my front as we came off the slip road. We were travelling at a good speed and we had bullied our way into the centre lane of the carriageway, forcing the other vehicles on the road to push left and right of us. Hearts and minds were not in our thoughts at that point, getting to safety was.

The tree line was more of a sparse wooded area with houses amongst it. I could see people moving about, but I saw nothing that I considered a threat. I watched the vehicles that had gone static at the side of us and everywhere my eyes went, my weapon pointed in the same place, ready to fire.

The lead gun truck of the Mosul team was now passed the woods and approaching a bridge that ran over the top of the road we travelled along.

"Overpass looks clear, passing now." They gave over the net.

We were close behind.

"That's us going under the overpass now lads." Sean shouted over his shoulder.

Chubbs repositioned himself in his seat so that he could have a good angle with his SAW on the overpass above us once we were clear to protect the rest of the team from any threat from above as they passed under it.

We were clear of another tricky area. The ground to our left and right opened up again to wasteland dotted with houses, and irrigation ditches that fed in to the fields. We came to a cross roads and zoomed straight across, relying on the sirens to keep the traffic static. As we crossed, if anything had approached from left or right, it would've been lit up by the side gunners. It would be treated as a threat.

We came to a point where there were more houses and blocks of flats on our right hand side. They had the same look about them as all the other residential areas in Iraq. Dirty and run down, with broken windows and makeshift air conditioning units hanging here and there. Between the buildings, large piles of rubbish and filth lay rotting in the midday heat while people walked by and ignored it.

I found my eyes and body moving in a sort of figure of eight motion as I tried to cover every possible position, from the road, the streets, the windows, to the roof tops and back down to the road. There were possible firing points everywhere.

As we cleared the houses on the right, we passed a small side street running along the side of the flats at a right angle to the road we travelled along. After that it was open waste land that was used as a football pitch.

About ten metres off the main road and parked by the wall of the flats, sat a white minivan, with five men sat inside it. All of them were watching us. Within a second though, they were gone from my arcs and I was facing the open football pitch area as we approached a large bend to our right.

A massive bang went off just to our rear. I quickly glanced back and saw a huge plume of dust and debris as our second client vehicle was swallowed up in the explosion. Immediately, I thought the vehicle, and everyone in it, had been wiped out. To my amazement though, I saw it emerge through the smoke and continue to follow us. It was weaving and swerving as it powered through the grey cloud but it was clear that the driver still had it under control.

I couldn't believe it. I thought we would be scraping up bits of them for sure.

As the IED was detonated, we heard the crack of bullets hitting the armour of our vehicles. From my position, I couldn't see the firing point but Chubbs had already started to return fire.

"White minibus Luke, white minibus," Chubbs screamed back at me over his shoulder.

He fired in short bursts from his SAW into the minivan I had seen just a couple of seconds earlier. From my position though, they were out of my arcs and so I couldn't get an aimed shot on them. I looked to my left and saw the bend up ahead and I knew I would then have perfect line of sight on them once we turned to the right. Just another second or two, I thought to myself.

Chubbs stopped firing as they left his arcs.

"White minibus Luke, small arms in the white minibus," He continued to scream at me.

I could hear the rear gun truck also opening up from within the blast area, which they were shrouded in.

"Yeah I got 'em."

I had my weapon jammed in to my shoulder and I was aiming down my sight, waiting for the minivan to come into my arcs. Chubbs had managed to get a few bursts off at them before they were out of his field of fire, and now it was my turn to give them our response. We travelled further round the bend and the white minivan floated, beautifully into my arcs.

I squeezed the trigger and began pumping rounds into them. They were still firing wildly towards us at that point, the whole call sign was taking fire and from what I could guess, one was at the wheel and there were at least four AK47s sticking out of the windows firing at us. None of their shots were accurate or consistent. Some would hit our vehicles and others, were clearly going over us or thumping in to the ground between us, splashing chunks of dirt and tarmac in to the air.

I felt the butt of the weapon thump into my shoulder as I fired round after round into the people inside the minivan. They were about seventy five metres away from me, across open ground and slightly lower than us; a perfect angle and range.

I watched my tracer rounds zip into the soft metal of the minivan and I could see the debris and dust kicked up from one or two rounds that fell just short of it.

I kept the rate of fire up and within a couple of seconds, the enemy fire had ceased. I carried on firing and looking for targets still moving within the minivan and making sure that our call sign could make a clear getaway.

Pete was firing from his vehicle and now that they were clear of the IED area, I could see the muzzle flash from his weapon. The minivan was caught in a cross fire with no way out.

"Magazine," I screamed as I reached my last round, informing everyone that I had to change magazines and that I couldn't continue firing.

I quickly pressed the magazine release catch with my right index finger, the magazine dropped to the floor and I quickly slammed in a full one with my left hand and I sent the bolt forward again, chambering a fresh round and all the while, I kept the van in my sights.

I continued firing and I saw my first few tracer rounds smash into the side of the minivan. I managed to get a few more bursts off and then, they were gone from my line of sight as we passed over another bridge. I could still hear Pete firing, along with Cach who was the rear gunner in the rear vehicle.

By now, the call sign was complete on the bridge. In the lull, everyone was doing a quick assessment, checking for injuries and slapping fresh magazines into their weapons. We weren't in the clear yet and we had a mile or so to go through more bandit country.

"Vehicle three is dead, it won't go any further." We heard over the radio.

Vehicle three had been caught side on in the blast, taking the full force of it and a hundred and fifty metres further on, it had finally given up and the engine cut out.

"Roger that, we'll push you in." Brian sent from the rear vehicle.

They travelled bumper to bumper for the next mile with the client vehicle being pushed from our rear gun truck until we reached the Mosul FOB.

We stopped to take stock once we were safe within the base. No one had any injuries to speak of. A couple of bruised heads and ringing ears and that was about it. We all debussed and gathered around the damaged truck.

A female client, who had been in the first client vehicle behind us and away from the blast, seemed rather pleased about the whole incident and, with herself.

"That's the fourth IED I've been in now. That means I qualify for the combat medal." She said, smiling and looking rather excited about the prospect.

Brian scowled at her. "Would you be this pleased with yourself if someone had been killed? You should try being in a gun truck when an IED goes off at the side of you. I wouldn't want to wear a medal for being a passenger."

She looked at him sheepishly and quickly walked away in the direction of their office.

"Fucking dicks, they get medals for fucking medals. They probably get one for standing in the scoff queue for too long. "

The second client vehicle had bore the brunt of the blast into its right hand side. All the windows were either blown out or, severely damaged. Shrapnel holes ran the full length of the truck and the tyres on that side were destroyed, it had come in on its run flats for the last mile.

If the IED had been better placed, then I'm pretty sure it would've caused maximum damage and we would have been carrying a couple of full body bags back to base. As it happens, the insurgents who had planted it were amateurs, and a lot of the shrapnel travelled straight up instead of into the killing area. If it had been angled right, then large lumps of metal would've punched through the armour of the vehicle and killed the people inside.

On that occasion, the shock wave had done most of the damage.

When the IED had gone off at the side of it, the fuel pump cut off switch had been triggered and that was what had caused it to die, there was no more fuel being fed to the engine. We hadn't realised that at the time, but once safe in the FOB, the switch was flicked back and the engine roared to life.

However, with the amount of damage done to the shell, and possibly unseen damage to the engine, we couldn't risk using it to get us back to Kirkuk. We swapped over with one of the Mosul team's spare vehicles and prepared ourselves for round two.

Before we could go anywhere, we had to get an initial report sent out on what had happened and a more in-depth one would be sent later, when we were back in Kirkuk. Chubbs and I had seen most of what had happened and done most of the firing, so it was us that would give the initial report. We had to head to the Mosul Op's Manger's office and give a rough statement for their records.

Before we were going to do that, we needed a brew.

Toad came up to me and Chubbs as we stood having a cup of tea and a cigarette. "Fucking hell Luke, from the angle I was at, I could see the rounds flying into that minivan. It looked like a tea bag; it had so many holes in it. I could see the rag heads inside it taking hits. They were bouncing about all over the place."

Toad had been driving the rear gun truck and as I was firing into the minivan, he was at a right angle to it, still in the area of the IED. He had been able to see from just twenty metres as my tracer rounds punched holes into the vehicle and the people inside.

"Nice one, did they look like they were having a good day out?"

Chubbs chipped in, "I think I got most of them though, cause I was the first to get rounds down"

"Bollocks, you only got a few bursts then he was gone from your arcs and into mine. I got a mag and a half into them."

A magazine carries thirty rounds but you never completely fill them. You normally keep just twenty eight in them to save the pressure on the spring.

"We'll split them between us, but I think I should have three and you have two." I offered as a compromise to Chubbs

He wasn't happy and the argument continued between us as we walked towards the office to give our statement. We were still in heated conversation as we stumbled into the Op's Room with our brews in hand.

"Okay then, well you can have two, I'll have two and we will give Pete the other one cause he did a fair bit of firing as well."

"Fuck Pete, he couldn't even see most of the time, he was in the IED cloud. He just fired in to the dust." Chubbs exclaimed.

In the end though, we compromised and took two kills each and donated the fifth to Pete.

We gave a rough verbal statement of the incident and our actions following it. We described what we had seen and what we had heard. We told them how, immediately following the IED explosion, we were opened up on from the white minivan.

"Well I shouted to Luke, 'look at them people in the white minivan, they all have small arms', I meant as in thalidomide people, but Luke decided to shoot them all." Chubbs couldn't help but make a joke of it. A joke that the Op's Manager took too seriously until we told him we were winding him up.

Once we were finished, we were ready to head back to Kirkuk. We had all restocked our ammunition and the replacement vehicle was prepared and ready.

Si walked over to me to shake my hand, "Good luck getting back mate. Keep your head down and don't be a hero."

"Fuck that mate. I'm only in it for the money."

Den had a son on the Mosul team. Leigh had originally been sent to the Kirkuk team for a week, and then he was transferred. I think the reasoning was that the son and father would be too concerned about each other, rather than getting on with the job. But as it turned out, they had just been in an IED together, but on separate teams. They spoke quietly to each other to one side and I watched as they gave each other a hug and Leigh waved him off as his father, Den, mounted up for the return trip to Kirkuk.

We headed south along Route Tampa and turned onto Richmond towards Kirkuk. We were expecting to be hit again at some point, and everyone was on edge. The route was long and pretty straight open road. We could see for miles and with very little traffic to negotiate around, we made good time. It was touching darkness by the time we made it home.

We had run the second stretch without being hit again.

Fifi had a big order of pizzas waiting for us. Everyone congregated around the benches outside my room and began cleaning their weapons and eating pizza. It wasn't long before beers were cracked open and everyone began gobbing off about the day's events and who had done what.

We nicknamed Pete, 'Bushwhacker Pete', because he had fired two hundred rounds and most of the time, he couldn't see anything from within the cloud of debris from the IED.

As always, the evening turned into a piss up as we celebrated another close shave. Den and Fifi had ensured that the clients wouldn't request a mission for a couple of days, on account of the vehicles needing a good service and check over and the so called concussions sustained from a couple of the blokes.

There were no head injuries but it looked good to have it on paper so that the colonel couldn't question it. He did though.

Den took him the Medical Centre report, explaining that two of the men had mild concussions and were on two days light duties, meaning we were unable to go out on task.

"This is no good to me, I can't understand what it says." The colonel threw the medical report across his desk towards Den, expecting him to pick it up and come back with a better one for his pleasure.

"It's not a fucking letter from my parents saying that I'm excused football training. It's a report from a medical examination, on two of my men, and it says they're hurt. So whether you like it or not, we can't go out for two days." Den walked out of his office and left the colonel fuming, knowing he couldn't do anything about it.

The man still hadn't learned that he couldn't win.

HQ had gone very quiet about the contract and what was happening. We were hearing regular rumours about who had won it and by now, it should've been announced to us who would be taking it over. According to the guys from the other competing company, they had won the contract and they had already been told by their head shed.

When we queried this with our own management, we were either met with hostile emails or complete information black outs. At one point, we even received an email from the bosses, telling us that the negotiations had gone back to the table and there would be a delay in awarding the contract, and that our company were still the favourites to win.

We didn't know what to believe, but there was no smoke without fire and the other company wouldn't have been told they had the contract if there was no truth behind it. We knew not to believe our own management because they had already proven themselves to be full of shit.

It was pretty much confirmed for us one day when the colonel that commanded the northern region came to visit from Tikrit. He told us that we had lost the contract and the changeover was already underway. Everyone went ape shit and stormed into the office.

Fifi was bombarded with questions and ranting. The management had lied to us and Fifi immediately sent an email off to Baghdad, demanding a 'non waffle' reply, explaining what was going on. He mentioned in the email that a colonel from USACE had told us that another company had won, so it was pointless trying to bluff their case.

For a couple of days, we had no reply then suddenly, every station in the country was informed of the loss of the contract.

They had kept the truth from us for a couple of months, and many believed it was in fear of men jumping ship. Regardless, because they had bull shitted over the whole thing, people nevertheless jumped ship in their droves just to fuck the management over. Teams were unable to go on tasks in some areas through lack of manpower.

The way I saw it though, the sooner the contract changed over and we swapped uniforms and became part of the other company, the better.

In the meantime, I would crack on and continue to take the money each month.

Ramadan, EFP and Vodka Protein Shakes

The attack in Mosul was confirmed as an IED, followed up by small arms fire, known as a complex attack. Often, it would be just a road side bomb and that would be left to do the damage. The insurgents on that day however, had been slightly braver than usual and as a result, six were confirmed to have been killed by our team.

So with one kill being donated to Pete and Chubbs and I having two each meant that one was left over. The argument of who got the most kills continued between Chubbs and me. Even to this day, it is still brought up from time to time.

In movies, you see people having flash backs and crying at night, waking up soaked in sweat, remembering the faces of the people they killed. I saw their faces that day as we drove past them. I remember each one of them, watching our convoy, and I had eye to eye contact with all of them. I can even describe them in detail. I can still see their eyes and the colour of their hair. I remember which of them had beards or moustaches, what styles they trimmed them, and I can still see their expressions as they waited in anticipation.

Fuck them. I've never lost a moment's sleep, or felt even the slightest pang of regret for the fact that they are dead due to my actions. I couldn't care less if they left wives and children behind and that they would be mourned and missed. They made their choice; to attack our team, and they came unstuck in the end.

Maybe if I was to undergo a psychiatric evaluation, the results would come back saying that I'm mental, or maybe completely unstable. Maybe, even a sociopath? If so, then there are a lot of sick puppies working in the Private Security Industry.

My own opinion on it is; that we who work in these environments are more tuned in to how life really is. It's cheap and it's brutal. You only have to watch CNN and the countless thousand's dying in Africa, the babies being discarded on the street in China and left to die, or the Palestinians and Israelis people battling it out in the Gaza Strip.

On the other hand, you could look a little closer to home and watch and read about the drug wars and gang killings going on in the streets of Britain and America, the kidnappings in South America or the people trafficking from Eastern Europe.

I've been accused in my time of being heartless and cold and having no conscience. That may be true, and if it is, then I prefer it that way. If I was a bleeding heart, trying to make the world right and wanting to save every life I could, then I would never sleep at night. As it is, I sleep like a baby.

Everybody had a secret stash of booze in his room. Myself, I kept mine in the fridge for all to see and didn't bother to try and hide it. Others found ingenious ways of either hiding it or, disguising it to look like something else.

Sean went as far as digging holes around the compound and burying crates of beer. Toad, even though his room was considered the team bar and it even said so on his door, had hiding places all over, including inside his walls, furniture and even beneath his room. Considering most of the drinking was normally done in my room or his, it was virtually impossible to find a single bottle in Toad's room.

Vodka was easy to hide. It was just a case of emptying a two litre bottle of water and then, refilling it with vodka. To the unsuspecting eye, it just looked like every member of our team had a dozen two litre bottles of water in his fridge.

It was inevitable that it would back fire at some point.

Rick, the only American on the team, went to the gym every day. He was keen on his fitness and never missed a session. One day, he came back to his room after a hard work out, puffing and panting and soaked in sweat. Part of his post gym routine was to make a protein shake, with water.

He filled his beaker with the correct amount of water then, added his scoops of protein powder. Only then did he realise that he had used the wrong bottle, and what he thought was a pint of water, was actually a pint of vodka. He had already gone to the trouble of shaking the mix and it was now ready to drink.

Rick now faced a dilemma, either poor it away and waste fifty six grams of protein and more importantly, a pint of vodka or throw the whole lot down his neck and deal with the aftermath. After hanging around with British guys for so long, there was only one real option.

He downed the lot in one go.

Andy was sat in his room watching TV when, there was a knock at his door. He answered to find Rick standing on his step, swaying and looking a little worse for wear.

"Rick you okay, what's up?" Andy asked, concerned at the appearance of Rick.

"Hey man," Rick's usual Texas accent was slurred as he stammered his words, "you aint gonna believe this, but I accidently drank a pint of vodka just now."

Andy was confused at Rick's statement, because let's face it, how do you accidentally drink a pint of vodka?

"Eh, how do you mean, accidentally? Like, you slipped?"

Rick explained the whole thing to Andy, who then ran from room to room, telling everybody else. He was still in stitches when he got to my door to repeat the story for what must've been the tenth time. I cracked up too and I needed to see for myself, what happens to someone when they hammer back a pint of vodka in one go.

I walked to Rick's room and knocked and as I expected, there was no answer. I opened the door and the vision that greeted me was something that will haunt me for the rest of my life; a little fat American guy, completely naked and sprawled out in the shape of a star fish on his bed, covered in his own piss and sick.

Rick was an empty wetsuit and, safe to say, out of action for the rest of the day. We had to keep checking on him throughout the night to make sure he hadn't choked on his own vomit, or swallowed his tongue. He woke up with a killer of a hangover the next morning and from then on, he discreetly marked his bottles so that he didn't make the same mistake again.

Our family of pet cats had grown by this stage. Obviously there was Woolfy, but now there was a mother cat and her litter of kittens hanging around the Op's Room too. There were six little balls of fur in the group, and being the animal lover I am, I wanted to make friends with them as quickly as possible.

To do this, I had to win over the mother first. At first she was wary of us but, when she realised we meant her no harm, she enjoyed the tuna we gave her and her babies three times a day. The kittens were a cheeky bunch, just like Woolfy, and would be sat on the wall of sand bags outside the office, waiting for us every morning, afternoon and evening calling for us to come and play with them and most importantly, feed them with tuna and milk. We spoiled them rotten.

Woolfy still came to visit us every night, doing a circuit of our rooms until he decided which he was most comfortable in, and bedded down for the night. He kept away from the mother and her young kittens in the area of the Op's Room. All our cats were wild and feral and it took a lot of coaxing from us to get them to allow us near. But towards other cats, they still behaved as though they saw each other as a threat, especially the mother. She would attack any other cat that came near, seeing them as being potentially aggressive toward her and her young family. To us though, they were little angels with fur.

It was that time of year again and Ramadan was about to begin. Every year, companies would try to go out beyond the wire as little as possible due to the increase in terrorist activity during certain periods of Ramadan. It became common practice that only mission essential tasks would be carried out, in order to avoid unnecessary risk to the teams or the clients.

"Yes well 'unnecessary risk' depends on how you interpret it," the colonel had said to Den. "All our missions are essential, and we need to be visiting these sites every day." He was back to being his usual self after their last running and once again, determined to be a thorn in our side.

It was obvious that the guy didn't have the slightest idea of what he was doing, and the fact that every member of the team had forgotten more than he could ever possibly dream of knowing, was a direct reflection of the chips that he seemed to carry on both shoulders.

"Unnecessary risk means, there is no need to go out on any missions that can be dealt with either by, the site managers or from here in the offices. If we travel out during Ramadan, when it's non mission critical, we are failing in our duty of care to you; the client, and putting my team in a possible situation of unnecessary risk." Den was quite straight forward in his explanation of reasons for prudence.

"I thought Ramadan was a peaceful time anyway?"

"Colonel, if you had been in country during Ramadan last year, you would know it is anything but peaceful. You only have to read the reports from that time period to see that it's a volatile time."

We had all been with the company during that time and all across the country, teams and military call signs were being hit regularly.

"Oh, it's just that you and your team are scared and lazy." The colonel accused.

Den hit the roof.

"You fucking what, we've been involved in more shootings and IEDs than you will probably claim to have been in yourself when you're home and gobbing off to you Red Neck buddies about how much of a warrior you were out in Iraq. It is fuck all to do with fear or laziness colonel, its professionalism and experience, two things that you are severely lacking. Now if you have a complaint, then send it to Baghdad."

Once again, the colonel was left speechless and confused about what to do next. He took the best option, and stormed out, back to his own office.

Den was stressed. He took the job and the care of the team seriously and as far as I was concerned, he was constantly haunted with the prospect of having one of us hurt, or killed, while he was the Team Leader. Maybe it was because he was much older than any of us and more experienced, that he saw it as a fatherly like responsibility to us. Either way, if anyone was hurt, I know that he would've taken it badly and he would've blamed himself. That's the kind of man Den was.

Missions were still going to be conducted however, but it was the job of the client to make sure that they were important to the project and not just a jolly because someone was bored and fancied a change of scenery from the office.

A team had been hit in a rough area south west of Kirkuk. They had been attacked from a number of angles on an area of road that the insurgents had deliberately prepared to their own advantage. As a result, they found themselves pinned down, with two of their vehicles disabled and a team member dead, having been shot with armour piercing rounds.

It had only been a couple of days since and the colonel wasted no time in requesting a mission in to the same area. Even the American military call signs were avoiding the area and advising all other units, as well as Private Security Companies, to keep out.

One of two things was occurring, either the colonel was deliberately attempting to put us in danger, or he was a glory hunter, hoping to receive medals and awards for having been blown up in 'the Line of Duty'.

I suspected the same as everyone else; he was just a complete dick head.

His request was immediately thrown back at him by Den and Fifi. Naturally, he wasn't happy with the decision and once again, accused us of being scared and lazy. Rab being the people person he was, wanted to drug him, drive him out of the FOB in the middle of the night and dump him in the city. I actually found myself lying in bed at night, fantasising about such things. Obviously, I needed to get out more.

The FOB continued to get pounded by mortar and rocket fire on a regular basis. Every night, we would hear the low thump as a round hit somewhere in the base. It was around this time that I was told of an Urban Legend, involving an American Army General named, Black Jack Pershing.

Before the First World War, he had been based in the Philippines where there had been a number of terrorist attacks by Muslim extremists. Black Jack Pershing caught fifty of them and had them tied to posts for execution. Before they were shot however, he had a pig brought in and butchered in front of them.

The execution squad then dug a pit in front of the condemned and filled it with the pig's carcass and entrails. Then, they each dipped their bullets into the blood and loaded their weapons. The terrorists were horrified; knowing that having their blood contaminated with that of a filthy animal such as a pig they would be refused entry in to Paradise.

Each of the extremists was shot with the pig contaminated bullets, all except one, who was left alive to watch as his comrades were then thrown into the pit themselves along with the butchered pig and then buried as a whole, pig and all.

The surviving terrorist then went and did exactly what General Black Jack Pershing was counting on, he told everyone he could about the whole thing. After that, there wasn't another Islamic terrorist attack for forty two years.

Pershing clearly believed in fighting fire with fire and I couldn't help but wonder why couldn't it be done that way now? The only answer I could think of was 'Public Opinion'.

To me, the whole thing made perfect sense. If you have a problem with someone, and any kind of normal reasoning will not suffice, then take the fight to them and hit them where it really hurts.

Terrorists have discovered that blowing our buildings up, killing innocent people and soldiers alike, hurts us. So why not get every known terrorist and in return, hit them where it hurts? I'm pretty sure that the likes of the 'Shoe Bomber' and anyone intending on following his lead wouldn't like the idea of getting turned away from paradise and his seventy two chicks because his innards were part pig.

Whether the story is true or not, I'm not sure but either way, it's a different angle in how the problem could be dealt with.

Having extreme opinions like these are probably one of the reasons why I won't get very far in my election campaign but, personally, I can't think of a better way of dealing with the problem. Maybe extreme action is the only way to react to extremist behaviour?

A large American company had become, pretty much, a private army, and even had its own helicopters as air support. They were constantly flying in the airspace above Baghdad and a number of them had even been shot down by terrorist cells operating in the area.

We had seen their call signs moving about in the north and it had only been a couple of months earlier, that one of their teams had been hit on the southern outskirts of Kirkuk with an EFP, Explosively Formed Projectile; shaped charge IED. The entire truck had been destroyed and a number of men had been killed in the attack. It was a sobering thought to us; that it could've easily have been our team, because we often operated in that area ourselves.

EFP's are made by moulding a solid copper or, iron plate into the shape of a shallow dish, known as a liner, with the explosive charge packed behind it. Because the plate stays intact when the explosive is detonated, the whole of the force created by the explosion is concentrated behind it, giving it an enormous amount of velocity. When it's detonated, the liner is then forced forward and inverted and turned into a solid slug of shrapnel, capable of penetrating even the thickest armour plating.

Once the slug hits the target, it punches a hole in to the armour, through which it penetrates and the destroyed portion of armour plating, then adds to the spall effect inside the vehicle. So then, you have the EFP charge and solid metal slug, plus the fragmented armour plating bouncing around inside the vehicle. In short, if you get hit with an EFP, you're fucked.

Luckily, they had been adopted mainly in the southern regions of Iraq by the Shia Muslims who had a constant supply of weapons and explosives, as well as manpower and technology from Iran. In the north, the Sunnis concentrated mainly on large amounts of explosives in their IEDs, causing big bangs and damage over a large area, whereas the EFP was a more precise and concentrated weapon.

With the introduction of EFP in the area, as well as the usual threat of Improvised Explosive Devices, shootings, rocket attacks and kidnapping, it was a wonder why any of the clients wanted to travel out beyond the wire.

It was still Ramadan and the clients needed to visit a number of sites within Kirkuk. For the last week, they had been taking our advice and keeping the exposure to a minimum on the ground. However, the time had come when they actually needed to go out and it wasn't just for the usual 'I'm bored in the office, so I'll go for a drive tomorrow' routine. We understood the clients need to oversee the projects and so, when it became mission critical; we planned to hit all the sites in the Kirkuk area in one sweep, rather than over a period of days.

We had three locations to travel to and the mission was planned to travel to them systematically, moving from the northern most site through to the south and then, coming back into the FOB. We also planned it to coincide with the American clearance patrols early in the morning.

All the routes needed to be secured, so every morning, the American military would push out their teams to clear them prior to any of their other call signs travelling along them. This worked in our advantage for obvious reasons; if there was anything lay in wait, then it would be the military call signs that would take the hit, and they had the assets and support to deal with it.

On route to the second site we were travelling south along one of the main roads through the city. It had rained during the night and the city took on a more dreary appearance than usual. The filth in the streets had been washed into the inadequate gutters on the side of the roads by the downpour and mixed with the oil and mud. The traffic just churned it all up and scattered it around with the exhaust fumes and smoke they continuously pumped out creating a quagmire of shit and misery which the locals either worked amongst, or just travelled through, oblivious to the putrid smells that were a part of their daily environment.

The vehicles ahead swung out of our way as they heard our sirens and saw the red and blue flashing lights of the lead gun truck. It always reminded me of my own vision of Moses parting the Red Sea, like in the movie, 'Bruce Almighty', where he creates himself a path through a congested street, packed with static traffic.

We approached a junction with the traffic holding back to our left and right, leaving us a clear path across. On the other side, the volume of traffic on the road dropped noticeably, which wasn't completely unusual considering there were less shops and market stalls along that part of the route.

"Road ahead clear, keep centre, approximately two kilometres to the next target." Sean was reading his GPS and also working from memory, having travelled to these sites on numerous occasions.

We all knew the area, but for the side and rear gunners who only had a view of what they were passing from right angles, it was useful to have an idea of what was coming up.

Sean's vehicle approached what looked like a discarded oil drum set back from the side of the road. Oil drums were always a common sight in Iraq. They were used as bins, fire containers and even road blocks. It wasn't unusual to see and rusty old drum lying on its side with other bits of waste and debris around it. But on this occasion, it drew the attention of Sean in the lead vehicle as he gave his running commentary over the net.

"Oil drum on the right up ahead, push left, push left," he gave over the radio.

All the other vehicles followed suit and began to move toward the centre of the road to put distance between us and the drum. It was a standard drill. If there was something on the side of the road that you wasn't sure of, then you got away from it.

As Sean passed the oil drum he noticed the shape of the dish, pointed directly in to the road, "Stop, stop, stop. There's a fucking IED on the right." He screamed over the radio.

An EFP needs to be pointed and angled in to the exact area of where the terrorist want the slug to travel. And the area immediately in front of it needs to be clear of obstruction so that the forming of the solid slug can't be interfered with.

With the momentum of the team from the speed we were travelling though, it was too late for some of the vehicles to stop before they came close. The first and second vehicles were virtually on top of the drum. Unable to stop in time before it, they accelerated through, hoping to get clear before it detonated.

The third and fourth vehicles slammed on the brakes. I was jolted forward in my seat, the straps to the harness holding me in place tugging at my shoulders and neck. We had managed to brake in time and we began reversing away from the IED. The vehicle in front was doing the same and it took a lot of skill for the drivers to control their vehicles and avoid hitting each other or anything else.

Out of the corner of my eye, I caught a flash of white and yellow as the IED detonated. The bang and whoosh was like having someone clap both sides of my head simultaneously, causing my ears to pop, my eyes bulge and my head feel like it's about to burst. I felt the air get sucked from my lungs and it was almost like an unseen and unfelt force was pushing me towards the firing port on my side of the rear gun truck. In essence I was being sucked out of the window by the vacuum caused by the explosion.

Toad was still reversing at top speed, but I'm pretty sure he was doing it blind and with the rest of his senses impaired. I could hear voices but couldn't understand a word that was being said. Everything sounded low and distant, yet I knew full well that they were the voices of the rest of my gun truck, screaming commands and observations to each other. Toad began to slow down as we left the immediate danger area. We had travelled about a hundred metres, back the way we had come.

"Hold it here Toad. We've got a split call sign now." Brian said.

Vehicles one and two had pushed further along the intended route, doing the same as we had done, trying to get as far away as possible from the blast.

"Den, this is Brian, radio check," nothing. "Den, Sean, this is Brian, radio check."

I could clearly hear Brian now through my ear piece, but I was still seeing stars. Den and Sean weren't answering up from Brian's radio checks. Den had been in the second vehicle in the convoy, with Sean in the lead and either their radios were damaged or they had been caught in the IED.

Chubbs was covering the six o'clock position and making sure that no vehicles approached. Omar and I debussed to check the immediate area of where we had gone static, in case there were any secondary devices waiting for us.

I looked back in the direction of the blast, hoping to be able to see any sign of the other half of the team, but all I could see was a cloud of smoke and debris. I could also hear shouts, sirens in the distance and the heavy crumpling sound of falling masonry.

I had already assumed that the second and maybe first vehicles had been wiped out. At that moment, there was no time to consider the people in them, even though they were friends of mine. I was thinking more about the team as a whole and of course, myself, and if there was any further threat to deal with.

I heard a faint crackle of static, then, "Brian you getting me?" Den's voice was clear on the net.

"Yeah Den, good to me, you still in one piece, any injuries?" Brian answered, sounding relieved that at least some of the other half of the team had made it through.

"No mate, we're all okay including Sean's vehicle, but my vehicle is fucked. The back end is twisted and the wheels are gone. The lead gun truck is covering the twelve o'clock and the side gunners are checking the area."

"Roger that Den, Luke and Omar are covering the street at this end. What's the score with your vehicle then, can it limp back to base if we change the tyres with our spares?"

"No Brian, you don't understand mate, the wheels are actually *gone*." Den made a point of his statement to make it clear what his condition was, as in, 'the wheels are just not there anymore.'

I looked back up the street and now that the smoke was settling, I could just about make out the other two vehicles further up, about fifty metres past where the explosion had happened. Pete and Guy were patrolling back in our direction, with their weapons in the shoulder, flanking their gun truck on either side of the street, clearing the area as they moved.

Den's vehicle was stopped at the side of the road, looking worse for wear but from what I could tell, the integrity of the armour was still intact, with the clients being kept inside and out of any further danger. Den was stood by the side of his vehicle, already smoking a cigarette, and looking like he had just broke down at the side of the road on a Sunday drive. It seemed like it was more of an inconvenience to him than a danger.

"We're gonna push back towards you Den."

"Roger that Brian, once you're here, we'll cross deck the clients into the third vehicle so at least we can be mobile if need be."

Both our trucks started to push back into the area of the IED. It made sense to move in that direction because the explosion itself had cleared the vicinity for us. If there had been a secondary device close by, then the blast of the first would've either initiated it, or damaged it.

Den's vehicle was disabled and regardless, we needed to become a complete team again for mutual support.

As our gun truck slowly moved along the centre of the street, I scanned the buildings, rooftops and road. Every window in the immediate area had been blown out and no doubt, people had been injured from secondary debris inside the buildings.

By now we could clearly see the blast area. The road, pavement, and the wall directly behind where the IED had been placed, were destroyed. A crater now stood where the explosion had ripped up the road.

I followed the direction of the blast with my eyes, and the building directly across from it had a hole punched through it. It didn't look like there had been a wide range of shrapnel thrown out by the IED.

As I came level with the building, I could see pretty much straight through it. Something had smashed its way through one side and out of the other at about the three metre mark. The ceilings inside were collapsing onto the first floor and the building was becoming more unstable as more masonry fell inward.

"Lads, you got eyes on that building to our left?" I called through my radio.

I followed the angle of what would've been the trajectory of the debris from the blast. To me, it looked as though the IED had been angled from the ground so that it would've hit one of our vehicles at chest height. With the lack of shrapnel damage to the surrounding area and the size, height and angle of the hole in the building across from the explosion, I'd already come to my own conclusions.

I now needed to hear it from someone else.

"Yeah Luke," Toad replied, "Not as big a hole as you would've expected from an IED like."

"Looks like a fucking EFP to me boys." Brian had obviously come to the same conclusion.

"Fuck sake," rang out in chorus from a few of the team.

If the charge had hit one of our vehicles, it would've opened it up like a tin can and killed everyone inside. Luckily, it had missed and Den's truck had been caught in the edge of the blast.

It was now in our best interest to get out of the area as quickly as possible. It was clear to us that the EFP had been initiated by a command wire, meaning that someone would've had eyes on us and could still have. It wasn't a random bombing to spread fear and terror amongst the locals. No other vehicle had been targeted as it passed and it was specifically set for either us or a military call sign.

We came up level with Den, who was still puffing away on his cigarette.

"You okay Luke?" He asked as if it was an everyday passing event. He was leaning with one elbow against the hood of his vehicle and his M4 in the other hand, watching the rest of the team move in.

"Yeah mate, how's you? Clients okay?"

"Yeah, they're alright, stinks in there though. I think Joe or the colonel shit their pants."

I had to turn away from the vehicle so that the clients inside wouldn't see me trying to hold back my laughter.

By now, the team was together and a rough perimeter had been set up to cover the street and the vehicles. Crowds had gathered at either end, but they knew better than to approach us. After a close call like that, we would've shot anyone who came near. Already, we could hear helicopters in the air and a message had been received that a military call sign was en-route to our location to assist us.

As soon as the second client vehicle was in position, Den cross decked the colonel and Joe, shitty pants and all, from the wreck and into the still intact truck. We set about stripping all the sensitive equipment from Den's vehicle and loading it into the second client vehicle. It took just a couple of minutes to do then we were good to go again.

Of course, the mission was binned and a return to base, via the quickest possible route, was needed. But with the American call sign on their way, we couldn't just leave the area.

Brian prepared the Thermite grenade and had it ready to destroy what was left of the damaged vehicle. Dragging it back with us wasn't an option, unless the military were bringing a flat bed truck and a crane with them.

They arrived five minutes later.

"Fuck, you guys okay?" The young officer asked as he surveyed the damaged truck and crater.

"Yeah no worries mate. We're gonna blow what's left of the Excursion here and then head back to base. You fancy escorting us?" Den was still looking and sounding like it was all in his stride.

"Yeah, no problem, can I just get a few pictures first?" The young American already had his camera out and some of his men were beginning to pose by the wreck.

Brian came up on the net, "Fucking Yanks, they're on a different planet aren't they."

We waited patiently while the guys took their happy snaps and once they were done, Brian tossed in the Thermite grenade; another small fortune up in smoke.

We headed back, with the American lads providing cover for us from the ground and the air. We were leaving a scene of chaos behind us, as what was left of the building would surely collapse and an armoured vehicle burned in the street across from it.

"And the moral of the story is, fucking stay indoors during Ramadan." Chubbs voiced his wisdom over the radio. "Either that, or bring an extra pair of underpants, shitty shit pants."

No one cared if the colonel or Joe could hear us, laughing at their expense. Once again, they had been exposed as the clueless idiots they were.

A few days later, we returned from a mission to Dibis, after visiting the Water Treatment Plant there with a few clients. We hadn't seen much of the colonel lately, or Joe for that matter. I figured they were probably still recovering from shame after their joint trouser shitting.

One thing we did notice was that our cats weren't about. Normally, they would be waiting for us at the Op's Room when we got in. We just assumed that their mother was probably out with them somewhere, teaching them how to hunt and do the things that cats do. That night though, no one could answer when asked where Woolfy was. It was strange not to have seen him in and around the rooms, or curled up on someone's bed watching TV with a bloated stomach from double helpings of tuna.

I brushed it off as a coincidence and that each group of cats were off doing their own thing on the same night. But the days dragged on and still, no one had seen any sign of any of them. Even the guys in the team that weren't that close to them started asking after the cats because they had become such a part of our everyday lives.

We asked the clients and they didn't know either. Maybe they had moved on?

After a week, Rab bounced into my room, looking angrier than he normally did, "Have you heard about the cats?"

"No, why, have they turned up?" I was lying on my bed watching a movie. I pressed stop on the DVD player when I realised it wasn't just Rab being his usual larger than life self.

"Have they fuck, I've just been told by one of the mechanics that they're dead."

I sprang from my bed, "Who told you, which mechanic?"

"It was John. He said that a Health and Safety guy had come around while we were out on a mission. He captured them and took them away and gassed them." Rab's eyes were bulging and his face was red with fury. "He won't tell me who it was though who caught them. I'll skin the bastard alive if I find out."

The news spread like wild fire amongst the men and before long, everyone was in the Op's Room, demanding that Fifi find out who it was. It may sound trivial to some people that a bunch of grown men, hired to work in Iraq and risking their lives on a daily basis, were getting out of shape over a few cats. But in a way, the cats were a link to normality for us.

At home, most of us had kids, families, friends and pets and the way we treated animals, compared to how the local Iraqi people did, set us apart and therefore, made us feel some level of normality when near enough every day we were prepared and geared up for a fight. To come back and hear a bunch of kittens shouting for you, or have Woolfy curl up on your lap at the end of the day, helped us to escape from the world we had around us.

We all knew who had orchestrated the killing of our cats, the colonel. He wanted his own back, just like he had done with cutting the internet cables. Instead of being a man, and facing us, he played the coward card and attacked us from the rear.

While we were out on a mission to Dibis, he had called the administration unit of the base, and requested them to send down a pest control technician.

Being the red neck retard that the pest control guy probably was, he more than likely believed the propaganda that was shoved down his throat twenty four hours a day, seven days a week, over the TV channels and radio stations of the base, telling him that he was there to make a difference, and to help in the fight for 'Iraqi Freedom'.

Dutifully, he came down and murdered our cats and kittens, then no doubt, returned home to a hero's welcome, claiming to have been a great help to the American soldiers in Iraq and the 'War on Terror'. He would probably leave out the fact that he never left the base, and probably claimed to be having flash backs of war and its horror. At best and in truth, he could only claim that he was on a FOB when some artillery shells and rockets had landed.

Yes, he made a difference.

The only difference he made was, to allow the real pests to get out of hand. After the cats had gone, the mice and rat population exploded. It started out as holes in our kit and equipment in the morning. Then as their numbers soared, we would hear groups of them running around our rooms in the dark during the night, chewing cables, clothing, equipment and any food that we had in reach of them.

Eventually, it got to the stage that they couldn't care less about the fact that we could see them, and often they would scurry across the floors and furniture in broad daylight. Mice and rat shit was everywhere. Good call, colonel.

I was home on leave again, and I was now beginning to look elsewhere for work. I was still aiming for Iraq but, with the contract coming to an end, I couldn't be sure that I would be taken on by the next bunch. I put my feelers out to friends and contacts alike, to see what was available. A few prospects came back and alternatives were looking good.

Towards the end of my leave, my girlfriend and I went out for a drink. My sister had just come back from a holiday in Spain, and she made the mistake of bringing me a bottle of Sambuca back as a present. Between us, we drank the whole lot in less than an hour. We were fine, until we left the house and the fresh air hit us. After that, I can't remember a thing.

The next thing I do recall is, waking up in bed the next morning. I noticed blood all over the shoulder of my girlfriend. I flapped and thought something had happened to her.

"Jesus, what's happened?"

She rolled over and looked at me, still sleepy and confused from the sudden panicked tone of my voice. Her expression changed from that of a woman with a hangover, squinting in the light, to wide eyed terror.

"Fucking hell Luke, what's happened to you?"

I couldn't work out what she was asking, because in my head, she was the one that needed sorting out, being covered in blood.

"You're face is split open Luke, can't you feel it?"

"Uh . . . nope," I reached up to my face and realised it was me that had been hurt.

My eye socket and cheek bone was swollen and I could feel a large deep gash below my left eye and around the side of it.

"Shit." I jumped out of bed to look in the mirror. "Fuck me. What happened?"

"I don't know, we got split up in a bar and I couldn't find you, so I came back here. I didn't even hear you come in."

She had already started to relax, knowing that not all things in my life run smoothly and now and then, a random atrocity does tend to occur. When she realised that my face wasn't actually about to fall off, she helped to try and piece back together the events from the night before, as well as my face.

I needed to clear the dried blood from my face so I could see what damage there was and the extent of it. The warm water stung the cut and made me wince as I splashed away the blood, trying to avoid further damage. Once it was clear, I could see my cheek bone and the bone around the eye socket, through the gash.

I didn't have a clue how it had happened.

I looked at my hands and the right knuckles were swollen and cut, I'd been in a fight, I now knew that much. By the vision in the mirror, I wasn't sure if I'd done too well in it though. It became obvious that a glass had been used on me, maybe a tumbler or half pint glass. The circumference wasn't big enough to have been a full pint.

I shouted back into the bedroom, "Did we fall out last night?"

"No, I don't think so. Why?"

"Just wondering, it looks like a small glass was shoved in my face."

She bounded into the bathroom, while I stood over the sink looking at myself in the mirror.

"You twat, and you're saying I glassed you?" She studied my face and the damage, but her guard was up and I saw no sympathy in her expression for the trauma around my eye.

I had to laugh, "No, I'm just starting the process of elimination."

She relaxed a little and turned me to look at her so that she could get a better look at me, "Luke, that's gonna need stitches. Is your vision okay?"

"About normal for a Sunday morning after a monster booze session the night before so, no it's not really."

"You're a knob at times." Even though she was serious, she still found it funny.

I staggered downstairs to find a mate of mine sprawled out on my couch. The story he gave me was that, he was sitting waiting for a taxi, eating a kebab, and he saw me stagger past, leaking blood all over the place. He brought me home and threw me into bed and got his head down on the couch in the living room.

He didn't have a clue what had happened to me and no one was any the wiser until I got a phone call a few days later from a mate who heard what had happened. Apparently, he had even seen the CCTV footage of me brawling with a guy in a bar, and I had the upper hand, until his mate blindsided me with a glass.

A week later, I was sat in front of a manager from the company that was about to take over our contract, being interviewed for a possible position on one of their teams when the hand over was completed.

He was pleasant and professional, but I noticed him staring at my ripped face and slightly black eye a few times too often. I couldn't say I blamed him to be honest, because I would've been doing the same thing and asking myself, "Do I really want this dick head working for us?"

I was kicking myself for my timing. Just like when I had first come into country in early 2005, I was potentially setting a bad first impression. I had a cut on the brow of my right eye then, and now, I was sat there in the limelight of a company boss again, with an even bigger cut on my other eye.

Just my luck, if I fell into a barrel of tits, I'd still come out sucking my thumb.

CONVENIENT LIES AND THE INCONVENIENT TRUTH

On the 18th October 2007, a Private Security Company attached to the American Army on a government contract, travelling east from Kirkuk to Sulimania, opened fire on innocent civilians inside a taxi that were travelling in the same direction as the team.

The taxi, as it turned out, was carrying not just the driver, but his wife, sister, his children, brother in law and mother and father in law. Also, a female reporter, as luck would have it.

They must've either had a very comfortable roof rack, or they were trying to break a Guinness World Record by squeezing as many people into a car as possible.

There has been a number of stories and accounts of the event from numerous so called eye witnesses and victims of the shooting. However, a lot of these versions conflict with each other; some in small and others in large proportions.

Some, regarding the amount of shots fired. Others, on how many men opened fire. Details such as whether the taxi was mobile or static, where it happened, how many civilians were involved. How many civilians were hurt, and how. Whether the team was firing as they past them or after they past, was the team mobile or static?

One story is that the team had driven past the taxi and then they decided to open up on it with machineguns. Another is that they allowed the taxi to pass the convoy and then, decided to shoot as they came level.

Other accounts say that the taxi was just static by the side of the road and the children were waving to the PSD, who then opened fire. Even some Iraqi Police claimed to have been involved in the incident.

"I saw a convoy of three cars pass a taxi and one of the guards took his weapon and opened fire on the taxi," said police officer Hussain Rashid. *"I*

tried to stop the convoy but they didn't pay attention to me. They stopped about 300 metres from the scene. Then they moved away."

According to some witnesses, the journalist tried to get out of the vehicle at one point but was forced back in when the PSD members pointed their weapons at her. How could this have been true if the team had continued on their route and by now, must've left the immediate area?

"The private security team initiated escalating warning procedures under the rules for the use of force, resulting in an alleged injury to a civilian occupant of the vehicle," Was the report released by the American Military.

Yet another story tells of how the entire team fired their weapons, and every person in the taxi was aimed at and shot indiscriminately.

Some say that there were mass casualties, others say there was one. One account is from the sister of the driver who claimed that she received shrapnel injuries, causing her to pass out and when she came to, she saw her brother leaning over her with his eye hanging out if its socket, making her think that he too, would also die with her.

Another passenger of the taxi is said to have sustained severe damage to his ear, causing him to undergo extensive surgery and the loss of his hearing, while a female is still struggling to walk. And that's not to mention all of the psychological problems they are all suffering.

Still, it must've been a big car all the same.

A month earlier, an American security company had been involved in an incident in Baghdad that had left seventeen, supposedly unarmed civilians, dead. The security contractors involved reported that they had been caught in an ambush and they had responded according to the 'Rules for the Use of Force'. The Iraqi authorities and media however, claim that they had deliberately shot and killed the seventeen 'innocent civilians'.

This resulted in a back lash, causing all the security companies operating in Iraq to fall under the microscope and their procedures and conduct to be scrutinised by the entire world. From then on, we were the bad guys in Iraq and it was us, the Security Contractors that were causing disruption to the rebuilding of the country and the continued freedom and security of the Iraqi people.

The Kirkuk incident has been under investigation ever since and as far as I'm aware, it still is. Now and then, articles crop up in the newspapers and magazines, or reports on the news channels, telling their versions of events, or remaining neutral and just reporting the 'facts'.

Because the PSD Company involved was Western based and contracted out to the American government, it is Western lawyers that have taken up the fight on behalf of the Iraqi civilians involved in the shooting. The last I heard, the payout being demanded is in the billions. Whether this will come from the company or the American government, I'm not sure.

The following is a true account from an eye witness of the events of that day:

How do I know they're true? The witness is me.

As soon as I had come back from leave, Brian and Chubbs informed me that they had resigned during my absence and that they were due to finish their contract in just a week. Andy had also left the company by now, and I saw my little circle of friends getting that much smaller. I was pretty gutted to be honest.

They were guys that I had got to know really well and had worked closely with in a hostile environment for a long time. So, to suddenly be faced with being separated and our days as a team numbered, I sort of felt that all was lost.

The contract was coming to an end and another company was due to take over, and we knew that not everybody would be taken on by them. But I hoped for the best, and in my hopes and dreams, I saw Brian, Chubbs, Andy, Cach and Rab along with me, cracking on with missions in a different uniform but, together. Unfortunately it wasn't to be.

That's when Chubbs announced that his wedding party would be in early November. He and Mandy had gotten married in Las Vegas but they were having their wedding do in the UK in his home town.

By now, it was already coming up to mid October and I didn't like the idea of missing the 'Wedding of the Century', as Chubbs claimed it to be. Everyone who I was close to on the team would be there, but the contract wasn't due to finish until the end of November, so I would miss it.

For the next few days, I listened as Chubbs and Brian discussed the events coming up for the wedding bash. I was envious. It was planned to be a big do, and true to Chubbs' style, the PSD boys who attended would be playing a lead role in the celebration.

Worse still, one evening while I sat in my room with Chubbs and Brian, Cach bounded in looking rather pleased with himself.

"I've done it."

"Done what?" I asked.

He looked over at Brian and Chubbs, "I'm coming to your wedding mate, make sure I get a fancy invitation."

"You're not due to go on leave though are you?" I remarked. Cach stared at me shaking his head, but the penny still hadn't dropped for me. "How you gonna be at the wedding then?"

"I've resigned you thick twat." He said it with a touch of triumph in his voice, as though it was an obstacle he had been struggling with for some time, and in essence, he had. We all had.

I raised my fists and flung them back down to bounce off the arms of the chair that I sat in, "Oh for fuck sake, that's another one gone. I'm gonna be left on my tod like a fucking loser aren't I."

Brian tried to console me, "We'll send you some photos from the wedding. Look here Luke; at least you'll still have Rab, Toad and Pete to play out with." Now he was just rubbing it in.

"Like fuck he will, Rab has just resigned as well and I think Toad is following suit." Cach said rubbing his hands with glee. "It's a sinking ship mate, and you're the only daft fucker stupid enough to go down with it."

I felt abandoned, and unsure of what to do, "Ah, but what about the contract?" I asked.

"Bollocks to it, they can shove it up their arse, 'cause I've had enough of this Monkey Farm."

I moved over to my laptop as Cach helped himself to my Yorkshire Tea.

"Right Chubbs, put me down for an invitation too, because I'm coming as well and we're gonna have a dance off at the do."

Chubbs jumped up excitedly and clapped his hands as he shuffled his feet, "Hey hey, roger that sun shine."

It then occurred to me, "Hang on, how are we gonna be at Chubbs' wedding if we are half way through the month and need to give four week's notice? That would mean that we would only get home for mid November." I pointed out to Cach.

"That's why I've got Fifi to screw the nut for me," Cach was waiting for me to ask how Fifi was going to pull strings for him. "He's gonna make out that I resigned last week and that my letter of resignation got caught up in his junk mail box. So in theory, I resigned the day I got back from leave."

"Fucking hell, that's genius." I exclaimed, "I'll have a word and get it done myself then."

I wrote out my resignation and sent it to Fifi, with strict instructions to do the same thing for me as what he had done for Cach. I sat back feeling proud of myself and as though a weight had been lifted from my shoulders. I was still hoping that I would be brought back onto the contract once the changeover was done, but I also intended on casting my nets out to see what else would bite in the meantime.

Brian and Chubbs left and the team carried on without them. Two Americans were brought in as their replacements. They didn't replace them as such. No one knew navigation and all the different aids and mapping sources as well as Brian, and Chubbs had been our rear gunner. We used other, already existing members of the team, to fill their slots and the new arrivals were placed into the client vehicles as drivers.

We had a mission to drop off a client in Suli. The United States Corp of Engineers had a mini FOB there and the client was to be dropped off and picked back up a week later to be brought back to Kirkuk.

Suli was always a run of the mill style job. We had done it dozens of times and once we get past the Green Line, we would be in Kurdish controlled country and we would lower the aggression of the profile. By this, we would bring in the weapons from the firing ports of the gun trucks and vehicles would even be allowed to approach our convoy and overtake once the rear gunner had waved them on.

The Kurds tended to be on the ball with general security in their territory and very little tended to get past them in way of terrorist activity. At every major junction and on the outskirts of every town, there are check points, where vehicles are checked and searched as they enter or leave.

The Green Line though is roughly twenty five miles east of Kirkuk. This meant that until that point, we were to continue with our normal hard drills, such as keeping all vehicles back and at a distance from us, and weapons being kept visible as a deterrent.

Now and then, people would make the mistake of coming too close, but all it would take was a wave of the hand or flash of a light by the rear gunner or side shooter, then they would soon realise their error and keep their distance.

It was never a case of, any vehicle that you saw, light it up.

That's one of the reasons we kept them back no less than one hundred metres. That distance gave us the time to judge whether or not the approaching vehicle was a threat. If, by the time the vehicle got to the fifty metre point and still ignored all warnings and showed no sign of slowing, then warning shots would be fired, to either get their attention or to disable the vehicle.

We always looked forward to Suli trips for two main reasons, first it was a break from the threat that we came under constantly in places like Kirkuk, Tuz, Mosul and Tikrit. And secondly, we could always resupply our beer stock. I had a third reason, and that was that Liam was based in the mini FOB. I always enjoyed a catch up with him.

By mid October the weather was staring to cool. Not to the extent that I needed to wear a jacket, although Guy insisted it was. It was still like a good warm day in the UK as far as I was concerned.

It was early morning and the air was cool for the time of year, which I was pleased about because it meant that I wouldn't be sweating my nuts off too much in my body armour and kit like during the summer months. It wouldn't be long until the rains would start. The days were already growing shorter and before we knew it, winter would take its grip on northern Iraq again.

For now though, it was all rather pleasant.

We set out around nine o'clock, heading north into the city, with the intent of skirting around the Kurdish part of Kirkuk where, we were less likely to run into trouble. As always the morning markets were open, and the smell of fresh blood from the slaughtered animals hanging out in the morning air in front of the shops, joined with the sour fetid smell of rot from the mixture of decayed meat and waste from the days previous.

I still couldn't understand how the sheep; standing at the side of the road and watching their friends being beheaded and skinned, then hung up on display, didn't realise that maybe they should try and make a run for it because it was obviously their turn next.

As usual, we used our sirens and flashing lights as little as possible in the Kurdish area. We knew that there would be hustle and bustle in the streets and we pushed through as best we could with the occasional beep of the horn and blocking manoeuvre by the gun trucks.

Once we reached the outskirts, we were able to take the road for ourselves, keeping to the centre and away from the road sides and maintaining a gap between ourselves and the other vehicles along the route. The civilian vehicles always recognised us for what we were and would keep out of our way on their own accord. Only now and then we would need to use our lights or sirens on the open road.

Clear of the city, the country opened up into typical Kurdish terrain. One minute there would be flat open expanses to one side then it would be sheer cliff faces or deep dried up river beds. In some places, up on the high open ground that the road followed, you could see in all directions for miles.

To the north east were the mountain ranges that ran through the countryside between Erbil and Suli, showing up blue/purple because of the rock and distance. To the south were the open plains that led into the oil fields in Kormor, with villas and small farms scattered here and there. In all, the scenery was always picturesque and pleasant to watch as we travelled through it.

About half way to the Green Line we came over the brow of the high ground where the road split around the summit of the feature, and then joined together again on the other side before it descended steadily into a small town. We knew the town and we had gone through it on many occasion.

It was a mix of half Kurdish and half Arab, but as far as I'm aware, they got on pretty well together with very little trouble. That doesn't mean that they loved the coalition forces though. We were still on the bad side of the Green Line by about fifteen miles and even once passed it, we always kept our eyes open.

As we descended into the steady dip of the road that entered the town, the second vehicle had a blow out. The whole wheel exploded, looking like a grenade effect and going with a bang. We knew from experience though that it was a blow out and that we hadn't been hit with an explosive.

"Vehicle two has had a blow out," Den sent over the net.

Every one of vehicles within the call sign had tyre's that were fitted with run flats. A run flat is a wheel within a wheel to explain it best. But the inner wheel is solid steel rimmed and hard moulded rubber or plastic. This meant that, even with the air shot out from our tyres, we could still drive. The best run flats could keep us mobile, at a reduced speed, for up to forty miles. If need be, we could push our way through any danger or killing zone and on to safety for quite some distance before we needed to stop and change the wheel.

We were still on the outskirts of the town, so we decided to go firm and repair the damaged wheel. We had trained and practiced every drill we could think of, for every possible scenario, including tyre changes. With the equipment we had and the practice and skill of the team, we could lift a fully armoured Ford Excursion, weighing about four or five tons and change its wheel and be mobile again in roughly three and a half minutes.

Our normal drill was that with three of the vehicles, including the one with the damaged wheel, we would form a protective triangle in the centre of the road, with the damaged side of the vehicle on the inside of the triangle so that the people changing the tyre had the protection of the armour to work within, while the other team members would provide cover from inside the triangle.

The rear gun truck would keep itself at a distance of about fifty metres to our rear, covering the six o'clock and deploying its side gunners out to the left and right to help with controlling the traffic. All civilian vehicles would be held at a further one hundred metres, giving us a safe zone.

We automatically got on with the task, every man working like a cog in a machine and instantly knowing what his job was. Some got on with providing protection and covering their arcs with their weapons. Others would be slackening off wheel nuts, handling the jacks or unloading a spare wheel from the roof, ready to quickly slot it into place once the damaged one was removed.

A team of Formula One mechanics couldn't do the job better or faster in a pit stop.

About a minute into the tyre change, there was shouting and hollering from the gun truck providing our rear protection. A second later a voice said, "Stand by," over the radio net. We all knew what that meant. The warning was followed by the brief chatter of a light machinegun.

The firing stopped as quickly as it started.

To the rear of the call sign, the two side gunners had deployed to either side of the road to help the rear gunner cover the six o'clock position. They also acted as an extra aid to the civilian vehicles, giving them more of a visual warning to stop, with the presence of men on the road.

Naturally, if you were driving along and you saw a vehicle static in the centre of the road, you would consider stopping. With men on foot either side of it, there's even less excuse for not noticing the obstruction. On top of that, with a huge white sign with red lettering, warning you to stay back one hundred metres in English, Arabic and Kurdish and the men on the road carrying guns, then for sure, you're going to decelerate or hit the brakes well in advance.

Most people did just that.

All the civilian traffic came to a steady halt as soon as they saw the vehicles and men. They pulled to the side of the road, helping us to determine that they had no intention of approaching any closer. We had not stopped so close to the high ground that as soon as anyone breached the summit, they would be virtually on top of us. Our rear most vehicle was about five hundred metres past it so there was plenty of time to see the obstruction and come to a halt.

A taxi pulled out from the rear of the queue of static traffic, and began accelerating along the clear side of the road and heading straight for our rear gun truck. It was a typical Iraqi taxi, a Nissan saloon, with orange painted wings and white body.

The dismounted side gunners immediately recognised the potential threat and began waving and shouting at the taxi, hoping it would realise that it wasn't just a traffic jam and that it was actually a security team causing the hold up. The rear gunner was waving his luminous flag and even flashing his weapon mounted light to get the vehicles attention and force it to stop.

The vehicle didn't. It continued to drive straight for us and even began to gain speed. By now, the side gunners had stepped from the road and had taken up fire positions, aimed at the taxi. That was when the rear gunner gave the warning over the net.

"Stand by."

He aimed at the front lower part of the taxi as it approached at speed. By now, the speeding taxi had closed the gap from the rear of the static traffic, and clearly had no intention or desire to stop.

The taxi was about seventy five metres away now and the gunner squeezed the trigger once and only for a second. The rounds thumped out of the barrel and sailed at high velocity into the front of the car. All four rounds hit the taxi in the grill and hood, causing an instant loss of power, and the vehicle began to slow and veer to the side.

That was all that was needed and the threat was neutralised. It wasn't our job to approach him and detain him afterward, or even to find out what his intentions were. The threat had been dealt with and the client was safe.

When the vehicle had stopped, the gunners moved back on to the road to ensure that nobody else decided to drive at us. A steady stream of oily smoke rose from the hood of the disabled taxi and fluid leaked beneath from a ruptured hose or tank.

The driver slowly emerged from his side of the vehicle, first raising his head just above the rim of the door, and when he realised there was no more shooting to be done he stepped out into the open, watching in our direction. He probably wanted to make sure he wasn't going to get another burst from us.

He looked his damaged taxi over and stood with hands on hips, as if wondering what to do next. Looking in our direction, he raised his hands in resignation then let them fall to his side. He was clearly pissed off, but at least he was alive. The shots had been aimed to disable his vehicle and not to hurt or kill him.

When he was sure there would be no more rounds sent in his direction, he began gobbing off in either Arabic or Kurdish at our team, more than likely calling us a 'bunch of shits' for ruining his car. He carried on hollering and gesturing in our direction until, he realised his ear was bleeding. By now most of the occupants of the other static vehicles were out on the road and watching with curiosity. Others began approaching the road from the scattered houses to the left and right.

Further up in front of us, about a hundred metres, there was an Iraqi Police Station. IP began to drift out from within its walls and head toward the scene, taking great care to give our vehicles a wide berth as they walked by. All of them looked in our direction though, and it wasn't long before the road behind, and ahead of us, was packed with onlookers. Women, children, men, elderly people and dogs crowded the area, trying to get news on what had happened or at least hear the gossip.

Seeing that he had an audience, the taxi driver removed his hand from his ear to inspect the blood on his fingertips; all 0.5ml of it. He turned his hand so that the crowd could see his terrible wounds and blood loss, and that's when the dramatics began.

As if on stage, as soon as he saw that the civilians had noticed the blood, his legs turned to spaghetti. He staggered from one side of his vehicle, holding onto the hood for support and dear life as his life force slowly ebbed away, and wailing with great agony. He leaned against the passenger side door and reached out to the gathered crowd as if pleading for help. Clutching at the side of his head and holding his other arm to his chest, he staggered into the middle of the road, bent double, as though his strength was failing and his legs would give at any moment. He dropped into a semi seated position on the tarmac and cried out to the crowd and gesturing in our direction.

It was like something from Shakespeare.

By now, he had made his way to the curb where he lay, gasping his last breath, with the locals fussing around him. Then he was up again and full of rage, shouting in our direction and to the people around him. He obviously couldn't make his mind up whether he was dying or not. After a few angry sentences for the benefit of his audience, he dropped again, this time to his knees, with his hands on the ground to support him.

What had cut his ear was anyone's guess. Maybe a shard from the engine had ricocheted through into the interior of the taxi and nicked his ear, or maybe a piece of the dashboard? Either way, it wasn't the life threatening injury he made it out to be, I had received worse from shaving.

The team looked on bemused.

The taxi driver was enveloped by the mob and no doubt, rushed off to hospital to be resuscitated judging by his performance. It reminded me of an old silent black and white movie I once saw a scene from:

There was some kind of battle in progress and as the white puffs of smoke went off, indicating falling artillery, and horses charged into the fray, one actor; who was obviously the equivalent of an extra for the day, refused to just fall down dead in accordance with the script.

Even though his part was small, and the movie was filmed from a distance to give a more panoramic view of the battlefield and everything else that was going on with the cavalry charge being the main focus, this one guy insisted on making his death as dramatic as possible. He fell about all over the place, clutching his chest and reaching his hand to the heavens. It looked comical, and so did our little taxi driver.

There were no other passengers in the taxi.

Within a few minutes, the tyre had been changed and we were mounted up and moving on. I never gave the incident another thought during the journey. To be honest, I had completely forgotten it at the time because I had other things to think about.

We crossed the Green Line and drove through the town of Chamchamal and on towards Suli. I was still enjoying the view and watching the mountains and tree lines pass by. If I hadn't seen the heaps of shit and rubbish by the side of the road, I could've convinced myself that I was somewhere in Wales, where I spent a lot of my childhood holidays.

As we approached the final check point before Suli, we did notice that the Peshmerga guard force manning the check point seemed to stare at us in a less than friendly way from how they normally did. Usually, it would be all smiles, waves and big thumbs up, grinning to us retards. This time, they watched us with suspicion and looking back now I realise, a degree of anticipation with a touch of hatred. Though, it could've been fear. Those two emotions can be hard to distinguish on people's faces in certain situations.

Nevertheless, we drove through and onto the FOB just a few kilometres further on. Once in the base, we did our normal drill; we went in search of a brew. Everybody piled into the canteen, where we knew there would be hot water, coffee and tea. Me, I headed for Liam's room to see if he was in, I could get a cuppa at his place.

Some of the lads had dumped their kit, removing their body armour and leaving their weapons in the vehicles before locking them up. This wasn't a problem because we were in an American FOB, small as it was, but it was secure. I had left my kit on because I didn't think we would be there very long. I was still in my body armour and ops vest with all my ammunition in the pouches and my pistol on my belt, my M4 was left in our vehicle.

I rapped at Liam's door and walked in. Liam was sat on his bed smoking a cigarette in just his underpants.

"Hey hey, Frankie, I didn't know you were coming."

"Yeah, I can see that. Otherwise you wouldn't have just been sat there in your duds scratching your balls would you?"

"Nah mate, I'd have been sat here starker's (naked) with a tub of peanut butter and an apple stuffed in my mouth, waiting."

"Nice," I shuddered at the thought, "get the brews on Fatty and tell me what's been going on. What do you know of the contract? Any chance of me getting onto your team when the change over happens?"

Liam and I spoke for about ten minutes. One minute about work and anything related, and the next nine, women and partying. As always, I got an update on his love life and how his kids were doing and I was shown the latest pictures of them. James and Stewart were growing fast, and Liam adored them.

Sean banged at the door and stuck his head in. "Luke, everyone's wanted outside mate."

"Yeah, no worries, are we off then? I'll just finish this brew."

"No, we're not moving off Luke, but everyone is wanted outside by Den. Dramas mate."

My eyebrows met when Sean said those words. Immediately, I started to think back on what I could've done or, what I hadn't done that maybe I should have.

"Eh, what have I done?"

"It's the whole team mate, not just you. Some Yank Major is outside with a couple of his blokes, telling Den to get us all together."

Still, nothing registered. I looked at Liam as I gave him his cup back, "Right mate, I'd better go and see what they want then. I'll be back in a bit buddy."

I began to wonder if we were getting a bollocking from some new FOB Commander because we didn't follow his new protocol when we arrived or something similar.

I followed Sean out into the sun light and to the area where the rest of the team had assembled. They all stood in a semi circle around the American officer, who was speaking with Den about something. His other two men stood slightly back, with pistols in drop holsters on their legs, looking nervous as though it was going to be a re-enactment of the 'OK Corral'.

As I got there, I nudged into the group and whispered to Pete, "What's going on mate? What we done?"

He leaned in closer, keeping an eye on the exchange between the Major and Den, "We're in the shit mate as far as I know. That shooting that happened on the way here, it's been blown outta proportion and now it's all over the fucking news."

"Eh, are you serious?" I was taken aback by what Pete had said because to me, the whole incident had been yet another dick head who thought he had special permission to approach PSD teams on the road.

"Okay gentlemen," the Major turned to face us, "I need you to come with me now. The incident on your way here today has escalated to the higher echelons and has already been sent out through the media." He paused for a moment expecting some sort of reaction from us. The indifferent silence prompted him to continue. "The Peshmerga and Iraqi Police are after your blood and already, I've had phone calls from local government officials demanding that I hand you over to Iraqi authorities. I'm not willing to do that at this time." He made his last statement sound as though he was doing us a big favour, "So, if you will follow me, we will escort you into the compound next door, where we can keep you in protective custody."

The team was starting to grumble, "Why can't we just wait here then?"

"Because my men are based in the compound next door, and that's where all our administration is carried out. It would make it a lot easier for us to deal with this from there."

"Okay then, I see your point," Den said to the Major then turned to us, "Right lads, head to the vehicles and we'll follow the Major."

"Sorry sir, but you must come as you are. You are not to return to your vehicles and your vehicles must remain where they are. We will escort you in our vehicles." He had now taken on a tone of authority. "You must come as you are now."

I looked about at the faces of the others. Only a few of us still had our body armour and assault vests with side arms. I began to feel vulnerable and naked.

"Nah lads, let's get our kit on." I said shaking my head.

"Sir, I've already made this clear," The Major was now pointing in my direction, speaking directly to me personally. "You are *not* to return to your vehicle, you must come as you are, *now.*"

I saw a faint smudge of red mist descend in front of my eyes, "Fucking bollocks. We will go to our trucks, collect our weapons and every scrap of ammo we have and then, we will walk to your compound. We don't need you to escort us and we won't go defenceless." By now I had stared him down and my voice had risen to the volume that best made my point, "You have already said that you 'are not willing to hand us over *at this time*', so when you get the order from your bosses, you gonna feed us to the fucking wolves? Like fuck you will. As soon as you do get that order, I suggest you get the fuck outta your building 'cause I'll not be handed over to them cunts so that they can saw my head off on the internet or bang me up in a prison cell for the rest of my life. We're taking our weapons with us."

The Major was dumb struck for a second and then tried to recover, "But . . . but I can't allow . . ."

"Allow fuck all mate, but we are coming over ready for a scrap and you and your young gun slingers here won't stop us." I turned towards our vehicles and we collected our weapons.

We patrolled across the short stretch of open ground that led to the Majors small compound with our heads up, looking defiant. We carried our weapons, held in to the shoulder and ready to fire, in case anybody got brave enough to take us on.

As we walked, I looked about. Peshmerga and police had gathered at a distance and stood watching us. All were armed and I felt myself wanting to take them on. I wanted to goad them into firing at us. My blood was up and I was in serious need of a fight. I felt confident too that we would win.

Once into the soldier's compound, we were led into a room that was what appeared to be their games room. A pool table took up most of the space in the centre, with couches and chairs at the far end and to our delight, a kettle and brew kit was close by the door. Our first priority was to test the room and know our surroundings.

The walls felt like thick reinforced concrete, with the only windows at around twelve feet from the floor. They were small and narrow, so they weren't a possible route of escape from the start. A door at the far end of the room led up a short flight of stairs and ended with an iron gate set into the wall, chained and padlocked, preventing us from using that as an escape route also. I eyed the lock and the hinges, it was solid and we had no heavy duty bolt cutters. Locks don't fly off when you shoot them with one bullet like they do in the movies.

I walked back into the room and it was obvious, we were already in a cell. The only way in or out, was through the door we entered from. Blind us with kettles, pool tables and Monopoly board games all you want, a cell is a fucking cell. If it came to it and we wanted to leave, unless the Americans allowed us, we would have to fight them too.

I peered around the door to check for guards, there was. A young soldier, no older than twenty years old, stood at the bottom of a short corridor holding his M16 rifle. From what I could see, he had another two, maybe three magazines for his weapon attached to his belt kit and he wore no body armour or helmet.

I turned and looked into our play room.

Fifteen men stood or sat, wearing body armour and ops vests full of ammunition. We all carried either M4 assault rifles or the belt fed SAW's. Everyone had a side arm and we all had a grab bag full of extra ammunition. We had enough fire power, in my eyes, to take on the whole of the Peshmerga in the area. We were better trained, experienced, equipped and most of all, Chubbs' wedding was in just a couple of weeks and I didn't want to miss it.

The kettle was already boiling as we gave Den our assessments of the situation and immediate area. He needed to have a clear picture in his head of our surroundings, so that he could formulate his plans and alternatives.

"We've still got our vehicles Den, so if it looks bad, then at least we can make a run for it. Everyone has locked their vehicles down and kept the keys. Unless the Americans disable them, then they're an option."

"Yeah, good, at least we still have them. We could always swipe the American vehicles too failing that."

Until it got worse, we just decided to sit it out. The Major came in regularly to give us updates and to see to our needs. Everyone had had to go to the toilet at least three times each in the first couple of hours. The Americans must've thought we were ill, but what we were really doing was conducting recce's (recognisance) on the interior of the building. Den even got himself invited up to their Op's Room to speak with the Major, all the time, eying their set up and manpower.

We came to the conclusion that there were roughly twenty soldiers in the building. We had no intention of fighting them, they were still; in theory, on our side. But it is always handy to know your surroundings.

We could've turned the building into a mini fortress and defended it if we needed to. With the amount of weaponry we had; both our own and the Americans' supplies, we could've planted a flag on to the roof of the building and declared that little patch of Iraq as part of the British Commonwealth. The walls and windows were designed to last, they were strong and there were very few entry points to defend.

Guy and Omar found a Risk game board. That was it, for the next twenty four hours, we sat arguing and trying to dominate the world with our dice and little figures. Friendships were formed and destroyed during them endless hours of Risk. At one point, Pete threw his chair back and tossed the board and its contents into the air.

"Fucking stupid bollocks game, Omar you're a bastard. There's no way that your two battalions can beat mine. I had twenty on there and you whittled me down to three. Have you set the fucking dice or summat?" Pete didn't want to play anymore.

Guy called after him as he stormed off, "How about Monopoly then?"

"Shove it up your arse."

Sean added, "Cluedo?"

For three days we sat in that room, eating doughnuts and drinking coffee and tea until it came out of our ears. Liam came in from time to time to let us know the latest news he had heard, and to bring us in whatever we needed. He found the whole thing hilarious, as always.

"Luke, you know me mate, if they try to hang you out to dry, then I'm with you. I'll not let them fuckers take a friend of mine and I'll fight through with you if need be. The rest of my team are up for it too. I've already spoken to Jules, and he's told me to tell you, that if the shit hits the fan, he will rock up with our vehicles and help out."

Our strength had just doubled. I had known from the start that Liam would be onboard, even just for the sake of a good scrap, but I would never have asked him to get involved. Deep down, I knew I wouldn't have had to. Jules was his TL and a great guy of the same making as Liam. Our team and there's together could now conquer the Middle East, never mind Suli.

"What about our vehicles Liam, have the Americans tampered with them?"

"No mate, we've been stagging on them around the clock on the sly, keeping our eye on them."

Liam, as always, had proved to be the best friend I could need or want. Not only did we have him and his team to support us, they had also taken on a proactive role and seen to it that our vehicles were safe. If things went bad, then their team would mount up in their vehicles as well as ours and move to our location.

The American soldiers had even let their guard down and become more approachable toward us. They had grown a new found respect for us from what I could gather, and one or two even mentioned about fighting along with us. I couldn't help but laugh, we were turning into our very own mix-match army. I was wondering how many more days it would take before we had an Air Force and Navy. Then, we could establish our own government.

My family had heard virtually nothing from me. Our phones didn't work in that area and access to the internet had been stopped. In the first couple of hours, the soldiers hadn't seen the harm in allowing us to use their connection until they realised that we were sending out our own sit-reps to our HQ. The Americans wanted a media blackout from our end.

We wanted people to be aware that we were there and what had happened and that way, we couldn't just disappear.

I had managed to get a short email off, vaguely explaining that we were in the shit, and that the Americans may even try to hand us over. At least my girlfriend would know why she hadn't heard from me for a while.

On the fifth day, enough was enough. We told the Americans to either release us, or we would force a break out, back to Kirkuk. They tried to puff out their chests to say 'you aint going nowhere', but it didn't work because we had a much bigger chest.

In the end, it was arranged that we would mount up and head back to Kirkuk during the very early hours of the next morning. We made our plans and got some rest. I had visions of check points being extra defended and ready for us.

It was still dark when we pushed out. No one used lights, not even head lamps on the vehicles. Liam's team were up and ready to act as a QRF, should we need any back up. We all shook hands and they wished us luck. Liam gave me a huge bear hug, and even through his big daft bravado, I could feel the tension and knew that he was worried for us.

"Don't let them bastards take you alive Luke. And make sure you take loads of them with you first."

"Cheers buddy, a simple 'good luck and stay safe' would've been suffice but you had to go into the details." I was smiling as I said it, but we both knew that Liam was right, and I had already come to the same conclusions myself. There was no way in hell I was going to be held captive and auctioned off to a terrorist cell to end up on the internet, begging for my life.

Our plan was to head west from Suli, as quickly as possible, with the lead gun truck smashing its way through any check points or road blocks that tried to stop us. Extra ammunition and medical kit had been given to us from Liam's team and it was all placed in easy to reach areas around the vehicles. Everybody was pumped full of adrenalin, ready for the possible fight ahead.

Once we reached the western edge of Chamchamal, we would be met by two support helicopters from the Kirkuk Airbase. They would then escort us in the rest of the way. There, we now had our own Air Force; we just needed the Navy now. Once in Kirkuk, ground call signs would clear us a path through the city, giving us a clear run to the base.

A good plan and it all went perfect.

When we reached the first check points on the outskirts of Suli, the guards were literally caught sleeping and all they could do was look on, slack jawed, as we thundered through their positions. None of them even attempted to stop us, and luckily for them, no one was foolish enough to reach for a weapon. We wouldn't have hesitated.

It was a similar story for the whole route back to base. We reached Kirkuk, having met up with our air support and we raced through the city with sirens blazing, mainly to piss people off and rub their faces in the fact that we were back and unscathed.

Safe, we closed in on our compound and parked up the vehicles. Fifi stood waiting, "Like the retreat from Stalingrad there lads. Good to see you back." He said shaking our hands.

"Yeah, but they didn't have gun trucks in Stalingrad."

"Fair one, everyone needs to get into the office for a hot debrief, there's a shit load of reports and stuff that need to be sorted out and Baghdad have been on my case all fucking through this, wanting info that I didn't have."

We piled into the office and a huge sigh of relief was heard from all around. None of us realised it, but we all must've been holding our breath since the minute we left Suli. We couldn't believe that we had made it through without a single shot being fired.

Fifi gave us a heads up on what had been going on. The story had been in the papers of all major countries, and even some reported that we had killed a dozen people, all women and kids of course.

The lads were furious.

"Fucking lying bastards," we sang out in chorus.

During our debriefing, it was unanimously agreed that Suli should be avoided for the foreseeable future and the dust be allowed to settle on the matter.

As Den sat explaining what needed to be done, the office door opened. In walked the colonel, clutching a piece of paper. He kept his face pointed to the floor as he crossed the room, avoiding eye contact with any of us and he approached Den, seated on the corner of a table.

Den looked up just as the colonel handed him the piece of paper, and without a single word, he turned and headed for the door. As he passed me, I noticed a shitty wry little smile on his face.

Pete also noticed and before the colonel could reach the door, he asked loudly, "Let me guess, a fucking Suli run?"

The colonel didn't say a word or look back as he left the room, but when we turned to look at Den, the expression on his face told us that Pete was right.

Den let the paper drop to the floor as we looked on in silence.

"Fucking prick," Den hoarsely whispered, staring down at the floor as he shook his head.

THE END OF AN ERA AND THE KIRKUK BAD BOYS

<hr>

The Suli mission request from the colonel was dismissed out of hand. There was no real reason why he had wanted to go there. He was just being his usual self. Den pretty much told him to shove the mission up his arse and no more consideration was given to it. In fact, not much consideration was given to any missions for the next week.

Debriefs were held, questions asked and reports were filed for reports. The Suli incident had put an enormous amount of pressure on the Coalition in Iraq. Not that the incident in itself was to blame, but it was the proverbial straw on the camel's back.

Since the end of the war in 2003, many companies had been considered unaccountable for their actions. Many people, on both sides had been killed and the number had continued to rise each year. By 2007, the Western governments, as well as the eyes of the world, were hoping to have seen a difference being made in Iraq since the invasion, for the better. But from where they were seated, all they could see was chaos and some blamed the foreign military occupation and the Private Security Companies.

Since the shoot out in Baghdad that had left seventeen Iraqis dead, as well as many other incidents, security companies were having pressure put on them from all angles to be held accountable for their actions. This led to companies becoming scared of reacting to incidents and threats, causing more confusion on the ground as to what they could or couldn't do.

Every member of our team needed to write a lengthy report on what he had seen and done during the shooting of the taxi. It was becoming bigger than 'Ben Hur', 'Gladiator' and 'Gone with the Wind' all rolled in to one.

Once the reports were collated, we then had to be interviewed by the Special Investigation Units. When it was my turn to be called forward, I went up to the office and sat in a small room with two Military Police and what I can only assume, must've been a member of the CIA.

I've always hated Military Police. Whether American or British, they were all the same to me, jumped up arseholes on a constant power trip, and they would stitch you up at the first opportunity.

The two MP's stood either side of the civilian clothed man, wearing sun glasses with their arms folded across their chests, trying to look hard as nails. In my book, wearing sun glasses in the dark or indoors doesn't make you look tough, just stupid. But obviously, no one had told these two bad arses.

They stood staring at me from behind their dark glasses, trying to show no emotion on their faces, as though I was supposed to be intimidated by their 'Terminator' style efforts of an appearance.

I gave a slight shake of my head and chuckled. They didn't seem to react, but I could feel their stares intensify on me. The civilian man seemed to be much more down to earth, and I got the feeling that he knew I wasn't impressed with his two companions.

This is where I needed to be on my guard. The two would be 'Terminators' were clearly MP's and from the start, I knew where I stood with them. They had shown their hand just by their appearance and body language and I could deal with them. They wanted me to be intimidated and scared of them. But the civilian guy, who appeared hospitable enough and more in touch with reality, hadn't yet given me any inclination of how he intended to conduct the interview.

He cracked on with the questioning and it was all very pleasant stuff. He asked me about times, dates, routes and even what the weather was like on that day. I answered everything truthfully and as accurately as I could. If I didn't know the answer to one of his questions, I would say, "I don't know," and the interview would carry on from there.

He knew what I would answer anyway, because he had a copy of my statement in his hand and he read through it, and flicked back and forth during the questioning. I was beginning to think that maybe it was just a routine interview that needed to be conducted as part of the paper chase, until we got to the part about the shooting.

"Okay Luke, tell me about the taxi, how many people did you see in it?"

"One," I was adamant about the loan driver.

At first, I thought he was going to move onto the next question.

Then, one of the MP's barked at me, "Then why are there numerous reports from eye witnesses stating that there were multiple casualties from within the vehicle?" He spoke in a strong southern American accent and he pronounced the word vehicle as, 'Ve-hicle'.

I looked at him, "Dunno mate, maybe it's because they're full of shit and want a big hand out from your government as compensation?"

He stepped forward and unfolded his arms, leaning closer, as if expecting me to squirm in my seat, "Well, what if we think that it's you who is lying? If you don't cooperate, we can have you thrown off this base."

"Crack on pal, because I'm going home in less than a week anyway." I turned to the civilian who sat watching quietly. "Look mate, you've got the report in your hand and you know what my answers will be to the questions. If you wanna play 'good cop, bad cop' then you can crack on. I'll even play along if you want, but my report or story isn't gonna change. I'll answer all your questions truthfully and to the best of my knowledge. I've nothing to hide and I think your guy here," I nodded in the 'Terminator's' direction, "has watched a few too many movies." The MP scowled at me from behind his sun glasses.

"He just wants to make sure you answer truthfully Luke," Answered the civilian in a mild manner. "Okay then, let's get on with the interview."

We sat for another half an hour or so, with him asking the questions and me giving the answers. At the end, he shook my hand and I was free to leave. As I walked out I caught the stare of the hard arse MP who had done the gobbing off.

"See you later Robo-Cop." I said as I moved to the door.

He stiffened and gave a mechanical nod in my direction, and I swear I saw the civilian smile.

The next day, we went into another debriefing. This time involving the clients as well as the FOB Intelligence Cell Liaison Officer who happened to be an officer from 1 Para, on attachment to the American Army.

I didn't bother to try and speak to him. Even though I was an ex member of 1 Para, I didn't recognise him from my time in the army and I was in no mood for chit chat with him at that point. I sat and listened to the debriefing and so did he. Everything that was written in the reports from the team members was read out. Maps were hung on the wall and diagrams drawn to show where we were and who did what.

The 1 Para officer listened and took notes intently and was fully aware of the events of that day, which would excuse my confusion and anger on our next meeting.

I had just a few days to do and then that was me finished with the team and the company. I was hoping to go home and after a few weeks, I would be called back to work for the next bunch to take over, on the same contract. Just in case things didn't work out as planned though, I had been in touch with a couple of other companies, and one of them was based in the city of Erbil. They were ramping up on a new contract and so I got in touch. Immediately, they showed an interest in me, so that was an option for me to cross deck.

In Kirkuk, we began the process of handing in our kit and tying up our loose ends before the end of our contract. I couldn't wait to be out of there. The possible contract based in Erbil was even looking more attractive than coming back to Kirkuk with the takeover company. I'd had a belly full of living on a FOB. Even though we had the best facilities, accommodation and kit, it was a constant pain in the arse dealing with the inflexibility and silly protocols of the American Army.

On top of that, I'd had enough of the likes of the colonel, and clients like Joe. Every day was a battle of wits, trying to aim off or counter their stupidity. I needed the work and I needed the money, but I was wondering if maybe it was time for a change of scenery and contract type. The Erbil job sounded like it offered something similar to my first contract, where we were completely independent from coalition forces and the bases.

I would wait and see what came my way first. The current contract offered longevity and job security, with an annual salary. All my needs would be taken care of if I went to work for the company that was about to take over, but I wasn't sure if I wanted to continue with the strict military style of PSD on an American Airbase, something that I had been a part of for the last couple of years.

Cach, Rab, Toad and I were to leave on the same day. The rest of the team organised a leaving party for us in the form of a barbeque. Unlike when Brian and Chubbs had left, I decided not to drink too much the night before my flight and end up waking late the next morning, covered in my own piss, with no time to shower and dress properly before my flight.

Toad followed the path of Chubbs and Brian though. Late, he arrived at the car park in the morning by the office, and he too stank of piss and stale booze. He didn't seem to mind though.

The team drove us to the air field and waved us off as we boarded our flight to Kuwait. I was sad to say goodbye to the gang, and it really did feel like the end of an era to me. We had been a close team and everyone on it had been strong members and characters. It was unlikely I would find a bunch of guys of the same calibre in any other job I did. But still, all good things must come to an end.

The political environment was also changing. PSD teams were no longer free to act as they saw best in the protection of their clients and themselves. Even going by the 'Rules for the Use of Force' that was laid down by the coalition forces, the game had changed. Every round fired needed to be accounted for, every incident reported and scrutinised, it was becoming harder and harder for security teams to operate in Iraq, especially as high profile.

I received my final pay from the company, it was short. A lot short in fact. Immediately I got onto them, demanding to know why I had only been paid a third of what I was expecting. Their reply was that, I was contracted to work a twelve week on and four week off rotation and during the last couple of years, I had done one or two short stints in country.

By short stints they meant, I had been sent on leave a couple of weeks before the twelve week mark on one or two occasions. And as a result, they deducted the money from my final pay. They had gone through my records and realised that, in their eyes, I owed them four week's worth of my salary.

I argued the toss by explaining that, it was never me that decided on when my leave dates were and that it was driven by the administration. They decided when I went home and came back. But they dug their heels in. Knowing they were thousands of miles away in Baghdad and out of harm's way, the management and administration staff decided to fuck us over one last time to gain a feather in their cap for saving the company some money.

What they didn't realise though, was that there were still teams to come in from the outer base locations of the country. Most had to travel via Baghdad on the final close down, to hand in kit and equipment before they finished their contract. So when their queries of why they had been paid short that month were met with emails telling them to basically, 'put up and shut up', they could be forgiven for being slightly upset towards the company office staff.

As these teams approached the Baghdad Company HQ, many of the administration and management staff suddenly realised that they had been gobbing off at people who were still in country, and conveniently made themselves scarce. Some thought that their positions would protect them, and stayed around to brave it out when the teams came in.

When you've been at the business end of a contract for a while, by 'business end' I mean the guys on the ground who work their socks off and take the risks, losing friends along the way, while the soft and podgy administration staff sit in luxury and their biggest danger is falling off a chair, you're bound to be upset at being ripped off with what you're owed.

So when one or two people were throat gripped, and from the story I was told, flung across the office with a bloody nose, they got the least of what they deserved. Surprisingly, the teams that went to Baghdad before flying home were all paid in full and, in cash.

I could just imagine a team member, fresh from the ground, forcing a tubby office worker to open the safe and pay up.

The wedding was a great do, and many of the lads attended, including members of the Tikrit team. Chubbs even said thank you to George Bush in his groom's speech for providing us all with a good living. Pink Champagne was handed out like it was going out of fashion and by the end of the night I was a drunken mess.

By now, the contract was firmly in the hands of another company, and even though I had been assured that I would hear something soon, I still hadn't.

The company from Erbil were asking me for deployment dates and so I needed to check in with my potential new employers on my old contract to see what was going on. I sent a few emails, but heard nothing in reply. Eventually, Martin sent me the number I needed to get in touch with the London office and hopefully get some answers.

I called them, explaining who I was and that I had gone through the interview process in Kirkuk with a member of their management.

"Unfortunately, we cannot employ you. Sorry, but it says on your record that you are not to be invited back to work for our company."

I was dumbstruck and I couldn't understand why they wouldn't take me on. I had a clean criminal record, which is something that particular company insisted on, and I had already been cleared by the American Military to work on a U.S government contract; the same contract I was supposed to be going back on to.

"Well, can you explain why? I was working on this contract anyway and I've already gone through all the compliancy that is needed."

"Sorry, but we can't give the exact reason," the female voice at the other end of the phone answered, "it just says that you are not to be re-employed onto the USACE contract, and that it's a request from the client."

The penny dropped, "Ah you mean the colonel. Well to be honest love, any company that takes the advice and recommendations of a man who couldn't find his dick with both hands and could fuck up a microwave meal, isn't worth working for anyway." I slammed the phone down.

I was fuming. The colonel had managed to stitch me up one final time.

I sent out emails to a few of the lads and soon, I discovered that I wasn't the only one to get shafted. Den and Brian had been black listed too. They had both always stood up to the colonel and obviously, he had his grudges with them.

Me however, as a team member, I rarely had any direct contact with him other than the odd passing in the office. I had never had a direct confrontation with him personally. I wondered whether it could've been my conduct in the interview.

Either way I thought, "Fuck em."

Not long later, Pete got in touch with me. He told me that he was working for the new company in Kirkuk and that the Op's Manager there couldn't believe that he had managed to get re-employed.

"Ah, so you're one of the Kirkuk bad boys are you?"

Pete had found the name hilarious and made a point of telling everyone that he could get hold of about it.

We had become infamous.

THE FOREIGN LEGION OF PSD

I returned to Iraq to begin my new contract. I had been brought in as a Team Leader. I was picked up at the airport and taken from Erbil to Suli in a soft skin, non armoured SUV. As far as the company were concerned, there was no danger in the north and our teams wouldn't be operating in any high level threat areas. I wasn't happy because, after all, it was still Iraq.

The project was a huge oil and gas contract, based mainly in the southern area of Chamchamal near a town named Kormor, east from Tuz. To me, just because there was a ridge line of mountains between the oil and gas fields we would be working in and Tuz, it didn't mean they couldn't get at us. Mountains can be crossed on foot, or driven along the roads and tracks. But still, I thought I would see how the job panned out. Surely the head shed would know what they're doing.

When I arrived in Suli, I soon realised that the teams were based in a hotel on the outskirts of the city, and commuting daily to and from Kormor. Very little existed in the way of alternative routes to get to the oil fields and it was apparent, at least to me, from the beginning that by default, we couldn't help but set patterns.

I always remember what the instructor said to us on the first day of my Close Protection course. "Trust no one, suspect everyone, and avoid setting patterns."

The clients needed to be working everyday to get the project up and running and a ridiculous amount of money was expected to be made off it. So right away, the pressure was on us to make sure that the clients could do their jobs. This meant setting out early every morning and returning late in the evening, running the same routes there and back.

It was promised to be a temporary measure and a new camp was being built in the oil fields themselves, but construction had only just begun and so for the immediate future, we would be driving back and forth every day on the three hour journey; a journey that would suck the will to live from me and anyone else who travelled it after a while.

I knocked at the door of what I had been told was the company Op's Room on the top floor of the hotel. A big guy who was introduced to me as the Op's Manager stuck out his hand.

"Hi mate, it's good to have you onboard. Everything is up in the air at the moment because the company have gone from just a couple of teams, to about thirty, virtually overnight, but we will get you squared away and briefed up as best we can."

I reported to the Quarter Master to be issued my kit. He answered the door and first of all, handed me a key as though I was supposed to automatically know what it was for.

"It's for the hotel room you'll be staying in." He told me after a while of me studying it.

I decided to go and drop my baggage off in my room first, and then return to collect the equipment I would be issued. Being the TL, I expected it to be quite a lot so I needed my hands free.

I returned five minutes later to the stores and what I was handed, I assumed was a joke. In my arms, my bundle of kit consisted of an AK47, six magazines and a mobile phone with no credit.

"Where's the rest of it?" I had a smile on my face thinking it was some kind of wind up.

The Quarter Master looked at me, straight faced, "Um, that's it at the moment. We haven't got anything else to give you."

I looked at my minute pile of kit, "Nah, you're winding me up aren't you?" To me, it was clearly the trick they liked to play on the new guys. It had to be.

"Honestly, that's all we have at the moment. We are waiting for more kit to come in."

I walked away with my hands nowhere near as full as what I had expected them to be. If I had a third hand, I would've been scratching my head in wonder as I studied my kit. I dumped the small bundle in my hotel room then, I stood for a few minutes, staring at the equipment before making my way back to the Op's Room.

I knocked at the door.

"What's the score with the kit? I've only been given an AK and a phone."

The Op's Manager looked up from his desk and sighed, he had obviously been expecting me to come back with questions.

"Sorry mate, but it's all we've got at the moment."

That phrase seemed to be part of the management 'welcome onboard' spiel.

"So where's my pistol, my vehicles, my radios, my tracker, actually, where's my team?"

"Well you're gonna be starting up a new team. They've not been recruited yet, but if you know anyone that needs work, then you can bring them in yourself and start putting it together. As for vehicles and all the rest, then there's none to give you yet. You're call sign will be Lima Two though."

I felt like saying there and then, "Oh, Lima Two, that's okay then. I don't need anything else as long as I have my call sign, happy days."

Instead I opted to return to my room and have a think. I came to the conclusion that I was being paid for nothing. I wasn't going to go and make a point of the fact though.

I spent the next two weeks mincing about the hotel doing my own thing. Nobody seemed to notice that I was just a loose wheel and so, I kept out of the way. Spike, who I had worked with on my first contract was there also and as always, constantly complained about how shit and cowboy it was. I had to agree with him.

It soon became apparent that the left hand didn't know what the right hand was doing. People could've just walked in off the street and claimed to have been recruited by the company and that's all it would've taken to get on. It worked in my favour though, because I was my own boss and slowly but surely, I was able to recruit my own men and gather my own kit. There was no pressure on me to get the job started. So at least I wouldn't be going off half cocked.

By now, I had managed to scrounge together my team radios and I'd secured a pistol for myself and plenty of ammunition. I had even been waiting in the car park on the day that I knew a fleet of new vehicles would be arriving. Because we had no Fleet Manager to take care of the vehicles, and the Quarter Master had left it to his Iraqi assistant to organise and oversee, I helped myself to the two best SUVs that arrived.

I just told the assistant that two of the vehicles were to be given straight to me by order of the head shed and without any question whatsoever, he let me take them without even having to sign for them. I could've driven them to the nearest garage and sold them for fifteen grand each and no one would've known, but I wasn't so bold at that stage. Instead, I parked them out of the way and locked them up for the time being, so that no one else could claim them.

The company was a mixed bag of nationalities. There were British, Americans, Canadians, Kiwis and Australians, French, South African, Dutch, South American and even Swedes. I had never come across anyone from Sweden working on the circuit before. But this company had a dozen of them, apparently all ex Special Forces. I didn't know that Sweden had Special Forces and for the life of me, I couldn't understand why they needed them. What would they be used for? The Swedes that we had with us, looked like they were no older than early teens.

Two of the main characters, Igor and Mica were from Eastern Europe. One was a Serb and the other, a Croat. Both were best friends and had been for many years. But they had fought against each other in Bosnia.

Mica had been a sniper in the Serb army during the siege of Srebanitsa and Igor had been running around in the city, dodging his bullets as they pinged around him. Both were well known for having their fingers in a lot of pies, both on the circuit and locally, so I decided to get friendly with them in order to help my logistics problems.

By becoming friendly with men from the Balkans, a by-product was that on a few occasions I would be staggering back to my room in the early hours to collapse on my bed with the room spinning, after spending all night drinking Slivovitz and vodka with them. Nevertheless, it was worth the headaches because before long, I had the weapons I needed and any other equipment I was short of, all paid for by the company.

I had collected a complete set of kit for myself and my team, including weapons, vehicles, and communications and medical kit. All I needed now was a team. Every team consisted of five Iraqis and an ex-pat as the TL.

I set about finding good, trained Iraqi guys to make up my team and I had a few in mind from my old days in Erbil who had worked with me a couple of years earlier. I brought in Ahmed, who had been my driver on my first contract and he would be my driver again. He lived in Kirkuk, just an hour or so drive away from Suli, so I allowed him to commute daily or whenever it suited him. That way, he would never need to go on leave unless he specifically requested it and so, he would be paid for every day of the month and pretty much working a normal, nine to five.

After a week of training, my team was ready to start the job they had been recruited for, but the clients hadn't come in yet, so there was nothing for them to do other than sit around. Instead, I sent them home to be on standby, and full pay, ready to come in when I called them. I knew that no one would notice because of the system being in such turmoil.

In the meantime, I got on with doing not much at all. Each day I would train in the gym and spend the evening, either drinking Slivovitz or watching cable TV in my room. I had gotten what I needed from the Eastern Europeans, so to save my liver; I made sure that the booze sessions were less frequent.

"Luke, you know Kirkuk pretty well don't you?" A big Kiwi came and asked me one day.

"Yeah, I know it like the back of my hand actually. Why?"

"We need to go to the airbase there and meet with their Int Cell. While we're there, we'll see what mapping and med kit we can scrounge."

I was actually looking forward to the prospect of getting out and doing something other than bumming around the hotel.

"Righto, when we going?"

"Tonight mate," he said while fumbling with a map of Kirkuk. The idea of running around Kirkuk in the dark didn't really appeal to me. "We'll be alright mate; we're going in armoured vehicles."

To me, it didn't matter whether they were armoured or not. I'd seen what can happen when you're hit with an IED.

I was expecting there to be some sort of plan to the mission, but I was hugely mistaken. The only plan was that, me the Kiwi, a Swede and an Australian would travel in two vehicles through Kirkuk, and that's where the plan ended.

"What route we taking?" I asked, hoping for a logical answer.

"You know," shrugged the big Kiwi, "we'll go direct."

"Yes but, once we get into the city, which route will we take? What will be our alternative route? What are the actions on break down, check points, IEDs, casualties, what if we are separated or roads are blocked and the rest of it?"

The other three looked at me as though I was mad. What I had asked was basic stuff. They are things you need to know if you're going to be travelling even the least hostile of routes. But going through Kirkuk, even though nothing was likely to happen, we still needed to be on the same song sheet.

No one had practiced SOP's or rehearsed for any possible dramas. I hadn't yet seen the vehicles we were to take, or knew what kit they had in them in the way of break down kit, medical kit or even communications.

I quickly grabbed my map book and before anyone could recover from my crazy little outburst of professional concern, I launched into a brief set of orders. I went over the route that I recommended and the alternatives, pointing out any vulnerable points in our path. Then I went into the SOP's of how we would move as a team in the vehicles, then the actions on and what if's of the task.

I was convinced that the Swede didn't have a clue what I was on about and he even looked at me in contempt for having rocked the boat. No one else seemed to care, but for my own piece of mind, I wanted to make sure they knew what to do. Up until that point, it had been a cowboy job, now it was slightly better organised, but we were still wearing spurs and big hats.

We drove to Kirkuk and it was dark by the time we had reached the outskirts. I had taken the lead, knowing that the others would probably get us lost and in trouble in no time. At least with me leading us in, I had control over events. We travelled through the city and over my old stomping ground. The last time I had travelled through there, I had been with a professional bunch and well equipped, now I was travelling by the seat of my pants, and in the dark.

The streets were eerie and quiet and we couldn't help but be noticed, even in the dark as the only two SUVs on the road, even though we tried to lower our profile by keeping a bit of distance between us. Still, we made it to the FOB.

Once in, we headed for the Intelligence Cell. It was a good job I had come along because nobody knew where it was, another great piece of preparation and planning. They must've been hoping for sign posts.

When we got into the correct compound, we were guided in by an American officer who looked at us as though we had come from another planet. We did look like a rag tag bunch. The Swede looked like a perfect candidate from a Hitler Youth poster, and I had to wonder whether or not he had permission from his mother to work in Iraq.

The Kiwi was big and had a rugged face and bent nose from years of playing rugby, and the Australian looked like someone from the movie, 'The Hills Have Eyes'. Bald headed with lob sided teeth and pointed ears, he was an oil painting from hell.

Me, well I looked like a tramp, having not shaved for nearly a month and wearing local style clothes. We looked like anything but a PSD.

In the briefing room, we grabbed a brew and waited for the Intelligence Officer to arrive. Ten minutes later, in walked the officer from 1 Para I had met on my previous contract on the FOB.

A typical British officer; tall, gangly and in a world of his own, he smiled, "Hi guys, hope you haven't been waiting long. I'll crack on with the intelligence brief then sort you out with what mapping I can."

We all closed in around a large map of the northern regions of Iraq that was taped to the wall. He began by telling us the military dispositions, including Coalition and Iraqi forces, and then followed with the ethnic breakdown of the area. From the outset, I realised that he didn't really know much about the ground, but he carried on with his waffle.

Cities like Kirkuk and Erbil are made up from Arab, Kurdish and Turkmen ethnicities and those groups are broken down again in to their religions and tribes. Sunni Muslim, Shia Muslim, Christian and I think there were even one or two groups who worshipped fire and peacocks. All the groups tended to settle into their own areas and keep to their own regions when it came to buying properties. The British officer was getting them all mixed up, and claiming Kurdish areas to be Arab and Turkmen to be Kurdish. I made a mental note to put the guys right at the end, but away from the officer to save him any embarrassment.

I was more than willing to screw the nut for him until he moved on to the Significant Actions, sig-acts. He began to tell us of events that had happened in the area over recent months in order for us to make our own risk assessment on the information he gave us.

"Yeah, be careful in this area guys," he said sweeping his hand across an area east of Kirkuk and speaking in a tone of voice that made him sound arrogant and all knowing, informing the new kids on the block about the do's and don'ts of the street. I looked up, my ears twitched and my eyes focused.

"Yeah fellas, just be careful in this area here," he continued, "they're not very impressed with Coalition forces at the moment and are pretty hostile toward us. It was only a few weeks ago that a team passed through here and killed a load of civilians, including women."

He was about to go on when I spoke, "You what? Say that again please." I had stepped a little closer and my eye brows were firmly knitted together.

He looked back at me, chewing a piece of gum, with one leg raised onto a stool looking as casual as he could. He looked at his hand and brought it across the map again, this time with hesitation in his voice, "Uh yeah, just last month, a high profile team drove through and shot some civvies."

"You waffling cunt." I snapped. Everyone in the room turned to look at me in shock horror, but before they could speak or lift their chins from the floor, I continued, "Obviously you don't recognise me behind the beard do you?" He looked confused and shaken. He tried to reply but I cut him off, "You know exactly what happened on that mission and you know that no one was killed. So why you gobbing off now saying there was?"

"I'm just going by the intelligence that came out from the reports." He was struggling for words now and he had removed his foot from the stool, dropping his arrogant, all knowing appearance.

"Well, I can't understand how you have such bullshit intelligence on it mate. I was on that team and I was here when, you," I pointed to him, "sat in on the debriefing and listened to the reports of what happened that day and why. And from what I remember, it was never mentioned once that a load of civvies were killed."

"You were in that team?" He was studying me, trying to recognise me.

"Yes, I was. And I remember very clearly that you were a part of the debriefing." I was fuming and I was almost growling my words. He had nothing else to come back with now and I could see him trying to think of a way to dig himself out of the waffle hole he was standing in. "Oh and you've got all your regions wrong too."

I received a slight nudge from my right, trying in vain to silence me, but I was on one.

"Obviously you're not much good as an Int Officer because you've got the north eastern part of Kirkuk as being Arab, when everyone worth his salt knows that it's Kurdish. And what you say is Turkmen, you'll probably find, if you ask about, that it's actually Arab."

I turned on my heel and stormed out of the room. I headed out the main door and walked toward the vehicles with steam coming from my ears.

What a wanker.

I wondered what would happen next after my little outburst. Would I be sacked? Would I be arrested by the MP's for threatening behaviour? Ten minutes later, I had my answer. The other three members of my team appeared in the door, walking towards me, I could see that they had their arms loaded with maps and aerial photos, beaming from ear to ear.

I was told that the British officer had made a sharp exit shortly after my rant and hadn't returned. The big Kiwi pulled me to one side, "Quite a temper on you haven't you Luke."

"It's not that, it's just that he's a waffle monkey, trying to give it the large one to us. Just makes me wonder how many others he's waffled that same shite to and they've swallowed it." I had calmed down a little by now, "On top of that, they were my team mates that he's dragging through the dirt with all that 'killing civvies' bollocks."

A few days later and my clients finally arrived. Their job was to travel to Kormor on a daily basis and begin preparing the well heads to be reopened and to start pumping oil and gas again. The wells had been closed twenty years earlier by Saddam Hussein. I'm unsure why he had closed them, but the reason I was told was that he was getting all the resources he needed from the southern part of the country, and didn't want to leave the Kurds with a bargaining chip in the north.

Another TL named Quintin would lead the second team on the project with me. With his strong Southern Irish accent and my north western English, our American English speaking Arab clients struggled to understand what either of us was saying. I found myself speaking in strange accents and pronouncing my words completely different than normal. I must've sounded like an Italian speaking in slow motion with a bucket on his head.

For the next few weeks, we were up and down from Kormor to Suli every day, and every day, I voiced my concerns about the pattern and routine that we were setting. None of my objections were ever given more than lip service. The only reason I cracked on was because we were promised that it would be a temporary measure until the accommodation and security base in Kormor was completed.

During a visit to the well heads one day, I left Quintin in charge to oversee the client security, while I went to see what stage the base was at. It was a mess. The perimeter walls were all over the place and the accommodation, plumbing and electrics all looked like they had been installed by a DIY nut who insists that he can do anything with his hands, and then fucks it all up.

It was to be expected though.

The company had contracted a local construction group to build the camp, rather than bringing in western workers. Naturally, being Iraqi, they cut as many corners as possible and worked at the speed of a stunned slug.

Deadlines and schedules mean nothing when speaking to an Iraqi, even when millions of dollars are riding on the job being completed on time. It didn't help that the Site Manager and Construction Chief Engineer were as bent and corrupt as a politician from a small African country. They didn't bother to hide the fact that they were skimming from the tops of the piles of money given to them to get the job done. Best of all, the Site Manager was an American and I've heard since, that the little weasel was arrested and charged with millions of dollars worth of corruption and fraud.

As I walked around the camp, I noticed that for every one person working, there was at least another six or seven stood watching him. Breaks were more frequent than working hours and the building of an accommodation camp to house five hundred people that should've taken roughly three months, ended up taking eighteen months. With constant rebuilding and planning, the construction alone ended up costing more than four times the original quote.

But as Chubbs would always say, "Buy shite, buy twice."

The clients, while setting up the well heads to begin pumping again, also needed to release the excess gases that had built up over the years and test the levels of gases to fluids and so on. How they did this, was by burning it off.

A flare pit was made at the back of each well head and the gases would be forced through the pipes and ignited.

"Each day we do this Luke," one of the clients informed me, "we are burning fifty thousand dollars from each well head."

The mini calculator in my head began doing the math and I had to ask if there was another way of releasing the excess, mainly one were the money wasn't burned and could line my pockets instead.

"Well, if you can organise a fleet of tankers to come and take it, then you could make a fortune from it on the black market." He told me.

I couldn't exactly see myself selling fuel at the side of the road in Kirkuk, so that idea was out of the window.

One night, back at the hotel as I lay on my bed watching TV, a huge bang rocked the whole building, causing the floor to shudder and the windows rattle.

At first, I thought that we had been targeted. I walked into the hotel corridor and the place was in panic. Obviously the Swedish and French guys had never been in an IED or rocket attack before. I could see bare arses running up and down in a flap. Some even carried weapons, as though they're going to fight Al Qaeda with their dicks hanging out.

There was no sign of damage and no smoke in the hotel, so I soon came to the conclusion that, we hadn't been bombed and that maybe it was somewhere close to the building. I quickly counted my clients and gathered them all into one room, instructing them to stay there and not to leave the room under any circumstances unless I specifically came to get them. They were shaken and frightened; just how I like them to be at times like that. They would've smeared themselves in Marmite and sung 'ten green bottles' had I told them to and they thought it would keep them safe.

Once they were secure, I reported to the Op's Room that all my clients were safe and accounted for. They had no further information on what had happened, so I went back to my room and continued to watch 'CSI Miami'. I wasn't going to get into a flap and start running around the hotel, semi naked with my body armour on, adding to the general confusion.

My clients were safe, and if we needed to evacuate, then the word would be given and I could grab them and escort them to another location with little fuss. In the meantime, I'd crack on with watching Horatio save the day.

As it turned out, the Palace Hotel further into the city had been hit with an SVBIED, Suicide Vehicle Born IED. The Palace was surrounded with high walls and military security and a car had driven right into the outer cordon and detonated, causing mass casualties. Even in Suli, it happens now and then.

Soon after, we moved to Kormor to live on the accommodation camp that had been semi-built. The security emplacements were a joke. The area was bisected by a road than ran straight through the middle of the site, splitting the well heads and the accommodation area. The local guards on the gate spent more time smoking and sitting in gaggles chatting, than they did actually checking vehicles and maintaining the security of the area.

We decided that the clients wouldn't move out of their rooms, even to go for a shower, unless we knew about it. I kept myself armed even during the night, sleeping with my weapons at the side of my bed. It was only when the operations staff and more teams began to arrive, that the security situation improved at all.

Brian had gotten onboard with the company and was sent down to Kormor to set up the base security. It was good to have him about, not only as a mate but, because he was more professional and switched on than most.

The guards were trained up and the defences of the site improved. Still, it was a ridiculous set up in the eyes of security and I was sure that a gang of army cadets could've stormed the position, overwhelming the Kurdish troops that were apparently defending it.

But we had very little in the way of choice to use them. A company that was all powerful with the Suli government and was pretty much owned by the Iraqi president's wife, insisted that we use local security forces provided by them to take care of the general defences of the area.

If we didn't comply, then they would close us down and throw us out of the country. Naturally, the company I was working for bowed down to the pressure, and the original plan of using Ghurkhas as the guard force was thrown out. The problem was though, when you've given in once without much of a fight to that sort of organization, they strong arm you even further.

Soon, the Iraqi company directors were demanding that our local PSD teams should be replaced by their security forces, and again, my company complied without a fight. The Iraqi head shed had clearly realised how much money there was to be made in a contract as big as the one that we were running and obviously, they wanted a much larger slice of the pie.

The main problem was though, what they were supplying us with in terms of manpower and equipment, could only be described as shit. The so called PSD were not even trained in basic military tactics, never mind our security procedures and SOP's. They were just Iraqi Policemen.

Their rank structure relied mainly on who was the biggest and could grow the best moustache. Their weapons were in shit state and best of all, they wore camouflaged uniform. Up until that point, we were trying to move away from the military appearance (some management even claimed that we were low profile, but we were anything but that, even before we took on the Iraqi Police bunch) then suddenly, we were given a group of untrained retards who all thought they were Rambo.

The first Iraqi Police team that was given to me looked like they had been sleeping rough for the previous month. They were a mess. Their commander, a young tall thickset man, approached me and peered down his nose at me as he spoke.

"I am Iraqi boss. I am Captain in Peshmerga." He informed me.

A Captain in the Peshmerga was roughly the equivalent of a ten year old school boy with a plastic gun in the UK.

"Okay," I smiled back at him, "I'm your Team Leader."

He seemed confused and then pulled a card from his pocket and informed me that he was in charge. He handed me the card and I burst in to fits of laughter.

The card informed me that he was the Arm Wrestling Champion for his unit, and by that, he believed that he was more qualified to lead the team.

I put him right with a polite, "Fuck off and get in your vehicle."

I had to let all my trained local PSD guys go, including Ahmed. It was a shame to get rid of them, because each one of them was experienced and reliable. Now I had to start from scratch, training my new team. However, this would prove to be a feat in itself.

They felt that they answered only to their Iraqi commanders and insisted on doing the opposite of what I told them. If I told them to stay in the vehicles, they got out. If I instructed them to keep their weapons out of site in the vehicles, they rolled down the windows and poked them out.

My hair was turning grey rapidly. Each week, the team that I had were replaced with a new bunch. The original plan was that we would be given the same guys working on a week on, week off rotation for continuity reasons. Otherwise, I would have to start from scratch every week with training them up.

Exactly what was supposed to happen, didn't.

I received complete strangers every Monday. The bullying Iraqi company didn't care though, they were being paid a fortune by our company to provide these men and in turn, they were paying the PSD teams a very small percentage of what they took from us, making themselves large profits in the process.

I walked into the office one morning ready to take the team and clients out, and the Project Manager, an ex officer in the British Army and complete oxygen thief, pointed at my pistol and proceeded to bollock me.

"You're supposed to be low profile you know, and weapons aren't to be on show." He wagged his finger in the direction of my hip and spoke in a tone of voice as though he was addressing a day one recruit.

"This is about as low profile as a circus driving through Baghdad." I waved my arm in the direction of my vehicles.

The five Iraqi Police guards, sat in their camouflaged uniforms looking back at us, their faces pressed up against the windows with their weapons clearly visible, grinning at us from within the bright white SUV. They stood out like a dog's dick.

"Your weapons are supposed to be out of sight though. That's what low profile is."

I looked down and shook my head, then looked back up to meet his gaze.

"You ever done low profile? And I don't mean this shite that we are doing here. I mean proper low profile." It was obvious that he hadn't. "Low profile is a completely different concept, and more than just wearing your body armour under your shirt and keeping your weapons covered up. For a start, the vehicles you use tend to look like any other vehicle you're likely to come across on the roads out here, not white SUVs with a bunch of cammed up retards in the back.

"Secondly, the tactics and SOP's are completely different. You go with the flow of the traffic, you make sure that you don't draw any attention to yourself; you dress like anyone else on the road or the street. Everything you do is kept on the covert side, whether it's comms or even the way you approach a check point. You make sure that if anyone looks in your direction, that they see nothing that would cause them to give a second glance. And that includes wearing a pair of big sun glasses that I saw you wearing just five minutes ago as you arrived, sat in the front seat of your big white SUV."

I looked at Brian who sat behind his desk with a big shit eating grin on his face.

"Just make sure you keep your weapon covered up Luke." He said to me as his way of getting the final word in as I walked over to my vehicles.

The Iraqi Police guys proved to be a complete pain in the arse. In the end, I turned to my civilian interpreter, Awat, who I had managed to keep hold of and told him, "Fuck it, they can do what they want because they clearly don't wanna play the game. If something happens, then it's down to you and me to take care of the clients. As far as I'm concerned, these half wits are just a pile of human sandbags to draw the enemy fire while we get the fuck outta dodge mate."

Awat grinned at this, "Roger that Luke. I'm a better PSD than them anyway and I've never even done this before."

Awat had lived in London for most of his life and still had a kebab shop there that he was making money from while he was in Iraq. Once a year, he returned to the UK for a month or two, and he planned to move back there one day with his wife and kids. He spoke perfect English and was keen as mustard to learn from me, so I took him under my wing and slowly but surely, brought him up to speed on the job. Within a month or two, he was probably the best Iraqi that had ever worked for me. He knew what I wanted done before I needed to tell him.

Kormor sits in a large bowl area to the east of Tuz. A couple of kilometres to the west of our base camp, a ridge line run from north to south with the town of Tuz just on the other side of it to the west. To the east of our position was open ground that led to another ridge line, roughly fifty kilometres away. In between these two ridge lines was open ground with the odd hill and ravine here and there. As the Site Security Manager, it was Brian's job to organise the defences and manning of the protection force.

He spent weeks travelling about the area, plotting positions and checking bearings, working out the best possible outer security perimeter for the base by using the ground and natural features to optimise an effective defence plan.

Once he was done, he drew it all up in a presentation pack to be sent to the Iraqi strong arm company who, insisted that they would provide the manpower. A list of equipment and numbers of men required to do the job was included in the presentation and it was their job then to give us the cost.

They dismissed the plan out of hand and instead, invited Brian and the Op's Manager to visit Suli airport and view the defences that had been set in place there by themselves and their military advisors. Their intent was to convince us that their set up would be the better option.

A brief word on defensive strategy: By no means would I consider myself to be a great General, or even close. However, I do know what is right and what, is a complete bag of bollocks.

When preparing a defensive line, the aim is to use the ground to its maximum potential. By this, you look for positions of vantage that overlook the approaches to your defences. You cover the dead ground that could be used as an unseen approach route or forming up point for enemy troops before they assault your position. You place your positions so that you naturally channel the enemy into your chosen killing area by utilizing the features on the ground, such as, hills, streams, marshy areas etc.

You ensure that you have mutual support and depth to your line, rather than just a single solid line of defence. That way, if the enemy did break through at any given point, they would be met by fire from further in-depth positions and counter attacks.

Advanced warning and observation posts should be placed out ahead of your defences. A system of resupply needs to be in place, communications set up, and the list goes on. All this should be done while using the manpower and available weapons to their optimum capacity.

Brian returned to Kormor shaking his head, "Ah Luke it was comical. They came up with a plan that a five year old must've thought up."

I listened slack jawed, as he revealed the Iraqi company plan to me:

They had given Brian and the Op's Manager a guided tour of the airport defences, hoping to convince him that his plan was no good. What Brian had seen, was a ring of Peshmerga soldiers placed at one hundred metre intervals around the entire airport complex and its runways. They sat in little guard boxes, like the ones you see at Buckingham Palace, facing outward into the open ground to the south or onto the main road north of the airport.

No observation or defensive positions had been placed onto the high ground to the south, or control points on the roads leading up to the airport. The defence had no depth, no mutual support and on top of that, to implement the plan in Kormor, Brian would need to have around one hundred times the amount of men down there than what he had requested. He would end up with an entire division of wannabe Rambo retards. As far as the Iraqis and they're advisors were concerned, they had a solid plan because it had been thought up by Peshmerga Generals.

The description that he gave me reminded me of my childhood, when I used to play with toy soldiers. I would line them up facing each other, and then shoot it out with no consideration to tactics and realism. That's pretty much the plan that the Kurds set into place for all their security instillations.

Brian, being the cool calm and collective objective thinker that he is, spent the rest of his time driving from one position to the next, kicking people to wake them up after they had got their heads down on guard duty and bollocking people for not manning the observation posts.

One of the positions was supposed to be a machinegun emplacement, overlooking the western dead ground that approached our site. Instead of a machinegun, Brian found what he described as a, "rusting blob of metal that had at one point, caught fire."

He went ape shit. The gun only had two hundred rounds; which would last just a few seconds on rapid fire, and when he test fired it, it shot three rounds then jammed continuously.

All his calls and requests to our head shed and the Iraqi company went unanswered. And when they finally did pay him some attention, he was told to make do with what he had and get on with it.

I wasn't surprised when a few weeks later, he handed in his resignation. He left and as far as I was concerned, our company became that little worse off for having lost him.

THE FEW BECOME FEWER

During one leave my brother, Martin, came to see me. We hadn't seen each other in a while, not since he had left the circuit six months earlier. He had decided that enough was enough and he fancied his hand at being a normal, nine to five kind of guy. He had a girlfriend and new born baby to think about and he didn't like the idea of being away from them constantly and risking being killed.

Soon though, he cracked and found himself yearning for, as well as the money, the life in Iraq. He missed the blokes, the banter and the adventure.

The life of a PSD isn't all action and none stop adrenalin rushes though, quite the contrary. It tends to be tedious and boring. Most missions go without a hitch, and it's only the odd time that you find yourself in a situation that causes your heart to race and your blood to pump through your veins.

A lot of the tasks we do tend to be driving from one location to the next and standing around, protecting the clients, while they go about their work. As PSD, we find ourselves wishing large chunks of our lives away, looking to the next leave and what we have planned for our time off. When I was based in Kirkuk, I was on a three month on and one month off rotation. Out of a year, that's nine months of my life that I would wish away.

So, Martin wanted to come back.

He had been working on the roads, digging holes, drinking tea and eating bacon sandwiches for the past six months. Some people are just born for certain things, and Martin wasn't a road worker. He had spent nine years in the Parachute Regiment with me and since leaving, he had worked the circuit in Baghdad.

To suddenly find himself getting up every morning, knowing full well that the highlight of his day would be reading the newspaper during his break, he realised that he didn't want to be doing it forever, and the sooner he got back to what he knew and did best, the better.

Like me, he had made very few friends in civilian life after leaving the army. He struggled with the mundane day to day goings on of catching up on the latest Soap Operas or going for a pint after work in the local pub. Most of all, he missed the humour that British soldiers tend to have. Near enough everyone on the circuit is ex military and the humour is brought across to the PSD. In a way, it isn't completely unlike army life.

He came to visit me at home the day before I was due to fly back to Iraq. My girlfriend, Lisa, was there and she would drop me off at the airport the next morning.

"He's after something, I know it." I said to her.

She had never met Martin, even though we had been together for nearly two years. "He probably just wants to see you because he's missed you."

"You're talking about our Martin here. I don't call him 'Black Beard' for nothing. The only time he bother's with anyone, is when he needs something. He's a complete pirate."

But that's just how he is.

Within minutes of turning up at my door he popped the question. "Any job slots going with your lot Luke?"

I looked at Lisa and smiled, "See what I mean, fucking pirate."

Martin looked at me confused, so I explained, "I told her that you was after summat, and behold, within a few minutes of being here, you're scrounging for a job."

"Fuck off Luke, it's not like that," I could see his discomfort now that I had placed him in on the spot and uncloaked him, "I just can't be arsed with civilian life. It's boring the arse off me."

I decided to make him squirm for a while, "Don't worry about it mate, I know how it is. I'll get you a job and then I'll not hear from you for a few months till you need something else."

"You're a knob aren't you, you gonna get me on with your lot or what then?"

I promised him I would fight like a Spartan to get him in with my company. Even though I call him a pirate, he's still my brother and I love him and I would do anything to help him out. I wrote a few quick emails to the bosses to warn them off and I advised him to do the same.

Two weeks later, while I was back in Kormor, he phoned me to say that he was on his way out to start with our company. I was over the moon to have him onboard and I was hoping that he would be based in Kormor with me. Unfortunately, it wasn't to be and he ended up working out of Erbil. Still, he was down my way from time to time and we would have a catch up and a brew.

Being Martin, everything he did, or got involved with, degenerated in to a Slapstick routine. He would be telling me about the comedy of errors that he and his team found themselves in on journeys to and from Erbil and I would be rolled up laughing at his descriptions. We never failed to have a laugh together.

I was leading my team in a usual Kormor day, travelling from one well head to the next with the clients while they cracked on with venting gases and taking readings. I was sat in my vehicle when my mobile phone buzzed.

It was Pete, who I had worked with on my last contract. I hadn't heard from Pete in a while but I knew that he was based in Kirkuk with the company that had taken over from us.

I opened the text, and it read:

'Luke, phone me ASAP. It's not good news mate!'

Because I had clients with me, I didn't want to start making personal phone calls, but my brain began racing, trying to work out what the problem could be.

Could it be something that had happened during our time in Kirkuk and had come back to bite me in the arse or was it something to do with my personal life that he had found out and wanted to warn me?

Deep down, I knew what the text meant, but I didn't want it to be the case. Someone that we knew had either been seriously hurt, or worse; killed.

I dropped the clients off and began trying to call Pete. I couldn't get through. I tried again and again and even used the satellite phone that had been issued to me. Again, I couldn't get through. It was either a problem at my end, with me being in a dead spot like Kormor, or it was at his end, on a FOB that is blanketed with Electronic Counter Measures, ECM, against frequency controlled explosive devices. Either way, I couldn't get the answers I needed and in the end, I text him asking him to call me back.

For the rest of the day, I heard nothing. I was constantly checking my phone, hoping that he would get in touch, but I didn't hear from him again. I was running through all the possibilities of what it could be and who. Then it dawned on me; Liam.

I had heard that Liam had been transferred from Suli to the Kirkuk team and that he and Pete were working together. Pete knew that Liam and I were close and to me, the pieces all seemed to fit.

Something had happened and Pete wanted to let me know.

I began to flap and my anxiety was made worse by the lack of information. I scrolled through my phone's address book and began texting and calling people that may have had some news. Nobody knew anything. I text anyone that I knew worked for their company and again, nothing.

I felt completely in the dark and helpless.

I spent the rest of the day wrapped in my own thoughts, and as soon as the clients had finished and I had taken them back to their accommodation, I began checking online news web pages and emailing people.

I got an email back from a couple of people, telling me that they had heard something had happened up in the north of Iraq, but they had no details as yet.

Cach was also working for the company that Liam and Pete were and I had called him earlier, but he had no information to give me at that time. My phone began to ring, it was Cach again.

"Hello mate, you got any news for me?" I asked, knowing that he must have or he wouldn't be calling.

His voice was quiet, and I could tell that he was struggling with his thoughts and how to best go about giving me the information I needed.

"Luke, I'm sorry, but it's Liam. He's dead mate."

My knees buckled and I involuntarily dropped into my chair. His word's had a similar impact on me as a punch to the chest. The wind was instantly knocked out of me, my breathing stopped and my throat closed up as though an invisible hand was squeezing it.

I could feel my stomach turn over, and after a long silence of maybe five seconds, "How?" I croaked. My voice cracked as I asked the question and tears had began to well up in my eyes.

Cach must've been able to sense how the news had hit me from his end, and his tone of voice became more subtle and comforting than I'd ever heard him speak before.

"I'm not sure of the full details yet Luke, but I'll let you know as soon as I find out. I'm really sorry buddy. I know how close you were to him."

"Thanks Cach." I was struggling to speak and needed to hang up.

I put the phone down and sat staring at the wall. Everything in my vision was a blur and as the tears began to flow down my face my head sagged into my hands. I wept like I had never wept in my life, and before long, I had dropped out of the chair and on to the floor on to my knees.

I had never felt pain like it. I couldn't control it, and the tears wouldn't stop. I tried to compose myself, but each time I tried, I would go into more convulsions of grief.

In the end, I just let it happen.

I don't know how long I sat in my room for, with the door locked. It must've been quite a few hours because it was dark by the time I emerged, having composed myself. I walked to the Op's Room and informed them that I would need a flight home soon and the reason why.

I was told that it wouldn't be a problem and that it would be squared away for me. Quintin also offered to take care of the clients for me for the next day or so, to leave me in peace. I was touched by his consideration.

I returned to my room and made a quick call to Lisa and told her about Liam. She was heartbroken for me, knowing how the news had devastated me.

After that I called Elaine, Liam's mother and Lyndsey, his ex wife. I spoke to them both for a while and during the conversations, we would all burst in to fits of tears suddenly.

They were hard phone calls to make, but I wanted them to know that I was there for them if they needed me.

Afterward, I reached into my kit and pulled out a bottle of Jack Daniels I had been saving. I hadn't yet opened it, but I decided to drink myself into oblivion that night. I sat in the corner of my room, with the bottle in my hand, and drank.

I woke the next morning with a splitting head ache, still dressed and sprawled out on the floor. I looked to my right; the Jack Daniels bottle was almost empty. I was confused for a moment, then my memory returned of the previous day's news; Liam was gone.

Liam and his team had been travelling from Kirkuk to Suli on a task when the vehicle that Liam was driving had a blow out in one of the rear tyres. Because of the speed they were travelling at and the weight of the vehicle, the explosive force of the burst tyre had caused the vehicle to flip.

Liam's door had come open and he was thrown from the vehicle, killing him instantly.

Five days later, and I was home again. Lisa met me at the airport and hugged me for what seemed like an eternity. We went to my house so that I could get my things together and sort myself out.

Liam lived in Newcastle, just a couple of miles from where my girlfriend lived, and his family all lived close by too. I decided that the best thing I could do, was to get up there as soon as possible and help out as best I could and lighten the load for Elaine.

I had known Elaine for a long time, having met her when I was in the army and she had come down to visit Liam. We instantly gelled and thought the world of each other. We had the same daft humour and she was able to talk for Britain. She always said that she looked on me as a son, and at that time, she needed the likes of me and Liam's other close friends around her.

The next day, we got to Newcastle and went straight to see Elaine and Liam's Grandmother, June. She smiled as she opened the door, but the grief in her eyes was unmistakable. I hugged her and before long we were stood in the hallway, bawling our eyes out together in each other's arms, rocking and sobbing. Liam's Grandmother, who I also called 'Gran' and his sister, Tree, joined us and we stood in the hallway for a while, just huddled together in grief.

Liam still hadn't been repatriated yet and funeral arrangements needed to be made. People who had known Liam started to arrive from all over the place. Quite a few guys managed to get themselves back from Iraq so that they could be there to say their final farewells, including Brian, Pete, Jules and Omar.

Dave Taylor was also there, another big daft pal of ours who sadly, isn't with us anymore. He was killed in Afghanistan in 2009.

The Parachute Regiment Association also offered to be present at the funeral and would provide a Guard of Honour from their ranks, as they had done for Swanny, bringing their Standards with them to present 'The Last Salute' at his funeral.

A week later, Liam's body was finally brought home. Elaine still had to officially identify him in the Funeral Home. She couldn't face it alone and asked if I would go with her. When we got there, we were led into the room were Liam lay.

I stayed strong to support Elaine, but inside I was a complete mess. I have seen many bodies, and made a few in my life, but when it's someone that you've known and loved, who died before their time, it's a different matter. I wanted him to wake up, to sit up and laugh at us for falling for his latest practical joke.

I just didn't want any of it to be real.

We went back to Elaine's home afterward and I had to get away and be alone for a while. I walked for hours then went to see Lyndsey and her sons. We sat and chatted for quite a while as the boys played.

Liam was buried a few days later, dressed in his Parachute Regiment uniform with his beret and medals. Marc, Steve, Ollie, Scott, Wes and I, all close friends of Liam, had the honour of carrying him to his final resting place led by Gaz, another great friend.

The Parachute Regiment Association provided the Guard of Honour as they had promised and his coffin was draped in the Parachute Regiment Colours. Liam had always been proud of being a paratrooper, to him, being able to call himself a paratrooper was better than being knighted.

As he was lowered into his grave, many of us rough tough soldiers and paratroopers fought back the tears, but to no avail. We all felt that the world had become a little more empty and worse off, having lost a great guy like Liam.

I did my best to comfort Lyndsey and her two young sons. James was old enough to understand that his dad was dead and I could see the impact it was having on his mind. Even though Liam and Lyndsey were divorced, Lyndsey was heartbroken and struggling to come to terms with the loss of the man she had loved and the father of her two young sons.

Liam Carmichael died on the 16th March 2008. He was twenty eight years old.

The last time I had seen him alive, was when we had made a run for it from Suli to Kirkuk after being detained by the Americans in October. He had given me a hug goodbye and wished me luck, offering to be the first to help should we get into trouble.

I loved Liam like a brother, and even now, I miss him greatly.

Lisa and I split up shortly after and I returned home to St. Helens feeling empty and lost. I still had four weeks left of my leave, but all I could think about was returning to Iraq. People had asked me at the funeral, if I was now considering leaving Iraq and looking for work in the UK.

313

To me, the answer was simple, "No."

Even though I had lost many mates, including my best friend, Liam, I still planned to work on the circuit. We all knew the risks and the dangers and people being killed wasn't exactly an eye opener to any of us. It wasn't a case of reality suddenly hitting home because, we knew the reality. We had seen it and been part of it on numerous occasions.

I wanted to be back doing what I knew best. I didn't want to be sat at home with my thoughts rattling around in my head and the time dragging by. I had lost my best mate and girlfriend in a very short period of time and I couldn't think of anything else to do to fill the hole.

Instead, I turned to drink.

I found myself staying up till all hours in the early morning, drinking whisky and cheap wine. Eventually, I would collapse into a pile of shit on the couch and wake up in the early afternoon, only to start drinking again.

I gave up shaving, and my appearance and bearing soon went downhill. I was hardly eating, and when I did, it tended to be junk and very little and more often than not I would be sick afterward. All I was bothered about was getting more wine from the local shop to numb my feelings and thoughts.

I sat around in my own drunken semi conscious world, wearing nothing more than just a towel wrapped around my waste and forgetting to wash on most days. My curtains were permanently drawn and the house was in perpetual gloom, with no fresh air or light able to get in. I had sunk to an all time low and had no immediate intention of picking myself back up.

I wallowed in my own grief and self pity for four weeks. Whenever people knocked at the door, it either didn't register in my alcohol soaked brain, or I just ignored them. It could've been someone coming to tell me that I had won the lottery and I couldn't have cared less.

The night before I was to fly back to Iraq, I got myself together, packed my kit and shaved the beard off.

Underneath the four weeks of growth, I looked haggard and worn out. I stared at myself in the mirror for a long time, studying the lines that had developed on my face and the dark rings below my eyes. I had aged twenty years in just a month. I emptied the last of my booze down the sink and vowed to sort myself out and get back to the old me. The only place I could do that at the time, was Iraq.

Kormor became busier and busier and the camp degenerated into a septic pit of bacteria just waiting for an outbreak of the 'Black Death'. The refuse system was based on the 'out of sight, out of mind' concept.

The leftover food and waste from the canteen would be carried across the camp and dumped over the side of the walls, where it couldn't be seen and as far as the locals were concerned, it was no longer a concern.

When the heat started to rise, the level of the smell, insects and rats went through the roof. You only needed to raise your head over the wall barriers and you would see an entire field of rubbish, food, dirty water, oil, medical waste etc. and it had developed its own eco-system. Black clouds of flies would be swarming around just above the ground, and rats and huge insects would be scurrying in and out of the rubbish.

They in turn, attracted their own predators such as snakes, scorpions and spiders. David Attenborough would've had a field day with his camera and microphone had he been there.

Inside the camp, was an open trough running along the road where waste water would run with bits of rotten food and garbage sailing along on a merry little cruise downhill to collect in a mini reservoir of shit at the far end of the compound.

We all had our own room and we kept them clean and hygienic, but we had to share ablutions with the locals who lived on the base. In the morning and evening, we would walk across to get a shower. The shower heads by that time had normally been broken off, or the hoses ripped so they were useless, and the sinks were either loose or collapsed, or full of phlegm and snot. I couldn't understand how the place could so easily fall apart and the Kurds happily live amongst it.

The toilets were always blocked and backed up, with shit and piss overflowing onto the floors and on more than one occasion, I found turds sitting in the shower cubicles. The place was disgusting and it was the locals that were causing it. It never seemed to bother them though.

Walking into an ablution block was always something that I dreaded. First of all, I would hold my breath, and then I would walk on tip toes to avoid too much human waste from covering my boots. If ever we saw a local in there, and tried to explain to them to clean up after themselves, they would pretend not to understand and look at us with stupid expressions on their faces.

One morning, I stood brushing my teeth and trying to see my reflection in the shit caked mirror in front of me. A Kurdish worker walked in, turned to the sink and lifted one leg and began rinsing his dirty fungus infected toes under the tap. I almost threw up as I removed the toothbrush from my mouth.

"Oi you dirty cunt, use the hose in the shower to do that." I barked at him.

My hand gestures, body language and tone of voice were a universal language in itself that crossed all barriers of origin, and it told him that I wasn't impressed. I even pointed at his feet and then to the hose in the cubicle.

With one leg on the ground and the other still in the sink, he looked at me with distain and babbled something in Kurdish, gesturing with his hands that either; he didn't understand me or, that I was to shut up and mind my own business.

The red curtain came down and before I knew it, I had swept his standing leg from underneath him. With his leg collapsed and his other foot still spreading bacteria around the sink for us, there was only one thing he could do. He crumpled to the floor that was awash with inch deep piss and excrement filled water. He lay, sprawled on his back, covered in 'cholera soup'.

He was spread like a star fish for a moment, stunned and before he could recover, I stepped in over him and planted a right handed punch to the side of his head, knocking his head back into the filth. I felt the hard bone of his skull against my knuckles and the shock wave travel through my wrist and up my arm. As the hit connected against and forced his head back down, it made a wet slap and a heavy thump when it hit the floor again.

I popped my toothbrush back into my mouth, slung my towel over my shoulder and walked out, smiling and greeting 'good morning' to the other locals who had now crowded around the doorway watching in horror as their friend flopped about on the floor like a fish out of water, trying to get to his feet and holding the side of his face.

I presumed there would be come backs, so I returned to my room and put my pistol belt on, picked up my AK47, and made my way over to the office to let them know what I had done. That way, they could aim off for it should any problems arise and it wouldn't be a complete surprise to them.

All I got was a grin from one of the blokes. "Fucking hell Luke, you're an unsavoury character at times."

I had always respected the Kurds. They had stood up against the Iraqis, Iranians and the Turks during wars and struggles. Even during the First World War, they had fought the British. But living with them was a different matter. As far as I was concerned, we should've had our own separate compound from them to save incidents like that.

I wasn't the only one to blow a fuse. Quintin had running's with them too over different matters and at one point, there was a Mexican standoff with guns drawn between them.

The more time I spent in Kormor, the more I found myself rebelling. Time and again, it was flagged up to the head shed that the living conditions were appalling and well below standard for ex-pats. The requests for better accommodation and separate ablutions were always ignored and we were expected to put up and shut up.

I just saw it as an excuse to cause more atrocities and take my frustrations out on people. I was bitter and twisted and in a way, I guess I wanted to blame everyone around me for the death of Liam.

I was slipping into a self destructive pattern.

On a trip to our new HQ; a large villa on the outskirts of Suli, I had a running with one of the local administration staff. I forget his name, but I'll call him Yasser for now.

For some reason, people walked on egg shells around this guy and in general, what he wanted, he got. He was supposed to be the company fixer, organising meetings and sourcing kit and vehicles from his contacts throughout Suli.

In reality, he fucked up everything he did. But he was protected.

As I walked in through the gate, I noticed a gaggle of our Kurdish security guards crowded around a shack and laughing at something on the ground. Curious, I stuck my head in through the group and saw, on the floor with a very short length of nylon cord attached to its leg and tied to a post, was a beautiful and powerful looking bird of prey; a Hawk or a Falcon of some sort.

The guards were prodding and poking it, flicking lit cigarettes at it and pushing it with the toes of their shoes, causing the bird to peck at them with its beak as it tried to back off.

Having a length of cord no more than three or four inches long tied to its leg, it couldn't back away too far and so it had to endure what the locals dished out for their own amusement. I also noticed that the nylon cord had cut into the skin around the bird's leg and it looked sore and swollen.

I lost it, "You fucking bastards. Get the fuck out of here before I kill the lot of you." I roared and I began grabbing people and throwing them back out through the door way.

I really wanted one of them to confront me so that I could've punched his lights out. The one nearest to the bird was in a crouch, having been distracted from his torture of the helpless animal by my ranting and raving but he had not yet risen to his feet, perfect for me.

I then grabbed him by the back of his shirt and dragged him five metres out into the open as he clawed at my hands and kicked his feet in the dust as they trailed behind him.

I dumped him on the floor and eyed the rest, "Don't any of you dirty bastards dare come near this bird."

I was stood glaring at them when they began gobbing off to Awat, who was now walking towards us.

"Luke, they're worried because that bird is Yasser's pet."

"I don't give a shit what they're worried about Awat."

I took off my shirt and wrapped it around my left hand for protection because I knew that the bird would try to attack me the minute I went near it. With my free hand, I slid the knife from its case on my belt and approached.

The large bird started squawking and flapping its wings, trying to claw at the shirt in my hand. That was exactly what I wanted it to do. I pinned the bird down and let it get on with pecking and scratching at my protected hand while I slipped the knife underneath to cut the cord from its leg.

Once I had done that, I wrapped the shirt across its talons and gently lifted it. It was screeching and trying to fly away. I walked into the open and pushed it into the air and once the bird realised it was free, it opened its wings and took off over the villa.

The guards stood watching me, with hatred burning in their eyes and quietly mumbling amongst them. I walked past them and headed for what I knew to be Yasser's office.

I got to the door and without knocking, I barged in, "I've set your bird free Yasser. I'm sure it's what you intended to do anyway. If it's not, then shit and fall in it."

He sat at his desk with the fat jowls of his cheeks hanging to his neck, looking at me but without saying a word. He knew exactly what I was saying because he spoke perfect English, but he didn't have the balls to do anything about it.

Instead, he rushed out of the side door to check if what I had told him was true and when he discovered that I wasn't lying, he ran straight to the Op's Room to kick off with the bosses.

I expected to be sacked, but once again, nothing came of it and I returned to Kormor feeling like I had actually made a difference that day, to a bird at least. I couldn't care less for the rest of the country.

Things carried on in pretty much the same manner down in Kormor. The more I rebelled, the more I hated everyone. I would go home on leave and get into states that even Oliver Reed and Keith Moon would've been proud of. I wasn't exactly a rock star, but I was certainly living like one.

If I had ever been inclined to dabble in drugs, then no doubt, I would've had sugar bowls loaded with cocaine around my house. Thankfully though, that sort of thing was never my scene.

I ended up living a life of extremes. While I was away, I would eat healthily, stay sober and train like a Spartan. At home, it would all go to rat shit.

One morning, the local police guys we had as part of our PSD team decided they would mutiny because they felt they weren't being given enough time off during the day. The fact that I had no time off myself and that regardless of what they wanted, the clients still needed to be protected while on site, didn't seem to have any impact on them.

Awat came to me looking worried, "Luke, they demand that you speak to them."

He glanced at the team and back at me, waiting to see what my reaction would be.

"Righty dokey then, let's go and see what the problem is."

It was Monday morning, and standing in front of me, was a fresh team who I had never worked with before. There were four of them, and the commander of the group was a skinny little bloke with a thick moustache and sunken cheek bones. He carried a pistol on his hip and he stood with his hand resting on the hilt. His body language told me from the start that he was after a fight.

To his right, stood a tall fat ginger Kurd with his AK47 in his hands, running his index finger over the trigger, looking at me as though he was thinking, 'I could easily deal with this little British bloke.' At least that is how I interpreted it, or was it that I wanted it to be that way?

Right away, they all started jabbering at Awat in Kurdish and gesturing in my direction. I stood watching for a minute, with my arms folded, trying to get a feel for what the problem could be. Awat turned to me, the look of concern clear on his face.

"Uh, Luke, they say that they are not happy because they want to be able to go back to their rooms at midday and have lunch and return two hours later. Also, they say that they don't want to work after five o'clock."

I had to laugh. I shook my head and turned to Awat, all the time keeping an eye on the skinny commander who still rested his hand on his pistol. Intimidation was clearly his aim, but it wasn't working. I'd already decided on my course of action should things go pear shaped.

"Awat, tell them that they will do as they are told and they will work for as long as I tell them to. If they don't like it, then they can fuck off now."

He looked at me, unsure of how to interpret what I had told him and I could see that he was trying to work out how best to put it across, without causing a drama.

"Just tell them *exactly* what I said Awat. Don't sugar coat it, 'cause I'm not gonna pussy foot with these wankers."

He told them, and immediately he was bombarded with angry Kurdish voices, mainly from the skinny one and the fat ginger guy. The other two stood in the background, watching and listening. I wasn't too concerned with them, they looked like they were just caught up in the whole thing and neither were carrying their weapons.

The two ring leaders shouted and ranted and threw their arms about, gesticulating like epileptic chimps. I got the feeling they weren't exactly happy about what I had said, so I decided to upset them a little further.

I removed my pistol belt and placed it on the hood of my SUV. I then stood in front of them, unarmed and with Awat translating; I offered them a chance to prove themselves as the rightful commanders of the team.

The look of shock and confusion was complete, and they struggled to understand how one guy could stand in front of four armed men, and offer to take the whole bunch on in a scrap.

Awat glanced at me in the same manner.

I winked at him, "Don't worry mate. Just keep your eye on the other two."

I stepped closer, bringing myself to within arm's reach of the skinny commander and keeping the fat ginger upstart on my left. The commander looked me up and down and turned his body slightly so that his left shoulder was toward me and his pistol and right arm were away from me in a sort of boxer stance.

The fat guy continued to finger the trigger of his AK47, which he had attached to a sling far too tightly, and held across his chest. He had a slight smile on his face, beaming with confidence. I smiled back and turned to the skinny guy.

I'm by no means fluent in Kurdish, but I knew how to best insult him in his native tongue. I called him 'a useless little girl' which, to a Kurdish man, is a huge insult.

His eyes widened and his body stiffened as he let out a low hoarse gasp that turned in to a roar. He tightened his grip on the pistol and began moving as though he was about to draw the weapon.

By now, I'd began to make my move and I had stepped in close and grabbed him by the shoulders, suddenly forcing him towards me as I brought my head in to connect with the bridge of his nose. I felt it give under my forehead and I heard the bones snap. I brought my head back and launched it forward again in to his face. Forgetting his pistol now, he brought both hands up to his nose as he sank to the ground, groaning and pouring with blood.

Awat, as always, could be relied upon to do the right thing. In the split second it had taken for me to drop the commander of the group, before the fat ginger one could react, he had lunged and wrapped his arms around the man's body, pinning his weapon to his chest and leaving him unable to use it. With the relatively small size of Awat compared to the much bigger ginger guy, it looked like he was hugging a bear.

They were still close on my left and as they struggled, I stepped across and threw a right hook into the jaw of the big guy. It landed in the area where the jaw bone turns upward toward the ear, causing it to jolt sideways and his teeth rattle. His legs fell from under him and he fell like a bag of shit, Awat and all.

Still holding his smashed nose, I disarmed the commander and Awat took the AK47 from the fat ginger one. I looked at the other two, who stood motionless and gave them the weapons and instructed them to pick the other two up and to leave. They hesitated, just for a moment then, went about scraping up their comrades.

Awat was straight on to his phone, because he knew that they would report straight to their commanders and to try and have me arrested. He had an uncle in the Peshmerga who was one of the Generals commanding the Suli region and he explained the incident directly to him.

After a few minutes, he turned to me grinning, "I'm my uncle's favourite nephew, and he's on his way to their barracks in Suli already to speak to their commander. I told him exactly what happened."

I reported the incident to the Op's Room, but I left out the bit about me dropping them both. I just referred to it as a bit of a mutiny so I had sent them home. My main client however, had seen the whole thing from the window in his office. He thought it was great.

I left the company just a few days before Christmas, well I say left; I actually managed to roll a vehicle with a bunch of us in it including my brother, on the way to the villa in Erbil. I went on leave and received an email a short time later telling me that, 'due to the scaling down of the company and the client requirements, your services are no longer required at this moment'.

I was happy to go.

It had been a long time coming and I now had the time to reflect and think about getting to grips with myself. I took some time out and spent much of it with my daughter, Leah.

Slowly but surely, I got over wanting to blame the world for Liam.

Soon, I was the old Luke again and I climbed back on to the horse and picked up where I had left off.

I returned to Iraq.

END

AFTERWORD

Iraq is still a dangerous country. I should know, because I still work in Iraq. Many of what happens now though, goes unreported. It has become old news and the public show an even lesser interest in the private contractors, such as me who work in Iraq, than they show in the military.

When a soldier is killed, it makes the news reports, albeit small and indifferent compared to the rumours of what certain celebrities will be wearing at the next awards ceremony. Then, there are the likes of Gordon Brown, when he was the British Prime Minister, either getting the names of the fallen wrong through incompetence, or just proving to the public that he couldn't care less.

The list of PSD killed in Iraq is also rarely considered. None of us ask for any recognition, not even from our own countries of origin. We don't do it for medals, God, Queen or country. I have only met one or two, mainly Americans, who claim to be doing it to make a difference and to bring liberty and freedom to the Iraqi people.

The majority of us are here purely for the money.

But something that should be kept in mind is that without the Private Security Teams operating in Iraq, the country would still be in the condition that it was in 2003, immediately after the war. The infrastructure had pretty much been destroyed. Power plants and bridges, as well as military instillations, had been targeted during the bombing campaign.

Once the invasion was complete, companies from all over the world rushed in to make their money in the construction and reconstruction that would follow in the wake of the war. It was and still is big business. The supply and demand of the security needed was too much for military forces to cope with, so Private Security Companies picked up the gauntlet and in a way, became troops in civilian dress.

The reconstruction still needed to be done, but the people doing it needed protection. The American and British governments couldn't supply the troops, so ex soldiers cashed in.

I've never bothered with the rights and wrongs of the invasion, even though I had been part of it as a serving soldier in The Parachute Regiment. War is human nature and always will be. I joined the army because I wanted to fight. I wanted to get stuck in. Has anybody ever met a little boy who didn't want to play with guns, to play war with his friends over the fields and run about, sounding off his own interpretation of what his gun sounds like?

Our soldiers have been fighting in Afghanistan and Iraq since 2001 and 2003 respectively, yet our governments still send them into battle with kit and equipment short falls. When they return home wounded and crippled, they are given the lowest and cheapest form of care that the men in power are willing to give, and the sooner they can palm them off with a small pay out, the better.

These men and women were sent into these places being fed lies from their governments about the reasons for going to war. Me; as I sat in Kuwait before the invasion, I considered the reasons for war. It all boiled down to money, in the form of oil.

There was no great rush or excuse to invade Iraq or Afghanistan before September 11th. Afterward, the Americans and British had just the excuse they needed. None of it was to find 'Weapons of Mass Destruction', or to rid the world of a tyrant, or even to bring liberty and freedom to Iraq. It was oil, plain and simple.

Personally, I never had a problem with it. Like I said, it is human nature to fight. Rarely in history have men needed much of a reason to invade a weaker country.

The Romans, Persians, Egyptians and Macedonians did it on a huge scale. Even in recent history, Great Britain had the largest empire the world had ever seen and the French, under Napoleon and the Germans under Hitler, had all had a crack at claiming Europe as their own.

So, in my eyes, I had no problem with going to war to steal a countries wealth. I just didn't like being lied to by politicians who believe us to be simple and incapable of coming to our own conclusions.

In my opinion, Al Qaeda doesn't really exist. Osama Bin Laden didn't sit in Afghanistan, giving out tasks to his troops who then ran around the world blowing up tube stations or flying planes in to buildings.

The governments of the west would have us believe that there is a set enemy to fight, like it was in World War Two against Germany and Japan. They do this because it is easier to gain support and no one is then likely to ask, "Who exactly are we fighting then?"

But in reality, the whole Al Qaeda thing is a belief or a movement, not a terrorist organization.

The Muslim extremists believe they are fighting a Holy War, Jihad, and that it's their duty to join the fight against the West, the infidel. No one gives them particular orders to attack specific targets; they do it on their own accord.

True, the terrorist cells sometimes band together in certain regions and call themselves the 'Army of . . .' or, 'Freedom Fighters for . . .', but in general, they act independently and the movement gains recognition for it as a whole.

I look back now over the years, and I remember the events during and after the war and up to this moment. I see the faces of the friends I have lost and I remember where and how they had died. Many have been involved with the Private Security Circuit and just as many, have been still serving soldiers in Iraq and Afghanistan.

Just a month or two before I had left the army Dave Taylor, Marc and Liam Carmichael had been sat in my room, having a brew as always. We were all due to leave at the same time and we planned to work on the circuit in Iraq. All of us were excited about our new career option, and we looked forward to living the highlife.

We joked and gobbed off about how great things will be, and I remember saying at the time, 'Yeah but there's a chance that a few years from now, some of us could be dead."

Marc and I still live.

Regardless of your stance on the war, whether you supported it, served in it, quietly objected or openly protested in the streets shouting, "Not in our name," and defacing war graves and monuments and attacking veterans, remember that these are your men and women, who are sent by your elected governments to fight on your behalf.

They deserve respect and honour by all and they should never be forgotten.

ABOUT THE AUTHOR

Luke Duffy was born in 1977 in northern England.

At the age of 18 he joined the Parachute Regiment and since leaving in early 2005, he has worked in Iraq on the Private Security Circuit.

He is a fan of many genres and in particular, Science Fiction, Military and History. With his love of literature and his experience in his subjects, Luke's ambition was always to become a writer one day.

Currently, he lives in the United Kingdom with his girlfriend Michelle and is the proud father of Leah and Manus.